Encountering the Dharma

For Dave Harris
with warm regards

Richard H. Seager

Encountering the Dharma

Daisaku Ikeda, Soka Gakkai,
and the Globalization
of Buddhist Humanism

Richard Hughes Seager

UNIVERSITY OF CALIFORNIA PRESS
Berkeley / Los Angeles / London

University of California Press, one of the most distinguished university presses in the United States, enriches lives around the world by advancing scholarship in the humanities, social sciences, and natural sciences. Its activities are supported by the UC Press Foundation and by philanthropic contributions from individuals and institutions. For more information, visit www.ucpress.edu.

University of California Press
Berkeley and Los Angeles, California

University of California Press, Ltd.
London, England

Library of Congress Cataloging-in-Publication Data
Seager, Richard Hughes.
    Encountering the Dharma: Daisaku Ikeda, Soka Gakkai, and the global-ization of Buddhist humanism / Richard Hughes Seager.
        p.   cm.
    Includes bibliographical references and index.
    ISBN 0-520-24576-8 (cloth : alk. paper)
    —ISBN 0-520-24577-6 (pbk. : alk. paper)
    1. Soka Gakkai.   2. Globalization—Religious aspects—Soka Gakkai.
I. Title.
BQ8415.8.S43 2006
294.3'928—dc22   2005006619

Manufactured in the United States of America

15 14 13 12 11 10 09 08 07 06
10 9 8 7 6 5 4 3 2 1

This book is printed on New Leaf EcoBook 50, a 100% recycled fiber of which 50% is de-inked post-consumer waste, processed chlorine-free. EcoBook 50 is acid-free and meets the minimum requirements of ANSI/ASTM D5634-01 *(Permanence of Paper).* ∞

For Tippy,
with whom I first crossed cultures

Contents

Acknowledgments   *ix*

Preface   *xi*

1. Mystic Opportunity   *1*

2. Creating Value   *21*

3. Mentor's Vision   *42*

4. Rising Star   *65*

5. Sea Change   *86*

6. Countervailing Trends   *114*

7. Zuiho-bini   *141*

8. World House   *171*

9. Intrepid Navigators   *202*

Notes   *213*

Glossary   *223*

Bibliography   *227*

Index   *233*

Acknowledgments

Many friends, colleagues, and associates encouraged me as I developed and completed this book, but a number of institutions and people deserve special acknowledgment for the specific contributions they made in assisting me.

First, Boston Research Center for the 21st Century provided financial support, administered through Hamilton College, without which I could not have undertaken the project. I want to thank its president, Masao Yokota, whose visits became a source of unexpected pleasure throughout the time I worked on the book, and Robert Eppsteiner, who lent me valuable aid during research trips and support when I encountered obstacles while working on the manuscript. I also thank Lane Zachary, who encouraged my creativity while fielding issues writers face in the publishing world today.

Hamilton College was generous in granting me leave to pursue this work. My colleagues in the Religious Studies Department consistently encouraged me to develop courses in which I was able to deepen my understanding of the Soka Gakkai. The librarians at Burke Library gave me valuable assistance in collecting important background material. Terri Viglietta was a great help in preparing the final manuscript.

Special thanks go to people in Soka Gakkai International's Office of Public Information for their work in coordinating research trips, providing translation services, and enlisting the cooperation of Gakkai members on three continents. In particular, I want to thank Toshinori Iwazumi, Ric Tsumura, Andrew Gebert, and, especially, Mari Shikoda, who sustained a transpacific correspondence with me that was vital to my work.

There are numerous individual members in the Soka Gakkai International movements in Japan, Singapore, Brazil, and the United States whom I would like to remember for their openness and interest in my work and for the entertaining times we shared together. For the sake of brevity, I extend to them all a collective thank-you.

And I send heartfelt regards to President Ikeda not simply for his support, without which this project would have been unthinkable, but also for the personal kindness he showed to me during a difficult transition in my life.

Preface

This book originated in a 1999 conversation with Robert Eppsteiner, at that time academic liaison for the Boston Research Center for the 21st Century (BRC), an activist group in Cambridge, Massachusetts, associated with the Soka Gakkai. From the outset, I had a strong professional interest in the project: I have long been preoccupied with the East-West encounter and have done sustained work on Buddhism in the United States. In a Columbia University Press book, *Buddhism in America*, I devoted a chapter to the Buddhist Humanism of the Soka Gakkai, the research for which piqued my interest in both Daisaku Ikeda, the organization's longtime president, and the remarkable history of modern Japan.

During research for that book, I came to see how scholars of American religious history are at a disadvantage for at least two reasons when studying the Americanization of Buddhism. First, we rarely understand the Asian background of groups before they arrive in the United States. Second, we do not necessarily look beyond the limited horizon of our own culture to locate the American experience in the broad contours of globalization. This project, however, gave me the chance to think about Japan, to immerse myself in at least one significant part of modern Asian history, and to get some sense of Buddhism around the globe.

From that preliminary conversation with Rob Eppsteiner, I was convinced that I needed to write a book in which there would be a degree of personal engagement with academic issues. That way I would be able to negotiate the fact that, while I have become a specialist in Buddhism coming to the United States, I am a nonspecialist in Japanese religion and history. I felt that a personalized narrative voice would enable me to wonder, ponder, probe, and struggle to make sense of the Gakkai and Japan in terms familiar both to myself and to the reader.

Such a voice would also give me an opening to investigate a fascinating dimension of the movement's history. Since its founding in the 1930s, the Soka Gakkai has repeatedly found itself at the center of controversies, some linked to major struggles over the future of Japan, others to intense internal religious debates that erupted into public view. Over the course of its history, however, it has also grown into a large, politically active, and very well established network of institutions, whose membership represents something on the order of a tenth of the Japanese population. One result is that there is a fractured view of the movement in Japan. On one hand, it is seen as a highly articulated, politically and socially engaged movement with an expressed message of human empowerment and global peace. On the other, it has been charged with an array of nefarious activities that range from fellow traveling with Communists and sedition to aspiring to world domination.

To varying degrees this fractured view has followed the movement overseas, where, despite its success at globalization, it has had to contend with both the legacy of Japanese militarism in Asia and the concerns of observers in the West that the movement was in some way an Asian cult. That the Soka Gakkai is a form of Nichiren Buddhism—a uniquely Japanese expression of Buddhism that evokes few of the romantic notions Westerners associate with Zen—has contributed to this misunderstanding. That since its founding Soka Gakkai has often been aggressive about proselytizing, rarely quietistic, and devoted to social transformation has also contributed to its reputation.

The complex image of Daisaku Ikeda, the charismatic teacher who has led the Gakkai for more than forty years, has also shaped its reception around the world. To Ikeda's disciples, he is an inspiring spiritual leader whose Buddhist Humanism enables them to engage with the modern world in individualized, satisfying, and socially productive ways. Some critics, however, charge him with being a controlling egotist and manipulator, a view long cultivated by Ikeda's enemies and those who seek to discredit the Soka Gakkai. This is particularly so in Japan, where the movement has a political significance that it does not have in the West or on the Asian mainland.

From the start of my research, I sought to understand this historical, yet highly subjective, dimension of the movement, which ultimately entailed my coming to grips with my own thoughts and feelings about Japan, Ikeda, and the Soka Gakkai. I also found myself thinking a great deal about both Japanophilia and Japan-bashing and the long, conflicted, yet creative history between Japan and the United States. In the last analysis, my way of making sense of these controversies was to look closely at what was being said about the Gakkai in authoritative documents published in English, whether from critics, policy makers, or scholars of religion. I also listened closely to what was said about Ikeda and the Gakkai both by observers and by members on three continents, always alert to how I might make sense of the substance of these charges. The narrator's movement from skeptical interest through doubt to appreciation mirrors my own journey during the years I worked on this book.

Two events also deeply shaped my engagement with the Soka Gakkai, the first personal, the second world historical. Between the first discussion with Eppsteiner of the BRC about this project and my agreeing to take it on well over a year later, my wife, Ann Castle, died very unexpectedly of leukemia, going from health to death in just five days. This was, to say the least, a profound lesson in what the Buddha taught about the impermanence of all things, a central tenet of Buddhist philosophy. As the reader will see, Ann's death became so inextricably related to my encounter with Ikeda and the Soka Gakkai that I felt as though I could not write this book without making reference to it, although I have chosen to hold the more intimate aspects of that story close.

The second, world historical, event is the terrorist attacks of September 11, 2001, and their aftermath. I began this project knowing I would need to come to an understanding of the social dynamics and spiritual intent of an international peace group grounded in the Japanese experience. When I began it, I assumed I would eventually adopt an ironic posture vis-à-vis a dynamic, high-energy movement devoted to the admirable, if quixotic, notion of world peace. Instead, I found myself having to wrestle with Japanese militarism, America's use of weapons of mass destruction at Nagasaki and Hiroshima, and the reality that Manhattan is not invulnerable to terrorists and that the United States was twice again at war. The story told in this book does not extend much beyond the onset of war in Afghanistan, but the narrator's point of view on Ikeda, the Soka Gakkai, and peace in general could not help but be influenced by the events of and around September 11.

Despite the fact that I have been concerned with developing a strong and engaging narrative line, I consider this an academic book. Throughout, I have tried to present a balanced, factual, yet interpretive account of the history and spirit of the Soka Gakkai, even as I will admit to having come to marvel at the movement's energy and intensity. At the same time, I have taken a few liberties in personal sections, conflating some experiences and ordering them in the name of narrative economy and style, even while remaining faithful to the spirit of my experience of events. My research in Japan took place in late September and early October 2000 and in late March and April 2001, when I also traveled to Singapore. I visited Brazil March 15 to 25, 2002.

Throughout the book, I am working out a central idea or thesis that the Soka Gakkai is best understood as a liberal and modernist religious movement, one marked by the self-conscious attempt to adapt Buddhism to the contemporary world. All three presidents of the Soka Gakkai have made unique contributions to this liberal modernism, each in dialogue with a distinct phase of the development of modern Japan, as it moved from self-imposed exile in the mid-nineteenth century to postwar globalization.

The Gakkai's full-blown Nichiren Buddhist Humanism, however, is directly associated with Ikeda, whose life and work are the heart of this book. Throughout the narrative, I try to keep Ikeda near center stage, knowing that even specialists who study the history of modern Buddhism coming to the West know very little about him other than his complex image. As I came to understand my task, my limits, and the material I had to work with, I saw it best to develop a picture of him as a leader who stood in succession, a man who received a legacy from his mentor and his mentor's mentor. How he worked with and added to that legacy is one kind of reflection on who Ikeda is—his aspirations, ideals, and personality.

Despite this focus on Ikeda, *Nichiren's Lions* was the working title for this book, an image chosen to emphasize the millions of Ikeda's dedicated disciples, without whom there would be no movement, no Buddhist Humanism. While this focus on the people of the Soka Gakkai remains central, I changed the title to *Encountering the Dharma* as I prepared the final manuscript for publication. One reason was to direct readers' attention to the modernist spirituality Gakkai members share in their globe-spanning community and to its foundation in the classic teachings of Mahayana Buddhism. A second was to suggest the power of the narrator's experience in discovering Ikeda's Buddhist Humanism at a time of personal crisis and disturbing social change.

There is also an underlying theme or conviction that runs throughout the text, one that reflects the point of view I eventually came to adopt vis-à-vis the Soka Gakkai and its history of controversy. Since its inception, the movement—like many if not most religions—has set out to transform the world, and it has not been afraid to take concrete action toward that end. In other words, there is a strong pragmatic streak in Gakkai spirituality that does not shrink from the fact that a movement needs dedicated members, a strong motive, solid doctrine and practice, focused leadership, social awareness, money, and political will to transform the world. That this has repeatedly meant that the Soka Gakkai has been embroiled in controversy seems simply to go with the territory.

CHAPTER 1

Mystic Opportunity

A cool spring has kept Tokyo's cherry trees in bloom for almost three weeks. One morning, I awake to see snow outside the windows of the Hotel New Otani. Later, walking in the hotel garden, I feel sure there must be a sequence of Japanese characters—gray sky, flecks of flying snow, pink blossoms—to capture the essence of the phenomenon, something literary thought to be "Zenlike" in the United States, where everyone knows cherry trees bloom in spring in Japan. But how wonderful to see them, especially amid billowy clouds of snow. *Such quiet beauty*, I think, *and such a sublime stereotype of "Japaneseness."*

But this is a workday, not a time for musing, so I use these moments to brace myself for another round of interviews and note taking. I flew into Narita a few days ago to learn about the history of Soka Gakkai, one of Japan's largest, most dynamic, and highly controversial Buddhist movements, and about Daisaku Ikeda, its president and the spiritual leader of some twelve million Buddhists in Japan and around the globe.

A historian of American religion, I'm a specialist in Buddhists in the U.S.—Tibetans, south Asians, Chinese, and Koreans; Zen, Pure Land, and Shingon Buddhists from Japan; and a wide range of different groups of Americans who are "meditating Buddhists," whose main practice is to sit in quiet contemplation. I also know many "chanting Buddhists" in the Soka Gakkai—artists, actors, lawyers, teachers, people in all walks of life; Caucasians, Latinos, Japanese Americans, and African Americans. I understand that their ideals fit comfortably into America's religious landscape, that Ikeda's Buddhist Humanism, which teaches individual initiative and social responsibility, is said to reflect values considered typically American.

"I still don't get a few things," I say to myself under my breath (a habit I've picked up from many months of living alone), as I sit with my notebook on a small bench nestled against a gnarled old tree, watching snowflakes melt on paving. In what way can values said to be typically American also be both Buddhist and Japanese?

The Soka Gakkai is a classic case of modern Buddhism on the move in the age of globalization, having found its way to more than a hundred nations, so I also need to know what propelled it out of Japan and how it is received in the West and on the Asian mainland. What's the appeal of chanting the title of the Lotus Sutra, an ancient Indian Buddhist scripture, in archaic Japanese for Brits, Brazilians, or Koreans?

"Nam-myoho-renge-kyo; Nam-myoho-renge-kyo; Nam-myoho-renge-kyo," I intone, tentatively and softly, just to hear what the chant sounds like in the cold Japanese air.

A clutch of Japanese guests enters the garden, which once was that of an old aristocratic family of Edo, Tokyo's name before Japan modernized in the nineteenth century. Like me, they are cherry-tree viewing and enjoying the snow, laughing among themselves as they negotiate the slick walkways, their exuberant intimacy reminding me of my more personal motives for coming to Japan.

At roughly age fifty, at the dawn of a new millennium, in the midst of a wildly euphoric bull market, I'm faltering. Just over a year ago, Ann, my wife, died unexpectedly. With intensely blazing grief now largely in the past, I find myself drifting, listless and unfocused, on a plateau of vague anxiety, not acute but threatening to become chronic. So I made this academic journey in the hope that Japan would distract and amuse me, give me some sort of an agenda, a jump start or some intellectual solace to help ease me into a new phase of my life.

I'm glad that Rob Eppsteiner—a charming American Soka Gakkai member with a warm heart and a good sense of humor, also about fifty—is traveling with me. Rob and I have now spent many hours together, day after day, without a tense word between us. I am easygoing, but Rob is a saint. He listens patiently to my endless fretting over the Soka Gakkai and its controversies. He takes charge of recording equipment. He hails cabs, hunts up subway entrances, and guides me through Tokyo's streets while I stand by often dazed and confused. He has become, in effect, my handler, enabling me to pour my energy into conducting interviews and indulging in speculation.

Rob and I are colleagues only now becoming friends, having met in 1993 in Chicago at the Parliament of the World's Religions, a rousing weeklong event where Buddhists, Hindus, Muslims, Christians, Jews, and New Agers from around the world engaged in what amounted to a mass demonstration of religious globalization. In our chats at the time, we discovered much in common. We both came of age in the '60s and both turned to the East, our lives transformed by the widespread vogue for Asian religions. We both have mellowed considerably, but still share many '60s-era sensibilities. Both of us continue to move in Asia-oriented circles, but he is a husband and father in a Soka Gakkai family. I'm an academic who studies the West's long fascination with Eastern spirituality, a history so creative, impulsive, and often neurotic that I've come to think of it as a passionate love affair. No small part of what I hope to accomplish is to see the history of the Soka Gakkai very clearly, which means piercing through American stereotypes about Buddhism and Japan.

Rob first pitched this trip to me as a quick one, just a few days to meet a few people, but somehow it has burgeoned into a major undertaking—multiple interviews each day; a crash course on the Lotus Sutra with scholars at the Institute of Oriental Philosophy; a visit to Kamakura, where Nichiren, the thirteenth-century reformer and inspiration behind the movement, narrowly escaped execution on the beach. The learning curve I'm treading is steep—Meiji-era modernization; Japanese militarism in the 1930s; the impact of the American occupation of Japan on the movement's history and identity.

But despite what amounts to very hard work, I am taking delight in my first trip East, my own little piece of the globalizing '90s and a dream long deferred, even though the East-West encounter has for decades been my academic meal ticket.

Much of this delight comes from the wonderful people I meet, who combine dedication, humor, and frank intelligence with startling amounts of energy, all of this tempered by a courteous formality I find appealing. But I also find communicating with them through interpreters exhausting. I must work to maintain my critical, scholarly poise while giving each interviewee 100 percent of my attention and energy. At the same time, I must keep in mind the charges of Ikeda's critics and enemies, must keep my radar up for signs of deceit or manipulation as I puzzle out what it all amounts to. This means I have to think on my feet during each interview, watch faces of interviewees and interpreters intently, and listen closely to their tone and inflection, all to gauge the import and accuracy of what they are telling me.

Fortunately, Japanese coffee is strong and I drink lots of it throughout the day. Weak coffee, I learn, is called "American." On postcards home I write: "Research goes well; Tokyo fabulous; am having a ball." But by seven each night I'm usually done in and long to cocoon in my room, to be offstage, to catch my breath and resharpen my wits, to rest up for the next day's exhilarating go-round with the Soka Gakkai and Japan.

.   .   .

By the time Rob and I leave the hotel for the train, the heat is up, the sun is bright, and the snow has melted, so we stroll slowly along a broad embankment past Sophia, a Catholic university, overlooking railroad tracks that run in a trough that was once the outer moat of the emperor's palace. Students spread blankets along the walk under arcing boughs of ancient trees, setting up daylong cherry-tree-viewing/drinking parties, with complete picnics from the look of their baskets. Shoes set neatly at the edges of blankets remind me I forgot to wear the loafers I bought at Takashimaya, an upscale department store near Shinjuku station, a busy commercial district. I like the stepping in and out of shoes one does in Japan and how it reflects a respect for public-private boundaries. But in the laced shoes I wore on the plane, I find it awkward and vaguely embarrassing.

Within an hour, Rob and I arrive by train in Hachioji, a Tokyo suburb, where we meet Rie Tsumura, a Japanese Korean woman who will be our guide and interpreter. A beautiful woman of about thirty-five, casually dressed, with long, straight black hair, Rie knows a great deal about the Soka Gakkai and speaks both formal and colloquial English. After many interviews, I've learned to depend on her skills and read her reactions. We have even brainstormed together how to handle interviews with elderly practitioners, so I can draw out from them what I need to make sense of the movement's early, controversial history.

The three of us cab up to Soka University, a flagship institution of the Soka Gakkai, where I am to attend the entrance ceremony for the class of 2005 and see Daisaku Ikeda in action. I am keen to watch him in public so I can begin to hone my judgments as to his character and charisma, to begin to assess just why it is that he makes social and political waves. Ikeda is loved by millions and held in regard by political and intellectual figures around the world. But that Ikeda is totally at odds with another, whose image and reputation as a cult leader have been shaped by Japan's tabloid press over the course of several decades. Some critics have raised legitimate concerns about Soka Gakkai and church-state issues as they are cut in Japan, but others seem to trade in rumors of thuggery, cronyism, and scandal and to damn him by innuendo.

Ikeda founded Soka University in 1971, and he and Soka Gakkai members devote immense amounts of money, time, and energy to its young women and men. Students have held a special place in the movement since its founding in 1930 by educator Tsunesaburo Makiguchi, the movement's first president, who laid the foundations for its unique form of Buddhism. Josei Toda, its second president, built the Soka Gakkai into a powerful mass movement during Japan's postwar decades. Ikeda became president in 1960 and has been the guiding force behind its globalization, a process he fosters by teaching Buddhist Humanism, a spirituality that rests on the pillars of peace, culture, and education—a noble-sounding, maybe somewhat vague philosophy that I must also puzzle out.

Makiguchi, Toda, and Ikeda have been deeply political, each in different circumstances and distinct ways, which has no doubt contributed to the many controversies in the Soka Gakkai's history. All three have also been lay leaders rather than ordained clergy. They are now seen as a lineage of Buddhist teachers, independent and authoritative in its own right—especially since 1991, when the Soka Gakkai was excommunicated from Nichiren Shoshu, a priestly sect with which it had been affiliated for more than six decades. This too is a controversy I need to figure out.

Cherry trees bloom later in Hachioji than in Tokyo, with about a week yet to peak, but pinkish-green buds frame the walks and plazas of Soka University, which, like most places I visit in Japan, is uniformly modernistic. There are no hoary temples or shrines, no burnished images of buddhas and bodhisattvas, no old mossy stone walls, nothing to suggest the romance of the samurai.

Like most things I've seen, the university is also comfortably familiar but oddly different in ways I find difficult to grasp and articulate. Wherever I travel in Japan, I attend to this uncanny sense of simultaneous sameness and difference. Japanese cities are much like those in the United States, but they are easier and safer to be in. I neither speak nor read Japanese, which contributes to this sense of being someplace I know well but do not understand. No stray conversations overheard on the street are ever understood; all signs are as delightfully opaque as Egyptian hieroglyphics. In Hachioji, a city with a bustling downtown of food courts and department stores, there's a view of Mount Fuji to be had, which signifies foreignness to me even as it is wholly familiar, the quintessential stereotype of Japaneseness.

But in most respects, Soka University is just another university. Students in T-shirts and windbreakers, packs on their backs, march from class to class or mill around making casual conversation. There is the familiar assortment of classroom, administration, laboratory, athletic, and dorm buildings, plotted out on the Musashino hills that surround Hachioji.

Still, I see clues embedded in campus architecture and design that suggest things familiar are here out of place and that this out-of-placeness is a key to understanding the Soka Gakkai and Ikeda. The facade of Ikeda auditorium where the entrance ceremony is to be held, for instance, has stylized Greek pillars and fronts on a fountain dedicated to Poseidon. A bronze Walt Whitman wearing a porkpie hat, a butterfly on his finger, lounges off to one side. Two grand statues, one of Victor Hugo, the other of Leo Tolstoy, flank the open staircase in the white marble lobby. Nearby, in the court of the Central Tower, stands a spectral Leonardo da Vinci. In the adjacent Women's College, there's a more modestly scaled statue of Marie Curie.

My sense of sameness and difference persists inside the vast auditorium. Seated on the ground floor, students in the entering class are fresh-faced but nervous. Neater and better groomed than most Americans their age, they are nonetheless familiar as young and idealistic. Parents, aunts, and uncles up in the mezzanine are proud and beaming. It could be matriculation at Harvard or the University of Wisconsin or Hamilton College, the old-line liberal arts school in New York State where I teach religious studies.

Except, of course, that everyone around me is Japanese. The fact that Japan is filled with Japanese people startled me when I first arrived in Tokyo, but I became accustomed to it quickly. Here in the audience I recall that critics would have me see all these people as cult members, either dupes of Ikeda or themselves treacherous schemers. So I play a game I will repeat frequently in the course of my journey. I first take in everything I see at face value—well-dressed middle-class people sharing a ceremonial occasion. Then I cast over the auditorium a net of suspicion: each woman then becomes a Tokyo Rose, each man a fifth columnist, the entrance ceremony itself a conference of conspirators.

It is an amusing, if ridiculous game, but with a serious intent. It's my job to sort through history, fantasy, mythology, and fact—no small matter for a historian of religion whose subject tends toward the imaginary, often extraordinary, and completely unseen. It demands a willingness to empathize with convictions that believers consider lofty and profound but others dismiss as outlandish, a capacity to entertain faith while remaining the skeptic.

But I'm surprised by the emotional flip-flop that accompanies my shift from taking things as they appear to viewing them with suspicion, a change in me from light to shadow, from trust to misgiving, from hope and goodness to distrust and bitterness. Since Ann died I simply don't know whom or what to trust, and my sense is that this emotional confusion has become more acute since my arrival in Japan.

The people next to me acknowledge my presence with courteous smiles, perhaps because I am obviously a *gaijin*, a foreigner. At five feet eleven inches, I'm not a tall man. When my weight is up, my Irish comes out, reflecting my mother's side of the family. When I am a little gaunt, I take on the Anglo-American look of my Protestant father. But here I feel large and clumsy, too conspicuously an American although I might be taken for German, English, or Australian. Many members have seen my photograph in the *Seikyo Shimbun,* the movement's daily newspaper, founded by Toda in 1951, which now has a circulation of five and a half million and is a major paper in Japan. They recognize me, I think, the American scholar who will meet with Ikeda-sensei. It is a fact that I am now known in Soka Gakkai circles and am treated a bit like a celebrity. But then again, maybe these people have no idea who I am and are simply casually polite to a foreign stranger.

I never quite know what is going on around me in Japan. Sometimes this is discomforting and feeds into my emotional flip-flopping. At other times, I enjoy it as an obliviousness to meaning and a refreshing new freedom, an escape from old habits of thought and personal identity, an unexpected opening for a process of reinvention.

I settle into my seat, positioning my notebooks and pens, fussing with earphones that will provide a simultaneous translation. But I'm soon preoccupied again by questions of sameness and difference, occasioned this time by the immense curtain that hangs at the proscenium. From where I sit, it has the soft sheen of frosted glass, but I learn later it is a woven silk tapestry donated by alumnae of the university. It recreates in fabric the famous painting by Raphael of Socrates and Plato, striding boldly together through the loggia of the Academy in ancient Athens, wrapped in flowing togas and engaged in philosophic conversation. I scribble notes: "Greek columns, Poseidon, Whitman, Hugo,

Tolstoy, Academy in Athens, etc. Book must be about why these at Japanese Buddhist-based university!"

Then suddenly, my curiosity about Japan and Ikeda is swept away. My cult-detection radar crashes. Disbelief fills an inner vacuum. My roof falls in again.

Ann is gone. In one rich flood, our entire life together comes alive in me—eighteen years of romance; ten solid ones of marriage; her oval intelligent face and wild blue eyes framed by brown-red hair. But then, as quickly and unexpectedly, she's gone. And I'm slumped in my chair, nauseous and teary, alone again, surrounded by Japanese, on the verge of becoming a sobbing gaijin in a sea of happy families. So by dint of will, I refocus on sameness and difference. Zenlike cherry blossoms in the snow. Fuji views. Socrates, Plato, Whitman, Leonardo, Curie: all of them unexpectedly, but apparently not inexplicably, Buddhist and Japanese.

· · ·

To my relief, the great curtain soon opens, revealing a scene familiar at any college or university: some eighty educators in academic robes walking onto the stage amid strains of lofty music and applause from the assembly. Some are Soka faculty and officers, others are professors, deans, and vice presidents from Universiti Putra Malaysia and China's Northwest University. References to the fragrance and fragility of cherry blossoms figure in their cordial, formal words of greeting. As the first order of business, delegates from Northwest University confer on Ikeda an honorary degree in recognition of his decades-long effort to foster amicable relations between China and Japan.

A short man with a round face and a spirit more gregarious than sage, Ikeda begins his address with banter and teasing. "So, how many of you think you will actually graduate?" he asks the incoming students. "Is this class any good? Did you get some live ones for us this year?" he asks, peering at the dean of admissions. He pretends to glower at the faculty—"Don't be arrogant. Don't be too stern. Serve students well; don't forget your income depends on their tuition."

Ikeda displays an almost maternal regard for the kids—behave but have fun, he tells them, get good sleep, eat properly. If you have no money for food, get treats from your teachers. Or write to me. But he also insists that they demand a good education. Learning is your "mystic opportunity," he counsels them, underscoring the central role played by education in the Soka Gakkai's spirituality. He then recites a poem of his own that I recognize as classic Ikeda, an expansive and romantic exhortation to victory.

My friends,
Absolutely never give up!
While sharing
    profound exchange
With new acquaintances,
While surmounting
    the wild flames
Of chaos and disarray.
Decisively seize victory
With voices raised in song
    infused with hope—
As heroes of learning,
As champions of philosophy!

Ikeda operates in a forthright style and strikes no overtly spiritual poses. He makes no cryptic allusions with koans, those cagey parables Americans associate with Buddhism. He makes no attempt to be "Zenlike" or to style himself a finger pointing at the moon. On the contrary: once he gets into the meat of his address, he lays out a stinging critique of Japanese nationalism that I find unusually hard-hitting for such a ceremonial occasion. Much to my interest, his remarks elicit rounds of applause from the apparently respectable audience of Japanese families. My radar goes back into operation.

One theme Ikeda develops throughout the address is that the spirit of the Soka Gakkai was forged in resistance. Today is the anniversary of the death of Josei Toda, his mentor, he reminds us, and also the anniversary of the founding of Soka University. Both events call to mind the heroic life of Makiguchi, the philosopher and educator who was branded a traitor by his country and died in 1944 after languishing in prison. That Makiguchi was imprisoned for noble ideas reflects the insularity of Japan, he tells us, "an island country whose people are plagued by jealousy and scheming." Makiguchi's "spirit of martyrdom" is the foundation for Soka education, whose mission is "to spread peace, culture, and education throughout the world, while forever battling narrow-minded nationalism."

Ikeda also develops a second theme, this one the violation of the long, deep relationship between China and Japan by Japanese militarists. China was the teacher of Japan for many centuries, he tells us, but then Japan turned on its mentor to inflict on it and other Asian nations unspeakable atrocities that "reveal the true nature of our country." Ikeda likens Makiguchi's work as an educator and his heroic resistance to that of Lu Xun, a Chinese scholar schooled in Japan in the early twentieth century who later fought the Japanese in China.

Going off text, Ikeda steps from behind the podium, looking down to speak intimately with the new students who sit directly before him. "Do not trust Japan. Watch out for any drift to the right. In the past that had dire consequences and fatal results," he tells them, referring to the rise of State Shinto and militarism in the decades before the Second World War. "Do you know what I am talking about?" he asks them, students born in 1983 or '84. "Do you understand what I am trying to tell you?" A few respond with a tentative "Hai, hai" ("Yes, yes"), but he remains standing before them, silent for a few long moments, allowing his remarks to sink in.

He then shifts gears, making a bold and expansive gesture as he exhorts the students to achieve excellence and transform the world—familiar, idealistic fare, even if expressed in metaphors almost unimaginable at an American university. Alluding to Xi'an, home of Northwest University and the eastern terminus of the ancient Silk Road that once linked China and Rome, he urges students to master foreign languages and to carry out exchanges for peace with other nations, each becoming a crossroads of East and West. "I want you to become people who can later look back and say, 'During my youth I gave it absolutely everything I had, and I succeeded in creating my own Silk Road!'" Emulate Zhou Enlai, first prime minister of the People's Republic of China, he tells them. Follow the three-point motto Zhou set down in his youth: be ahead of your times in your thinking; conduct yourself in the most up-to-date manner; keep abreast of the most current scholarship.

"Please strive each day to open up a new age of your own victory as a human being and of the victory of humankind," he concludes. "Cheerfully and tenaciously advance along the brilliant path of your mission—together with your professors, together with me, together with your irreplaceable friends."[1]

· · ·

Back in bright spring sunlight, Rie, Rob, and I mingle among parents and students on the plaza fronting the auditorium, within spitting distance of Whitman and Poseidon. Having translated for many scholars and journalists, Rie finds Ikeda's rhetoric familiar. Rob has been a member of Soka Gakkai for thirty-some years and has met Ikeda on numerous occasions but enjoyed the speech immensely, finding a great deal of inspiration in the words of a man he considers his mentor and teacher.

I'm preoccupied by how his remarks about Japan's insularity, his criticism of its past and its spirit, and his warning to students have put new, confusing blips on my radar. On one hand, much of what Ikeda said was surprisingly conventional and idealistic for a figure who seems always to be embroiled in controversy. On the other, I'm intrigued by his good humor, directness, and sharp geopolitical edges, none of which I had expected.

Ikeda's address also sheds light on the design of Soka University, helping me to make sense of things I'd only wondered about earlier, such as the Bridge of Literature spanning a campus pond. Rie had pointed out how the bridge is decorated with Chinese characters inscribed by Chang Shuhong, director of the Dunhuang Relics Research Institute. Dunhuang was a caravan stop on the ancient Silk Road, where a trove of Buddhist art and scripture was discovered early in the twentieth century. I now understand that the Silk Road is a metaphor to conjure with in the Soka Gakkai. *Great East-West stuff,* I think, jotting notes: "Silk Road = ancient East/West contact = Ikeda's aspiration for students – contemporary globalization."

Ikeda's remarks also provide a glimpse into the intricacies of the Soka Gakkai's relations with the Asian mainland. Earlier Rie had drawn my attention to a prominently placed cherry tree dedicated to Zhou Enlai, which had been planted in 1977 by the first class of students from the People's Republic of China. The university takes pride in having pioneered Japan-China student exchanges, so Ikeda's reference to Zhou suggests the tree's significance. Ikeda also met Zhou in 1974, their meeting leading to the forging of links between Soka University and educational institutions in China, ties that are now central to its special educational mission to northeastern Asia. These contacts and networks reflect Ikeda's concern both to overcome Japan's insularity and to rectify the damage Japan inflicted during its decades of military expansion.

Ikeda's speech also suggests why Raphael, Whitman, and others have so prominent a place at a university founded by Japanese Buddhists. His concerns about Japan's insularity help me to see the campus as a landscape that signifies a kind of cosmopolitan internationalism. Seen historically,

it is an architectural embodiment of the selective process of westernization and modernization that began to preoccupy Japan deeply in the
middle of the nineteenth century. The familiar but out-of-place quality
I sense here and in Japan as a whole is an expression of the immense
success of that extraordinary undertaking.

More specifically, I begin to see Raphael, Whitman, Leonardo,
Hugo, Zhou Enlai, and Madame Curie as people who are regarded as
among the best in the world by Ikeda and the Soka Gakkai. They are
paragons of a Soka University education, their presence on campus
functioning like the names of luminaries engraved on the friezes of old
neoclassical buildings, recalling to mind the work of great laborers who
built Western civilization. Here, however, they represent the ideals of a
liberal-arts education that is also both Buddhist and Japanese, their
out-of-placeness refreshing, even while perplexing to me.

Rob and I are soon on our way back to Tokyo, settled into a train
humming with speed, streaking through a broad rail corridor, dense
midrise exurbs extending on either side. It's years since I've ridden a
train, my image of them formed by traveling to Chicago from my
hometown in industrial Wisconsin on aging, swaying cars past abandoned factories and the backs of tenement buildings, their fire escapes
hung with wash. This is an altogether different experience—rails as
space-age transport. In Japan, it's said that if a train is to leave at 10:01,
don't bother to show at 10:02 because it's already far out of the station.

As Rob catnaps, I rework my thoughts about the Soka Gakkai and
Ikeda, casting about for an organizing principle that will help me to
sweep bits and pieces of information into a single idea or thesis.

My instincts tell me that Ikeda's Buddhist Humanism is kin to
modern liberal religions in the West. In particular, it resembles nineteenth-century liberal Protestantism, a broad reform movement in the
United States and Europe that sought—and still seeks today—to adapt
received traditions to the modern world. Like liberal Protestantism,
Buddhist Humanism is essentially a hybrid forged out of traditional
religious material and modern, secular ideas such as human rights, individualism, and democracy, and the scientific worldview.[2] It is a self-
conscious attempt to make ancient concepts and rituals potent and
relevant in a world dominated by self-interest and a capitalist economy,
by instantaneous communications, rapid social change, and teeming
megalopolises. In this light, Ikeda and the Soka Gakkai fit nicely on the
familiar side of the sameness/difference equation I sense everywhere
I turn in Japan.

This analogy may also shed light on some of the controversy. Protestant liberals were and still are a fairly benign crew, idealistic to a fault perhaps and too optimistic about the prospects for America and the world, at least for my taste. But their congenial reformism evoked and still evokes today snide assaults from secularists on the left who have no use whatsoever for religion. More vituperative attacks come from the Christian right, who consider liberals the real enemy, charging them with everything from plotting against American values to Bible-hating blasphemy.

But my instincts aren't yet honed enough to make sense of the cast of characters in Japan—militarists, Socialists, Communists, high priests, and divine emperors—which is why my learning curve is so steep. I can't seem to wrap my brain around the Japan-Buddhism-difference-unfamiliar side of the equation.

Arriving at a conceptual impasse, I decide to play tourist and enjoy scenes slipping past as the sun dips behind the towers of central Tokyo, now coming into view. The hum and shush of the train lull me into a haze in which I fantasize Ann in Japan, how I would depend on her to make sense of the people we'd be meeting together, her taste for power and politics so much more acute than my own. I always sought out radical alternatives, an idealistic streak leading me into "the '60s," Eastern spirituality, and the study of religion, all of which appealed to Ann despite her pragmatism. She jumped on board the entrepreneurial bandwagon of the '80s and began a business while I slipped into good-natured academic cynicism, the two of us quite happy with how we had differentiated.

"That balancing act is all in the past," I say aloud, rousing Rob as the train pulls into the station right at 4:47. He suggests we cab to the hotel, shed suits, slip into jeans, and head out for drinks and dinner in Shinjuku or Akasaka-Mitsuke.

• • •

A too-cheerful Japanese woman talks about light rain in Kuala Lumpur, overcast skies in Ho Chi Minh City, and full sun from Hong Kong to Hokkaido, a weather report I find fascinating, even though I make sense of it only by watching radar and graphics, another small, familiar-unfamiliar jolt to my consciousness. Notes and books are scattered about the room, some from New York, more collected here, my library on the road. Despite a good meal and an hour walking the streets with

Rob, I'm still restless. I need to bone up on Nichiren and the history of Buddhism in Japan, but fixate instead on the incomprehensibility of Japanese TV, zany talk and game shows all the wackier because I can't understand a thing.

Eventually, I turn off the TV and all the lights and sit in the dark, the twinkling, blinking lights of Shinjuku's towers inducing a calm in me I've not experienced all day.

"To study religion is your fate, not your passion," I mutter aloud, working my way into a plush armchair by an expansive window. To think critically about what most people take for granted, to focus on faith while not having one of my own . . . "I hate it."

I once relished cynical detachment from the spectacle of American "spirituality"—its born-again politicians, its New Age shamans, its cults of celebrity and civil religions, its self-serving worlds of profundity and weirdness. But my disdainful love for the over-the-top lost its savor when Ann died. Ironic hipness suddenly seemed a weak existential option, not a set of convictions but an attitude about those of others with no substance of its own.

It is, thus, a new thing for me to approach academic work in the hope of finding direction or solace, so I'm surprised to find myself warming to Nichiren, the Kamakura prophet, whose ideas form the basis of the Soka Gakkai and some forty other sects in Japan. A mover and shaker, a reformer both brilliant and irascible, Nichiren has been called the Martin Luther of Japan, even though he took on the Japanese establishment more than two centuries before Luther was born. So anti-authoritarian as to be foolhardy, so convinced of his unique grasp on truth as to be irritating, he also strikes me as a genuinely spiritual man. Given that confrontation, not decorous harmony, was one of his strong suits, Nichiren is often said to be not typically Japanese. His followers often embraced this quality by styling themselves "Nichiren's lions," their seeing in his passionate nature not hardheadedness but courage, fortitude, compassion, majesty, and courage.

Nichiren's Buddhism, like all forms of Buddhism, is based on the teaching of Shakyamuni, the *muni* or sage of the Sakya clan who lived in the sixth century BCE, north of what is now India. Shakyamuni identified life's central problem as *dukkha*—suffering, stress, frustration, that sense of things always being out of joint. He also taught that one can put an end to suffering by following what he called the *dharma*, the teaching or law that is the path to genuine happiness, wisdom, and freedom. As a result of this discovery, Shakyamuni was called *buddha*, "awakened," this state or quality becoming one of his many names—the Awakened One, "the Buddha."

The Buddha taught that suffering is rooted in false ideas about the permanence of the soul or self and of all phenomena. To cling to such ideas is to cling to an illusion, the futile defense of which is the ultimate source of dukkha. Another of his teachings is a sophisticated version of the biblical notion that one reaps what one sows, that "what goes around, comes around," which is described by Buddhists as the law of cause and effect or the law of karma. According to the Buddha, actions or karma born in false egotism, such as anger, craving, lust, greed, and the like, bind people to illusion, which leads to suffering as certainly as a cause leads to an effect. He further taught that people can free themselves from illusion created by bad karma in the past by taking positive action in the present, a process Buddhists often refer to as transforming one's poison into medicine.

Nichiren Buddhism is in the Mahayana tradition, a broad current of teaching that predominates in East Asia. As Buddhism moved from India to China, it absorbed aspects of Confucianism and Taoism, which gradually recast Shakyamuni's teachings. Scriptures that re-expressed his ideas, such as the Diamond, Pure Land, and Lotus sutras, became authoritative as new philosophical schools proliferated before taking root in Korea and then in Japan, where Buddhism also absorbed elements from their indigenous traditions.

Drawing on both Indian and East Asian sources, Mahayana philosophers developed an understanding of the universe and society quite different from that of theologians in the West. Both the universe and society are seen to have come into being not through the work of a creator but through the law of cause and effect, a premise that many argue makes Buddhism more compatible with modern science than is Western theism. For centuries, Buddhists have pictured the universe as infinitely vast and eternal, likening it to an interconnected net or web in which negative and positive karma work within and among the myriad beings inhabiting it. Society itself is essentially a network of spiritual and ethical relationships in which people's actions matter immensely. Both universe and society are driven not by fate, destiny, blind energy, or the will of God but by an endless, collective chain of causes and effects set in motion by the actions of individual people.

Within this framework, Mahayana Buddhists place a particular emphasis on the bodhisattva, an awakened being who makes a commitment to awaken others to the nature of suffering and freedom, thus exemplifying the essence of Shakyamuni's teachings. On the most exalted level, a bodhisattva is a mythological being and an object of veneration, an exemplary model of the wisdom and compassion of the Buddha who reincarnates through endless lifetimes, always aiding others to alleviate their suffering. On the human level, a bodhisattva is a person committed to becoming awakened in order to awaken others and teach them how to walk the path. Bodhisattvas demand of themselves a spiritual and ethical orientation to life that amounts to a vow to create good causes that make for good effects, thus doing their part to set in motion a positive chain reaction in the web of relationships that comprise our world.

Nichiren, the son of a fisherman, who pursued the truth through the dominant Buddhist institutions of Kamakura Japan, was one among many Mahayana teachers and reformers over the centuries to give substance to these ideas. "If Japan ever produced a prophet or a religious man of prophetic zeal, Nichiren was the man," writes Masaharu Anesaki, an early-twentieth-century historian of religion at University of Tokyo, in his classic study *Nichiren: The Buddhist Prophet.* "One of the most learned men of his time," he was "a strong man of combative temperament, an eloquent speaker, a powerful writer, and a man of tender heart."[3]

Anesaki's account makes clear how, seven centuries after he took up his mission, Nichiren could fire the imaginations of Ikeda, Toda, and Makiguchi and inspire a dynamic lay Buddhist movement dedicated to social transformation. Like many of his contemporaries, Nichiren understood himself to live in the age of *mappo,* the latter day of the dharma, a long era of turmoil during which Shakyamuni's original teachings had become corrupt and needed a vigorous restatement. Convinced he grasped the true essence of those teachings, he vigorously propagated his views, lovingly taught his disciples, and struggled against rival Buddhist schools for the soul of Japan. The record of his efforts is contained in his writings, or *Gosho,* the authoritative religious texts for all Nichiren Buddhists.

Nichiren was influenced by Shinto, Japan's indigenous tradition; Confucian social ethics imported from China; and a range of Japanese schools of Buddhist philosophy and practice then current. From these, he fashioned a unique understanding of the "mystic law," a phrase used within the Soka Gakkai today to refer to dharma. For Nichiren, freedom and happiness were not to be gained by rebirth into an otherworldly Pure Land, as claimed by the priestly Jodo sect that dominated the Kamakura government. Nor was it to be achieved through the contemplative detachment taught by Zen masters, or through the complex rituals of esoteric schools, or by adhering to the numerous rules of monasticism.

According to Jacqueline Stone, a Princeton University authority on Buddhism in medieval Japan, Nichiren developed his teachings in two interrelated ways. First, he preached a passionate fealty to Buddhist principles as expressed in the Lotus Sutra, a foundational scripture of Mahayana Buddhism. Second, he taught that not just monks, nuns, priests, and other clerics had the capacity to awaken themselves but also laypeople, who could do so in the midst of struggles they encountered in ordinary life. They could, in Anesaki's words, restore a "primeval connection with the eternal Buddha" as laborers, warriors, merchants, and farmers, as wives and husbands.[4] Nichiren understood the essence of this inner awakened nature to be expressed in the chant "Nam-myoho-renge-kyo," a phrase thought to embody the essence of the teaching of the Lotus Sutra.

Responding to the widespread turmoil in medieval Japan, Nichiren publicly criticized dominant Buddhist schools in his preaching and teaching and in his *Rissho Ankoku Ron*, a treatise whose title is often translated "On Establishing the Correct Teaching for the Peace of the Land." In it he charged that the government, by supporting corrupt forms of Buddhism, led Japan astray and drew down upon it many calamities. He prophesied that continued unrighteousness would draw down further disasters—more famine, war, rebellion, and even invasion by the Mongols, who dominated the Asian mainland—as surely as bad causes lead to bad effects. Nichiren's charges angered authorities, so he endured persecution and was exiled twice; but he remained certain to the end that he and his disciples were bodhisattvas with a mission to propagate true Buddhism and thus to renovate Japan.

. . .

Tokyo in the dark is much like Houston or Chicago or almost any large city—a vast plain of lights punctuated by clustered, half-dark towers whose mirrored skins reflect the city back on itself. From high in the New Otani, where I am nestled down with a drink from a basket of treats sent by Ikeda, the hieroglyphics I find so marvelous in their indecipherability lose distinctiveness; they become neon blur, just as our unique individualities dissolve into the mass when viewed from a distance.

In such moments of quiet, I can admit to myself that modern religion exhausts me—the daily assertion of our unique spiritual worth, our endlessly putting meaningful constructions on our being—Christian, Buddhist, Muslim, Jew; Marxist, patriot, rationalist, feminist, cynic.

Raised Roman Catholic, I'm mystically inclined and still appreciate a well-executed mass, but I don't believe in the Bible, even though the biblical worldview structures much of my thinking. I don't believe in the Lotus Sutra either, but I respect the fact that, over the centuries, it has played a major role in lives of millions, probably billions, of people in an East Asian, Lotus Buddhist tradition of great power and sophistication.

A compound of philosophy, parable, and poetry, the Lotus Sutra is a dazzling, sometimes maddening exploration of both the illusions that cause suffering and the Buddha's methods of healing. Its tales of children who escape from a burning building, its appearing treasure towers and disappearing cities, its poisons that turn out to be medicines are as central to East Asian Mahayana Buddhism as are the parables of Jesus to Christianity. Composed around the second century of the Common Era in India, this sutra is considered by devout Buddhists to be the last and most complete of Shakyamuni's teachings. Given a systematic, doctrinal interpretation in China, it was introduced into Japan in the ninth century by Saicho, who also founded a great monastic compound on Mount Hiei, where four centuries later Nichiren took up his studies.

Wherever I dip into the sprawling text—Shinjuku's cold lights becoming distant, a single reading lamp now lit, my hotel room becoming my cocoon—I see, once again, the alternative spirituality I searched for in my adolescent quests. The marvelous intelligence of Hinduism and Buddhism! The extravagant, yet persuasive and plausible, worldviews! All that led me to this problematic profession in which I make my money—the study of religion!

I am soon drawn into the universe of the Lotus Sutra, which is cyclical and eternal, the classic Asian Hindu-Buddhist perspective. In contrast, Christians tend to conceive of the world in a linear framework—an assumption inherited from the Bible, which begins with the creation of the world by God and ends with its fiery conflagration. The sutra, however, opens with an aged Shakyamuni gathering his disciples before him on a hilltop in India, Eagle or Vulture Peak, to give them a final teaching, a scene as well known to Nichiren Buddhists as the crucifixion of Christ is to Christians. But this scene soon explodes when a brilliant light bursts from Shakyamuni's brow to illuminate the universe in all directions. He then reveals to his disciples that he has been teaching them through many lifetimes in a universe that is uncreated and unending, in which past, present, and future are linked in what one academic called "the coincidence of the historical and transcendent."[6]

Like the Bible, the Lotus Sutra claims to reveal a universal truth, but it does so in its own unique terms. Christians find truth revealed in the Sermon on the Mount and the life and death of Jesus, which are the foundations of a universal ethic of love of God, self, and other. In the sutra, Buddhists find truth in the universality of the dharma. On one hand, this universality is expressed in the concept of nondualism—all distinctions such as body and mind, self and other, life and death are understood to be relative concepts. To cling to these as ultimate is to cling to illusions that cause suffering. On the other, universality is also expressed in Shakyamuni's teachings about the true nature of the Buddha. Buddha, he tells his disciples, is not the man who once taught in India nor a cosmic being, but an eternal essence or principle that pervades the entire universe. Thus, to live in oneness beyond dualism is to become awakened to the universal Buddha nature within all beings.

The Lotus Sutra also teaches that Buddhism, like Christianity, is a missionary religion. Jesus's injunction—"Go therefore and teach all nations"—has long inspired Christians to spread the Gospel and to build up the church progressively as a kingdom of God on earth, a process understood to come to its eventual climactic end in a final renovation of heaven and earth. The Buddhist mission in the Lotus Sutra, however, operates within Asia's traditional cyclical framework and is inspired by the Buddha's revelation on Eagle Peak. In the course of his preaching, Shakyamuni reveals to his disciples a great assembly of bodhisattvas arising from the earth. These are disciples he taught in the distant past, he tells them, but they are seen as they rise up to teach and preach true Buddhism in the future. These bodhisattvas of the earth have risen and will rise again and again, striving in each lifetime to fulfill their vow to aid suffering people.

Later that night, too tired to do more reading, lying in bed, still edgy with jet lag, I begin to flip-flop again, as I struggle with all that I'm experiencing and learning. When a sinister mood grips me, I look back on an unreal, surreal week, always at the mercy of the Japanese, lost in a forest of their hieroglyphics, with no reality check other than my gauging of facial expressions and my trusting to what seem to be their good hearts. I cringe, muscles cramping beneath the sheets—"You're a pigeon, a sitting duck, a way-overeducated gaijin ripe for the plucking."

But then I flip-flop and am buoyantly manic, chuckling with delight as I picture Socrates, Leonardo, Curie, Whitman—maybe even Zhou Enlai, who knows?—among the bodhisattvas of the earth revealed on Eagle Peak, all of them returning again and again from their journeys into death to teach and preach humanistic Buddhism.

Eventually, desperately in need of sleep and too tired to drive myself crazy any longer, I turn to Ann and try to imagine where she is and what she is doing, missing her, needing her on a journey I would never have taken had she lived.

CHAPTER 2

Creating Valuc

Many of the familiar elements in Ikeda's Buddhist Humanism can be directly traced to the philosophy of Tsunesaburo Makiguchi, whose life spanned the decades during which the Japan we know today came into being. Makiguchi was born three years into the Meiji Restoration, the beginning of Japan's rapid transformation from an isolated, tradition-bound island world into a modern, cosmopolitan nation. He died a year before its defeat in World War II, the opening of a second pivotal era in its making. Makiguchi dedicated his life to adapting humanistic values usually identified with the West to the needs of the Japanese, a passion he shared with many of his contemporaries during the conflict-ridden modernization process set in motion by the Meiji Restoration. But his first and greatest aspiration was to reform Japanese education, an undertaking inspired by modern Western philosophers and educators.

Many of the less familiar, Lotus Buddhist elements in Ikeda's humanism can also be traced to Makiguchi, the result of his attempt to realize his vision by turning to religion. At the age of fifty-seven, Makiguchi embraced the philosophy of the Lotus Sutra and allied himself with the seven-hundred-year-old Buddhist sect Nichiren Shoshu, one of forty-some Buddhist groups in Japan based on Nichiren's teachings. He then began to develop a philosophy that was a hybrid of West and East and in 1930 founded the Soka Kyoiku Gakkai, the Value Creating Education Society, a movement of reform-minded educators.

Makiguchi's hybrid of secular ideals and ancient religion form the core of a dynamic legacy he bequeathed to Toda and Ikeda, his successors as presidents of Soka Gakkai. Part of the dynamism in this legacy can be attributed to his ideas: his fusion of modern West and ancient Buddhism proved to be fertile ground on which to build a religious, political, and cultural movement in Japan, a movement that began to establish a global reach around 1960. Another part of the dynamism can be attributed to an unlikely alliance Makiguchi also bequeathed to them, one between lay educators, progressive and innovative in outlook, and Nichiren Shoshu priests, who often displayed deeply conservative religious and institutional instincts.

The controversies in Soka Gakkai's history begin too with Makiguchi and must be considered a part of his legacy. Throughout his life, Makiguchi's attempts to implement his ideas were blocked, first by a highly regimented education system, later and more seriously by the rise of a militaristic state. For both Toda and Ikeda, Makiguchi's persistence in the face of frustration became a model of endurance; his unwillingness to bend or break before the government, one of principled resistance; his death in Sugamo Prison, a powerful example of heroic courage in the face of tyranny. As the founding mentor of this teaching lineage, Makiguchi is also the point of departure for developments that would lead to the appearance of Socrates, Victor Hugo, Walt Whitman, and all the rest at Soka University.

.   .   .

I shower, shave, dress, and say good-bye to Ann, whose picture sits on my dressing table, then head down the hall to the elevator, giving nods and small bows in response to those of the young, bright-faced housekeepers. In the lobby gift shop, the woman who's there every day—some seventy years old, as heavily made-up, wizened, and urbane as her counterpart in a midtown Manhattan hotel—sees me coming and has a pack of cigarettes ready.

"Good morning, Camel Filter, soft," she says, each syllable resonant with the sounds of her native language. I pass her too many yen and she returns correct change in neatly arranged piles of coins, a transaction we negotiate with a small tray, not hand to hand. I had fantasies of quitting smoking in Asia, some vestigial romanticism still at work in me about Buddhism, asceticism, and purity until I discovered that Japan is very smoke friendly. Anyway, this is not the time to engage in austerities, on a journey I like to think of as my bull market perk, my own little go at globalization.

Rob is already out hailing a cab, so soon we are off to Shinanomachi, a busy, comfortably fashionable neighborhood in the Shinjuku district of central Tokyo, which is action central of the Soka Gakkai, the "Value Creating Society," often referred to as the Gakkai, the society, or simply SG. Most of its major institutions are headquartered in Shinanomachi, each with its own substantial building, all within easy walking distance, a formidable and most tangible expression of the legacy of the life and work of Makiguchi.

The headquarters of Soka Gakkai–Japan, an organization claiming some ten million members (roughly one in ten Japanese), are here, as is Min-On, the Gakkai's cultural affairs organization, and the substantial new building of the Women's Division, all of them a five-minute walk from the modest home of Ikeda and his wife, Kaneko. The office building housing *Seikyo Shimbun,* the movement's daily newspaper, and those housing Komeito, a political party founded by Ikeda, are about half a mile away. At the time of the break between SG and Nichiren Shoshu, the Gakkai was banned from the temple at Taisekiji. Since then, this area has become a magnet for members, who come for conferences and workshops, visit Gakkai bookstores, relax in its vest-pocket parks, and stop by headquarters to leave messages for Ikeda, who, I am told, attempts to answer each one himself.

Gakkai operations are larger than I'd imagined, my only previous exposure to them being in the United States, where the organization is comparatively small and, now at least, low key. The members thronging the streets create a festive air, but I wonder about the power all this real estate represents, given the charge that Ikeda works patiently to take over Japan. I also don't know what to make of Komeito or Komei, the Gakkai-supported political party. For decades, it was opposed to the conservative Liberal Democratic Party or LDP, which has dominated Japan since 1955. In October 1999, however, in the midst of major political realignments, a retailored Komeito joined with the LDP to form the current ruling coalition, a shift that seems to justify the suspicion of critics. That religion is deeply involved in politics I know from the history of the United States, but how this relationship plays out in Japan is another unknown part of the sameness/difference equation, one that feeds my suspicions and makes it hard to differentiate paranoia from critical insight.

I conduct most interviews in the Soka Gakkai International building where writers, administrators, and translators coordinate the activities of the movement worldwide. In free moments, I've gotten to know a few people, all of them raised in Gakkai families, and find their motives and spirit reassuring. Mr. Iwazumi, who heads the operation, graduated from Tokyo University and worked for a time in the shipbuilding industry, but came to the Gakkai in search of a more meaningful profession. Andy Sumimoto downsized too, moving here after graduate school at Columbia University and years in Singapore where he worked in financial services. I find Mari's work as a freelance interpreter particularly intriguing because she is privy to aspects of globalization entirely foreign to me. A woman of about thirty-five, crisp and competently professional, she sometimes pinch-hits for Rie, but she is always rushing off to other appointments to interpret for contractors working on missile defense research or for fast-food franchisers.

After days filled with back-to-back interviews, I have a day off with plans to combine tourism and research into modern Japan. I want to establish pictures in my mind that illustrate Japanese history, a subject that, like most Americans, I know very little about. I hope to educate my instincts so I am better able to assess what Ikeda and the Gakkai are really all about. So Rob, Rie, and I head off in a movement minibus to visit the temple complex at Asakusa, said to be the oldest in the city, and to take a look at the new Edo-Tokyo Museum.

I study vistas on the long drive from Shinanomachi to Asakusa—new spiking towers and shiny department store clusters; vast stretches of '60s-vintage midrise office and apartment buildings; intermittent glimpses into the greenspace in the heart of the city where the emperor's palace stands, hidden from public view behind banks of high trees. Since World War II, the emperor has been considered only human, not also divine, but he remains a symbol of tradition, special and newsworthy but also taken for granted, much like the British monarchy before all its recent scandals.

Occasionally, I peer from the elevated expressway into small Shinto shrines, quiet spots of dark wood and green in the dense concrete fabric of modern Tokyo. They remind me of Puritan graveyards, parklike with tombstones askew, unexpectedly sighted in America's gritty northeast cities. As a historian of modern religion, I know not to dismiss such antique structures as charming, but meaningless, flotsam adrift on sprawling urban seas. They are better seen as buoys marking shoals, submerged rocks, and deep currents of power that move just beneath the surface of today's ostensibly secular cities.

I again begin to work out an analogy in my notes. "Shinto is to Japan as Puritan/Protestant is to the U.S. Both form deep-structure values of a civilization. Both operate in public and behind the scenes. Both appeal to nationalist sentiments to buttress their authority. And vice versa."

Limits to the analogy log in immediately. Shinto, the indigenous tradition of Japan, has been a force for millennia, not a few centuries. It long ago absorbed elements from Confucian philosophy and Buddhist religion, both imports from the Asian mainland. It remains potent today thanks to its long association with Japan's folkways, social order, and emperor. Shinto and Protestant theologies also differ completely. The former is polytheistic, its deities or *kami* manifest in nature and social relations. Festive, at times bawdy, Shinto is comparable to the native traditions of North America, while American Protestantism is classically European, adamantly monotheistic, and set to the service of a New World nation-state. "Both still legitimate a modern civil religion," I scribble in my notes, peering at Tokyo as we creep through traffic; "both are cultural default positions on a meta-political plane."

. . .

The story of why Makiguchi—a man who began his professional life philosophizing about human happiness—was charged with treason and died in prison is a part of the epic history of the modernization of Japan.

Makiguchi and his contemporaries thought deeply about East and West, tradition and innovation, responsibility and freedom, but had to contend with a powerful authoritarian streak in their society with origins in Tokugawa Japan, an era extending roughly from the seventeenth century to the nineteenth. Under the Tokugawas, Japan's people were ranked hierarchically, with samurai, the society's elite, at the top. Throughout most of this period, Buddhism and Shinto functioned symbiotically, the government using both to suppress a small Christian community. Buddhist institutions became part of an extensive surveillance system, its priests charged with registering births and deaths and tracking people's movements in villages and towns. Eventually, Buddhism too became suspect because of its foreign origins, despite its many centuries in Japan—a trend that later accelerated. Seeking stability and conformity, the Tokugawa shoguns also closed Japan to the world, a seclusion that ended only in 1853 when American warships under Matthew Perry appeared in Tokyo Bay bearing demands for diplomatic ties and access to markets, an event that helped to precipitate the Meiji Restoration.

Meiji Restoration refers both to a coup d'état that overthrew the shogunate and restored the emperor in 1868 and to events that marked the next three decades. So called because the emperor and his reign took the name Meiji, or "Enlightened Rule," this was Japan's modern revolution, comparable to but different from and later than those in the West. Like them, it established a modern nation, revitalized a civilization, and created a national mythology or civil religion. Like them, too, its meaning continues to be debated. Scholarly, political, and popular evaluations of the Meiji revolution have shifted, often radically, during the past century and a half.

The twin tasks facing Meiji leaders were to forge a synthesis between elements of Western modernity and the traditions of Japan and to foster unity in what amounted to a new nation. That nations of the West dominated India, China, and swaths of Southeast Asia lent great urgency to this task, as did the expansion of Russia to the Pacific. As a consequence, much of the energy released by the Restoration was devoted to playing catch-up with the West in an effort to protect Japan's autonomy. In early Meiji, as delegations traveled west to study and bring home philosophy, technology, and political ideas, the Japanese first got their reputation as brilliant imitators. Catchphrases from this time—"Civilization and Enlightenment"; "Japanese Spirit and Western Techniques"; "A Rich Country and a Strong Military"—only begin to suggest the westernization strategies adopted and their political ramifications.[1]

The transformation of traditional Japan took place on many fronts and with an astonishing rapidity. Old feudal estates became transformed into prefectures, modern administrative units, almost overnight. The emperor and his household moved from ancient Kyoto to Tokyo, where the new imperial state was showcased in large-scale building projects inspired by European monarchies. The first railroad was constructed only in 1872, but by the turn of the century numerous industries flourished, often created by government fiat and subsequently privatized. Meiji marks the origin of the great *zaibatsu,* family-owned industrial and financial combines that came to dominate Japan. In 1889, a Western-style constitution was adopted that melded the sovereignty of the emperor with circumscribed rights for the people and new parliamentary procedures. The Diet, Japan's parliament, was established the following year, late by Western standards but the first national assembly in modern Asia.

A uniquely Japanese form of civil religion played a crucial role in forging a national identity among people who had long understood themselves in terms of region and clan. The emperor, for eight centuries little more than a figurehead, played a key role in this process, serving as a symbol of both Japan's antiquity and its modernity. The emperor's ancient authority, writes one historian, had been that of a "magical king in charge of the fertility of rice" and "chief priest for the important rite of the harvest festival." As revived by Meiji leaders, this role was reexpressed in the concept of *seikyo itchi,* the unity of ritual and government, a phrase that conveys the unique way ceremonial and political authority were fused in the person of the emperor.[2]

This restored emperor became the linchpin in a religious system designed to rally people to the cause of economic and political modernization, which was progressively institutionalized into what would later be called State or Shrine Shinto. Between the Meiji Restoration and World War II, the role of Shinto in the political life of the nation was central to debates over Japan's identity as a modern nation. In 1890, teaching it became mandatory in all schools after the government issued the Imperial Rescript on Education. This required the Japanese people to express morality and identity in the form of loyalty to the emperor, a dogma inculcated in students through memorization and ritual until Japan's defeat in World War II.

Social unrest accompanied these transformations, whose political meaning traditionalists and progressives hotly contested. The process was often infused on either side by a sense of loyalty to group and dedication to duty, lingering expressions of the samurai spirit of the Tokugawas. The result was that Japan became, in the words of Masao Maruyama, a leading postwar scholar, "the first centralized nation-state in the Far East," but one flawed with a "structural imbalance." A modernizing elite stood "at the apex of Japanese society, engaged in ceaseless struggle to reach the pinnacle of world prominence," while most people remained embedded in an older way of life in which "traditional forms of social consciousness were tenaciously rooted."[3]

Americans reading Makiguchi's philosophy today will find in it many of the familiar ideas found in Ikeda's Buddhist Humanism—the dignity of the individual, the cultivation of the whole person, an essentially optimistic outlook on life. So fundamentally sane and healthy are Makiguchi's ideas that without a grasp of the times in which he lived, it remains mystifying why he was ever charged with treason and imprisoned.

There are two distinct periods in Makiguchi's public life, each generating controversies that point to his tragic end. During the first he was a secularist, his passions the philosophy of education and teaching. This period was marked by his growing frustration with an educational system that valued competition and rote memorization and was devoted to shaping young people into loyal subjects proficient in the skills required for modernization. In the second, Makiguchi took up Nichiren's Buddhist philosophy and religion, a move that gradually transformed his frustration into religious resistance to Japan's imperial civil religion.

Makiguchi was born in 1871 in the fishing village of Arahama ("Desolate Beach") in northwestern Japan, where he was raised by an uncle. At fourteen he moved alone to Hokkaido, the northernmost of Japan's main islands, then a frontier region rich in resources and important to Meiji strategies of political unification and economic development. He studied at the Hokkaido Normal School, a teacher's college, graduating in 1893 at the age of twenty-two. He devoted much of the next thirty-five years to primary education as a teacher, administrator, and would-be reformer, first in Hokkaido and later in Tokyo.

During this time, he published respected works on geography and community while compiling extensive notes, drawn both from classroom experience and from extensive reading, for his theories of education. These consist of closely argued discussions of ideas that range from those of Socrates to the British utilitarians and German neo-Kantians, the latter two then in vogue in Japan. He also devoted much effort to proposals for educational reform, conceiving of his work as a systematic philosophy and a scientific pedagogy, and envisioning its eventual publication in twelve volumes.

The ideas Makiguchi developed at this time form the more familiar elements in the intellectual legacy he bequeathed to the Gakkai, where progressive education remains of great importance today. His arguments are often both subtle and dense, but three central ideas—happiness, value creation, and benefit—are disarming in their essential simplicity, closely resembling the humanistic ideal of an American liberal-arts education. It is not without reason that he is sometimes likened to America's own John Dewey and is considered the guiding spirit of Soka University.

Makiguchi saw as the goal of education human happiness, by which he meant neither self-serving egotism nor sensual gratification, but the satisfaction to be derived from responsible selfhood in the context of community. He considered happiness to be a lifelong process of creating such satisfaction, an undertaking he called "value creation," which he understood to be the essence of what it means to be human. Benefit factored into his theory as a kind of value-oriented decision-making—to be truly happy and to create value, one chooses to engage in activities that are life-enhancing and of benefit both to oneself and to the community. Teaching students to develop the capacity and intelligence to make such choices was, in essence, the goal of Makiguchi's value-creation education.

Makiguchi's theories were shaped by contemporary debates over the future of Japan, but there was always a universalistic element to his thinking, inherited both from his Western philosophical sources and from the cosmopolitan agenda of the early Meiji Restoration. Thus Makiguchi understood happiness, value creation, and benefit to apply to self and society—be that home, neighborhood, town, nation, or world community, a globalizing thrust in his thought later made far more explicit by Ikeda.

A dignified man with a special compassion for disadvantaged students, Makiguchi was also stern, stubborn, and uncompromising when it came to principles; this streak in his personality apparently contributed to his frequent transfer from one school to another. In 1932, he went into retirement and his career as a professional educator came to an end.

About that time, he also turned to Nichiren, a move of utmost importance to the legacy he bequeathed to Soka Gakkai, but one that dramatically increased the stakes in his personal life. As Japan moved toward the Sino-Japanese War of 1937–45 and war with the United States in the Pacific, Makiguchi's uncompromising nature and his Buddhist convictions set him on a collision course with State Shinto and the emperor system, the two pillars of prewar Japan.

. . .

I snap out of my reverie when we arrive in Asakusa, which was the city's adult entertainment zone in the Edo or Tokugawa period. Once a hot spot for the geishas and Kabuki theater favored by Edokko merchants, it is now a standard stop on the circuit of international tourists.

The Asakusa complex has both a Buddhist temple and a Shinto shrine, a typical arrangement that reflects how the two religions have long coexisted in a usually happy, but sometimes difficult, relationship in Japan. The main temple, Sensoji, is Buddhist and is dedicated to a Kannon or Kuan Yin, a female bodhisattva of compassion venerated in China and throughout East Asia. But the nearby Shinto shrine memorializes the temple's seventh-century founders as kami, in effect christening the temple and its Chinese bodhisattva with Japaneseness.

Sensoji's roots run deep into Japan's history. It was a center of the Kannon cult in the twelfth and thirteenth centuries, when typically Japanese forms of Buddhism that remain powerful today—Zen, Pure Land, and Nichiren Buddhism—first began to emerge. A major temple was built here in the seventeenth century under the Tokugawas, who ruled Japan with Edo as their capital city. Destroyed by American fire-bombs during World War II, Sensoji was later reconstructed.

Rob and I sit watching people offer incense to Kannon in Sensoji's forecourt and then walk to the nearby Shinto shrine, where they clap hands together to awaken the kami and take a small slip of paper, an amulet or talisman, a kind of spiritual souvenir, to be placed on a family altar at home. Rie looks bored by this too-familiar scene, but I take a moment to develop the Shinto-Protestant analogy. "Sensoji and its market streets recall Philadelphia's Independence Square or Boston's Quincy Market. Both rehabs of national ethos/mythology. Old history still potent today but with a tourism/nostalgia gloss."

"This makes it clearer to me why Makiguchi ran into trouble," I say to Rob, reading the scene before us against the books I've been study-ing on Japan's religious history. Shinto and Buddhism are so enmeshed as to be day and night, the first about birth, marriage, community, the second about the metaphysics and rituals of death and rebirth, the two for centuries complementary parts of a single system.

But Makiguchi balked and held fast to the dharma alone, placing the morality of its universal law above the claims of Shinto and the emperor. The Japanese have an expression—the nail that sticks up gets pounded down—which is often cited to describe powerful conformist tendencies in Japanese society. David O'Brien evokes it in his *To Dream of Dreams: Religious Freedom and Constitutional Politics in Postwar Japan* to illus-trate how Japan privileges collectivism and conformity over personal rights in matters of religion even today.[4] "Makiguchi was another nail pounded down," I say to Rob, who seems to enjoy listening to me struggle to hone a few academic insights.

Rie diplomatically interrupts our conversation to remind us that we should head to the museum, a striking, eight-storied, ultramodern building that houses exhibits that illustrate feudal Japan morphing into modernity. Its displays enthrall me—Western living rooms tacked onto traditional wood-and-paper homes; photos of the first Ginza district, which was built in brick, then a novelty, to showcase Japan's progress; the East-West mix in the artifacts of the lives of the *modan gaaru*, the "modern girls," of Tokyo, their styles setting off a debate over the morality of Japan's new modernity.[5] An entire history of similarity and difference!

I run through the museum quickly, absorbing visual impressions, storing up images of popular culture to flesh out academics, always with an eye to figuring out Japan and Ikeda. But I stop in my tracks before a video sequence of the firebombing of Tokyo that two elderly men watch intently, silent and pensive, their brows furrowed. I think I've seen the footage before but in a very different setting, in old episodes of *Victory at Sea*, maybe, or in a Hollywood movie about heroics and wartime romance. In this context, the images of urban conflagration are raw and alarming but strangely satisfying, their in placeness here in Tokyo a revelation of suffering and evil unvarnished by glamour and civil myths.

Later, we eat in one of the Tokyo shops that serve trim sandwiches— no half-pound of roast beef, just enough food, a discreet lunch like those served by ladies at bridge clubs in the '50s. *Ann would find this very civilized*, I think, eating the single caramel served for dessert. Rie and Rob are talking Gakkai and other conversations around me run in Japanese, so I tune out and fall into a reverie, a raft of images of old Japan soon sweeping over me. Cheap tin toys and transistor radios, crazed kamikaze pilots, Godzilla in Tokyo. Karate, kendo, ninjas, and judo. Tempura, sushi, sashimi, and miso. Haiku, koans, geishas, kimonos. Honda, Yamaha, Sony, Toyota. I'm shocked by the utter banality of my instinctual knowledge of a nation that has been America's greatest Asian ally for more than a half-century. "Not much to go on," I say aloud, which draws Rie and Rob's attention. "Oh. Nothing," I lie, unwilling to admit that I'm often stunned by my ignorance of Japan.

. . .

Like most Japanese, Makiguchi was exposed to Buddhism as a child and he later had some contact with Japanese Christianity, but his mature outlook on life was always that of a modern secular scholar. During the years of work on his pedagogy, he remained skeptical about religion's dogmatic claims, all the while respectful of humans' capacity for wonder, mystery, awe, and sanctity.

When Makiguchi eventually took Buddhism seriously, it was because it enhanced, rather than overturned, these convictions, as he found in Nichiren much that lent support to his educational theories. The Lotus Sutra's teaching that true Buddha is awakened wisdom fitted his own view that creating value is the essence of being human. The idea that bad and good acts reap their own punishment or reward gave a religious cast to his conviction that decision-making ought to be value-oriented. The connection he taught between self and society took on profound depth in light of Buddhist nondualism and moral heft with its ethical teachings based on the compassion of the Buddha and bodhisattvas. But even with his new religious convictions, Makiguchi remained a rationalist in outlook, rejecting mystical, otherworldly views of the dharma to understand it in terms of happiness on earth.

Makiguchi's Nichiren-based ideas are an expression of what Heinz Bechert called "Buddhist modernism," the self-conscious effort to adapt Buddhism to modern society, a movement that has surfaced in many parts of Asia over the course of the past century.[6] A fusion of modern, liberal pedagogical ideals with ancient Lotus Buddhism, Makiguchi's philosophy is a hybrid worldview that would be the starting point for Toda in the postwar years and, after him, for Ikeda. But the legacy Makiguchi bequeathed to his successors consisted of more than a modern interpretation of ancient Buddhist ideas. Four dimensions of his legacy suggest why Toda and Ikeda would need to clarify and interpret what he passed on to them, a trial-and-error process they took up in the midst of constantly changing circumstances in postwar Japan.

First, Makiguchi's conversion made available to Toda and Ikeda the resources of the Lotus Sutra—its compelling cosmic worldview, universalism, and sense of mission. All of these came to his successors tied to his ideas about happiness, value creation, and benefit.

The Lotus Sutra, however, also came tied to Nichiren Shoshu, an obscure, seven-hundred-year-old sect Makiguchi joined that claimed to be the only orthodox expression of Nichiren's teaching. As a result, Nichiren Shoshu doctrines, rituals, and institutions—traditional forms that often ran against the grain of Makiguchi's modernist spirit—formed a second dimension of his legacy. Tensions between the Gakkai and Nichiren Shoshu surfaced frequently under Toda and Ikeda but exploded in 1991, when the Nichiren Shoshu high priest, Nikken Abe, excommunicated the Soka Gakkai.

A third dimension consisted of three "secret" or "hidden" laws Nichiren discovered in the Lotus Sutra and expounded upon in his *Gosho* (Writings), the chief scriptural authority for all Nichiren Buddhists. These three laws shaped Nichiren Buddhist philosophy and practice for centuries and remain at the core of Gakkai spirituality.

The first is *daimoku,* the primary religious practice in the Soka Gakkai and all Nichiren sects. Daimoku is the chant "Nam-myoho-renge-kyo," a phrase that literally means "Hail [or Devotion] to the Lotus Sutra of the dharma." Drawing on ancient ideas about the efficacy of chanted words, Nichiren saw daimoku as a practice that restated the essence of both Shakyamuni's teachings and the Lotus Sutra in a way suited to the age of mappo. It is not a hymn of praise or prayer of supplication, but a means to awaken and express Buddha nature. Daimoku is usually followed by reciting selected passages of the Lotus Sutra in a daily liturgy called *gongyo*, a term that means "assiduous practice."

The *gohonzon*, a term usually translated as "object of worship," is the second hidden law. It is most readily understood as a symbol of ultimate reality, a mandala or map of the spiritual forces of the universe, which was devised by Nichiren himself. The most prominent feature of a gohonzon is an inscription in calligraphy of the phrase "Nam-myoho-renge-kyo," which is surrounded by signs for bodhisattvas and lesser deities drawn from Japanese traditions. The gohonzon is not an icon or a sacred image in the conventional sense of the terms but an abstract representation of Buddha as a universal essence or principle. It also evokes the vision revealed by Shakyamuni on Eagle Peak of bodhisattvas who rise from the earth on their mission to teach and preach to suffering people the path to happiness and freedom.

When used in practice, daimoku and gohonzon mirror in each other the essence of Nichiren's teaching. Daimoku is a verbal performance of Buddha nature, the gohonzon its graphic representation. The two are used together in practice in a way analogous to sitting in meditation before an image of Shakyamuni, the more familiar practice of Zen Buddhists. In some respects, Nichiren Buddhism is, like Zen, a *jiriki*, or "self-power," practice—it is understood that one must exert oneself to effect an inner awakening. In other respects, it is a *tariki*, or "other power," practice in that the power to awaken is inherent in both daimoku and gohonzon.

The significance of *kaidan*, the third of Nichiren's laws, is quite different. In Japanese Buddhism, kaidan has traditionally meant "ordination platform," the place at which a monk or priest is invested with the authority to teach, such as the great medieval monastic establishment on Mount Hiei. Additional ideas cluster around it in Nichiren's Buddhism because, while he established the first two laws himself, he prophesied that the third would be established in the future. As a consequence, kaidan has sometimes taken on a prophetic, even eschatological, cast in Nichiren Buddhism, signifying a sanctuary to be built when true Buddhism spreads throughout Japan. It also means a seat of institutional authority, such as the head temple of Nichiren Shoshu at Taisekiji, where the *dai-gohonzon,* the greatest gohonzon, is maintained by the sect's priesthood. Thus kaidan is a complex of ideas about authority and sacred space made all the more complex by carrying a sense of futurity. Debate over the meanings of kaidan would result in doctrinal controversies in the postwar decades that factored into the break in 1991 between the Gakkai and the priests.

A final dimension to Makiguchi's legacy is Nichiren himself, whose life as a reformer has given him a complex reputation—intolerant and combative for some, to others fearless and courageous. His disputes with Kamakura authorities add a powerful political element to his reputation, highly charged and open to conservative and liberal interpretations. These contrasting views would fuel further controversies in the postwar decades, when the Gakkai took as its platform Nichiren's political-spiritual tract, *Rissho Ankoku Ron* ("On Establishing the Correct Teaching for the Peace of the Land"), and set out to transform Japan.

· · ·

Rie preps me for a visit to Makiguchi Hall, an imposing ceremonial–office–meeting hall complex that stands adjacent to Soka University. "Some people find the building too grandiose for a religious organization," she explains. "Others imagine it's a reflection of Mr. Ikeda's personal wealth, which it certainly is not." She also assures me that the enthusiasm I'll see in a leaders' meeting should not be mistaken for fascist zealotry or fanaticism but is the kind of energy groups in Japan often display, whether at sporting events or corporate sales meetings.

I know why Rie is telling me all this. I've read reports of alarmed observers such as Polly Toynbee, a woman who was swept into the world of SG-Japan and, unable to process the experience adequately, imagined the worst. Her grandfather, Arnold Toynbee, a British historian who died in 1975, played a pivotal role in Ikeda's life, an episode to be discussed in chapter 6. But in 1984, the Gakkai invited her to Japan for a visit to honor her grandfather and, as she charged later, to enlist her aid in obtaining unpublished transcripts of a Toynbee-Ikeda conversation owned by Oxford University Press.

As she later reported it in the *Manchester Guardian,* Toynbee felt as though she barely survived the experience, seeing deceit and manipulation at every turn. The Gakkai entourage that met her at the airport, their photographers, the bouquets they presented, the greeting sent from Ikeda, did not strike her as a cordial welcoming, but as intimidation. She saw in Ikeda a man "without a whiff of even artificial spirituality" who "for years has had his every whim gratified, his every order obeyed." What she observed to lead her to these conclusions is not clear, but she left no doubt that she found the entire experience arduous and grating. Dinner with Ikeda and his wife, Kaneko, was an "ordeal," their small talk "excruciating." Describing Ikeda as a "small stout ball of power," she wrote that "something in him struck a chill down the spine."[7]

The odd animus of observers like Toynbee suggests that they ought not be taken too seriously, but I dwell on all of them nervously as I am driven to meet Ikeda, wondering if I'm about to encounter the embodiment of the Oriental potentate. And at a glance, I see why some people might find Makiguchi Hall intimidating. Its monumental historicity manages to evoke the nineteenth and twenty-first centuries simultaneously, capturing both the grandeur and the grandiosity of postindustrial cities. Its porticoes and colonnades are lush and yet too august, although I think they will age gracefully, like neoclassical courthouses that were too austere when new but are now oases of ornateness among the sleek towers of today's cities.

"Some people arrive thinking Buddhist teachers ought to live in huts," I scribble in my notes as we make our way onto a circular drive at the rear of the building. "Others expect ecclesiastical robes and are disappointed by well-cut suits and French cuffs." I know such orientalist romances well from the '60s, when I and many in my generation sought out the Asian mysteries. It had long been assumed that the West is all about ego and materialism but that the East remained a land of asceticism and spirituality. This kind of dualism allowed the West to have it all in the heyday of imperialistic thinking. We got to be rich, powerful, and arrogant but could take comfort in the notion that the spirit lived in the humble and benighted East. Such fantasies persist into this booming globalizing age even when we are all being thrown together and, theoretically, cannot afford such distortions in our thinking.

Ikeda's two sons, Hiromasa and Takahiro, greet Rob and me outside Makiguchi Hall at the sixth-floor entrance, its lower five floors angled into a ravine in the Musashino Hills. Takahiro, the younger of the two, handsome and charming, soon leaves, having to return to the Kansai region, where he is a teacher in a Soka school. Hiromasa escorts us on a tour of the ceremonial section of Makiguchi Hall, including several large, well-lit galleries of Ikediana—portraits of Ikeda alone and with

Kaneko painted by members, miscellaneous Asian and African antiquities, case after case of ceremonial medals and pins and trophylike awards. I feel like Madeleine Albright on a state tour, graciously taking everything in with no idea what it all means, so I ask Hiromasa.

"These are gifts given to President Ikeda by educators, intellectuals, and heads of state he has met in the course of his dialogues with people around the world. Members come here to visit," he tells me as we stroll past row after row of displays. "They come to see all that the Soka Gakkai has accomplished. Many understand all this as tangible benefit," he says, evoking one of Makiguchi's central concepts while gesturing to take in the contents of the entire museum. This is all "testimony to the value that can be created by ordinary people," he continues, using another.

Hiromasa is about forty-five, friendly but with a serious mien, and I try to decipher his grave manner as Rie translates. I recall hearing that Ikeda's nickname for him is "Stainless Steel," a father's teasing way to acknowledge that, while he himself is impulsive and romantic, his son is a hardheaded realist. In recent years, Hiromasa has represented his father at numerous Gakkai events around the world, which has led some to speculate that he may one day succeed him. But others say a father-son succession would be too typically Japanese for a movement that strives to be thoroughly internationalist in scope and spirit.

Hiromasa leads us into a small reception room where he introduces us to Roberto Baggio, a famous Italian soccer player who joined the Gakkai in the late '80s and is in Japan for a tournament. After he departs, Baggio and I exchange pleasantries through an Italian-English-Japanese interpreter until I am called to a top-floor reception room to meet with Ikeda, after which I will attend a monthly leaders' meeting.

When the elevator door opens, Ikeda embraces me with warmth and immediacy. "Let me express my heartfelt sorrow at the death of your kind and good wife," he says first thing, speaking through Rie. "Such a loss is life's greatest sorrow and a great test of faith." He then turns to introduce me to Kaneko, his wife, whom he laughingly refers to as "my sister." As she and I shake hands, I recall her having said that Ikeda's becoming president of the Gakkai was the funeral for her family because thereafter their lives were dedicated to *kosen-rufu,* a term I have yet to master but that seems to signify an era of harmony and peace. She looks tired, perhaps frail, and knowing that she lost her second son to a sudden illness, I wish I could sit and talk with her about Ann.

But the three of us are soon in motion, ushered down a hall by their handlers, Ikeda and I talking of education and religion, Kaneko a few steps to the rear, bulbs flashing as photographers snap picture after picture. I try to chat lightly but truthfully, with understated humor that seems to get lost in translation. "One of my personal struggles, President Ikeda, is that I've become overeducated and now find it difficult to be religious," I say, with an implied sigh and small grin, a comment that is meant to be ironic and charming but fails miserably as an icebreaker.

"Education is a privilege," he replies with determined gusto, "it enhances true spirituality." The comment makes perfect sense coming from a religious educator and teacher, but it feels a bit like a put-down, although I remind myself that it is not clear whether the brusque tone was Ikeda's or Rie's. After that, my memories of this interlude become blurry, but in all the photos of Ikeda and me walking together I am smiling broadly, looking uncharacteristically happy. Given that Ikeda is short, I also appear to be a very tall, rather formidable gaijin.

Ikeda and I are directed to paired easy chairs, Rie seated between us, Mrs. Ikeda off to one side, with Rob, reporters, and other observers on couches set around the huge, brilliantly lit room, decorated with what looked to be French or Italian antiques. I now can only recall lots of gold frames and high ceilings, a grand room but very comfortable, like salons I visited years ago while living with a government family in Mexico City. The room spoke of formality and authority yet efficiency, like the best meeting room in a fine hotel where people come together to do important business. I try to absorb as much as I can while young Gakkai women serve us lemonade, chocolates, and coffee. I notice great fabric on couches and chairs, the deep pile of the carpeting, and Ikeda's awesome cuff links. *Probably a gift,* I think, even as I covet them, the nicest of many I've seen since arriving in Tokyo.

Ikeda speaks first about Nichiren's passion and conviction, his struggles against authorities, his near execution on the beach at Tatsunokuchi near the city of Kamakura. It is more an oration than a conversation and, thinking of Polly Toynbee, I wonder if his intensity should make me uneasy, so I put myself on guard. *High-profile leader; passionate personality; well turned out, like everyone else I've seen in central Tokyo,* I think, enjoying myself. But then I flip-flop: *Overbearing; authoritarian; self-aggrandizing, down to the way he dresses,* a darker view that suggests I ought to shrink back into my chair.

Ikeda speaks in more intimate tones of his love for his mentor, Josei Toda, and how he had battled to build the Gakkai out of the ashes of a war created by militarists. Then, in a voice that seems to seek my understanding, he describes how he and the Gakkai were and continue to be vilified in the Japanese press for blatantly political reasons.

He changes tone again, now more effusive. "But Makiguchi Hall, all this," he says—looking me straight in the eye, making a gesture expansive enough to take in the room, the sixth-floor galleries, Soka University, even Shinanomachi, an hour away by train—"was built to honor my mentor's mentor, who died in a three-tatami-mat cell in Sugamo Prison."

Then suddenly the meeting is over, and he and Kaneko and I are saying our good-byes, the schedule tight because a leaders' meeting is about to begin; it is to be simulcast via satellite to Osaka, so it must begin promptly.

Within moments, I'm on the seventh floor of Makiguchi Hall, on the dais in a large auditorium, where I sit among forty senior leaders, mostly men, surveying some fifteen hundred juniors in the audience— Japanese guys, crisp and alert in white shirts and rep ties; young women in tailored suits of blue, soft pink, or lime green, most of them wearing a string of pearls. *They can't all be beautiful,* I'm thinking to myself, wowed by a sea of these outfits, cool, refreshing, and muted like pastel mints, the "Sunday dress" of young Gakkai women in Japan. I also see delegations from around the world scattered throughout the audience, from Kenya, perhaps, Korea, Brazil, the U.S., some in colorful national dress, some in unisex blue blazers, others dressed any old way, choosing not to stand on ceremony.

When the meeting begins, Ikeda works from prepared notes, but he is spontaneous and engaging: cajoling, teasing, and verbally poking and prodding the assembly, urging them on in their religious practice and varied pursuits. He reviews how the Komeito fared in a recent election, both encouraging and admonishing losers and congratulating winners. Throughout all this, I watch closely to gauge the tone of the rapport established between Ikeda, the mentor, and the assembly of his disciples, always alert to the charge that they are credulous dupes and he a manipulator.

The audience listens intently to Ikeda's remarks and claps at each of his encouragements. They love laughing at his jokes and teasing and are thrilled when he introduces Baggio, whom Ikeda has known for years, and the two dance a jig together at the proscenium. People seem to be enjoying themselves immensely, although I note a few young Japanese men, with hair dyed blond and multiple piercings, whose scowls suggest that they consider the proceedings wholly uncool. But even their slouches signal that they are at home, and I find myself feeling that I'm being made privy to the gathering of an immense and rather intense international family.

When the meeting ends, everyone stands, all of us on the dais turning to face an altar at the back of the stage, which is dressed simply with
offerings of oranges, grapefruits, and water. Above is a tabernacle,
whose doors swing open slowly to reveal a large gohonzon, brown,
black, and green in hue, as I now recall it. The calligraphy is meaningless to me but I know that it reads "Nam-myoho-renge-kyo" and that
I should see in it the revelation of Shakyamuni on Eagle Peak. Ikeda
then strikes a small gong and announces that the assembly will chant
one hundred daimoku for the repose of the soul of Ann Seager Castle,
a gesture that comes as a complete surprise to me.

Ikeda begins the chant slowly, in the rich, deep-throated tone cultivated
by Japanese men—earthy, organic, corporeal, almost bullfroglike, wholly
unlike the celestial piping I did as a young boy singing Gregorian chant:
"Nam-myoho-renge-kyo . . . Nam-myoho-renge-kyo . . . Nam-myoho-
renge-kyo." I gaze up at the gohonzon in silence, feeling it's not my
place to join in, hardly knowing how or what to think, as the auditorium begins to pulse with fifteen hundred voices sounding what I know
they take to be the awakened heart of the living universe. I attempt to
deploy my radar even while knowing it's a graceless thing to do, but
fail. And the nausea that still accompanies my recollections of Ann's
death is soon dispelled by "Nam-myoho-renge-kyo, Nam-myoho-renge-
kyo, Nam-myoho-renge-kyo," quickening in pace, droning insistently,
yet calming, ninety-four times more for the repose of Ann I know not
where.

A few minutes later, I decompress in a nearby room after the meeting, where Rie asks me point-blank: "Well, what did you think?" I can't
possibly be put on the spot so soon, so I mumble something vague
about the Versailles look of the reception room, saying I'd seen that
kind of thing before in Mexico City, then change the subject.

"What's a tatami mat," I ask, "and how large is a three-tatami-mat
cell?"

"You know," Rie replies, "a woven floor covering used in homes and
restaurants. Three-tatami is about the size of a big walk-in-closet."

We sit for a few more minutes waiting for our car to arrive, so I begin
to pick my experience apart in silence, trying to figure out if I'd experienced a form of Japanese Buddhist grace or had just been outrageously
manipulated, trying to size up Ikeda the man and the movement
Makiguchi created.

. . .

Events during the last phase of Makiguchi's life can be sketched in quickly. Financial crises in the '20s, Japan's takeover of Manchuria in 1931, and the assassination of the Japanese prime minister in 1932 set the stage for a militaristic elite to assert control of Japan. One tool at their disposal was the Public Security Preservation Law of 1925. Designed to control anarchists, Communists, and radical students with threats of imprisonment, it was later emended to apply to religious dissenters and to mete out the death penalty. This law became central to a system of ideological oversight that led to the arrest of some seventy thousand people over the course of two decades. As wartime pressures increased, additional legislation gave the government power to ban religious groups refusing to worship at Shinto shrines and to require all households to venerate amulets from Ise, the shrine of kami-goddess of the sun Amaterasu, the mythic progenitor of the imperial family.

During this time, Makiguchi steered Soka Kyoiku Gakkai in a direction that emphasized Buddhist elements in his synthesis. In 1936, the group held its first summer meeting at Taisekiji, the head temple of Nichiren Shoshu, setting a precedent that would become an important one for Toda and Ikeda in the postwar years. Between 1937 and 1940, Soka Kyoiku Gakkai was launched as a formally incorporated organization with Makiguchi as its president. As war escalated and the government tightened its grip, Makiguchi felt increasing urgency to broaden the movement's appeal and to attempt to propagate it among the urban poor, another precedent of importance to his successors. Throughout this period, Makiguchi viewed militarism as an expression of state egotism, and war as a slander on the Buddha's true law. His greatest crime, however, was that he elevated the Buddha dharma above the law of the state, an act of conscience expressed in his refusal to recognize the emperor's divinity. When questioned by police, he insisted that "the emperor is an ordinary man, who went to school as crown prince to learn to be emperor. The emperor makes mistakes like anyone else."[8]

These opposing forces collided directly in 1943 when Makiguchi was summoned to Taisekiji. Nichiren Shoshu, like virtually all religious institutions, had capitulated to the demands of the state. In the presence of the high priest and his predecessor, both of whom remained silent, Makiguchi was urged by the temple's chief administrator to recant his convictions through the simple act of accepting and venerating an amulet from Ise and to encourage Soka Kyoiku Gakkai members to do the same. Whether their insistence was motivated by cowardice, pragmatism, abject fear, or overt nationalist sentiments is difficult to say, but Makiguchi refused.

The end came quickly. In 1942, the government pressured the Soka Kyoiku Gakkai journal to stop publication. The society disbanded in 1943 after the arrest of Makiguchi and nineteen other leaders. Makiguchi was charged with lèse-majesté—affronting the dignity of a sovereign—by denying the emperor's divinity, and with slandering the shrine of Ise, charges that amounted to blasphemy and treason. A *shiso-han* ("thought criminal"), he was imprisoned, one of a motley assortment of Communists, anarchists, Buddhists, Christians, and other wartime resisters, and there he died in 1944, apparently from exhaustion and malnutrition.

CHAPTER 3

Mentor's Vision

Josei Toda plays a crucial role in the Gakkai teaching lineage, but little work on his life is available in English. More is known about Makiguchi thanks to Ikeda, who cites him so often in his writing and speeches that it is easy to lose sight of the fact that the two never met. Ikeda's attention to Makiguchi reflects the need to establish a clear line of authority in the Gakkai after its break with Nichiren Shoshu in 1991. It also reflects Ikeda's conviction that Makiguchi's life was a heroic example for members of a man who faced formidable, real-life obstacles with courage and persistence, who turned the poisons of disappointment, frustration, and oppression into the medicine of fortitude and resistance.

Subtler and more intriguing is that Ikeda's devotion to Makiguchi is also an expression of his love for Toda, his own mentor. For Ikeda, to honor Makiguchi is to acknowledge his role in forming Toda's spirit and character. This honoring implicitly acknowledges that Toda, in turn, poured himself, with everything he learned from Makiguchi, into Ikeda. The passing on of wisdom and experience from one generation to the next is the core of the mentor-disciple relationship and the chief building block of a spiritual teaching lineage, both means of propagating Buddhism with an ancient and important history in Asia.

Toda's place in the Gakkai lineage is crucial because the movement he received from Makiguchi was very different from the one he passed on to Ikeda. After the war, Toda transformed a disbanded group of educators into a mass movement devoted to personal and social transformation, which he renamed simply Soka Gakkai. He reshaped Makiguchi's philosophy to address the needs of postwar Japan under the American occupation. He strengthened the Gakkai's links to Nichiren Shoshu, encouraging members to study its doctrine, to take on its rivals, and to defer to its priests. All of these initiatives generated rounds of controversy quite different in character from those that plagued Makiguchi.

One can think of Makiguchi, Toda, and Ikeda as links in a presidential chain of cause and effect, the work of each giving rise to that of the next. Makiguchi's philosophy and his convictions are a cause whose effect is Toda and the postwar movement; Toda a cause of Ikeda and Soka University; Ikeda's politics and philosophy the effects of the work of his predecessors. But Toda's position within this chain is unique because it was he who formed the living bond between Makiguchi and Ikeda and it was his work to revive the movement in the crucial postwar years that secured for the Soka Gakkai its significant place in modern Buddhist history.

. . .

Our car slowly cuts a tight curve in the road as we descend into Makiguchi Memorial Garden, which stands in a winding ravine in the Musashino Hills, adjacent to Soka University. Rob, Rie, her husband, Koji Shibata, and a few others form a small party that accompanies me on my quiet quest to honor Ann by planting a cherry tree in her memory.

Upon my arrival in Tokyo, Ikeda sent me a message at the hotel: "Would Doctor Seager permit a cherry tree to be planted in his wife's name in the Makiguchi Memorial Gardens in Hachioji?" Taken by surprise, I was delighted to have Ann in Japan but knew accepting would trigger bouts of self-doubt and skepticism. Alone that night, I pondered Ikeda's motivations. *A gracious act of the sort you've been told about by American members? Or buying my sympathies?*

I'd anticipated that my personal stake in the project would be raised as research progressed, but I hadn't factored Ann into the equation. But in the many months since her death, I'd come to think that I might as well throw my usual reticence to the winds, now having so little to lose. "She was so willing to see goodness in the world," I recalled while running my fingers over the thin silver frame in which I keep her picture. Her faith allowed me to indulge cynicism, but now I have to go it alone, to cultivate good-mindedness on my own, to give the world a break. So I'd decided to cut Ikeda some slack and accept his offer. I'd just wait to see what happened.

The driver parks in the bottom of the ravine, where pine and spruce, still-bare trees and lightly greening shrubs, and a canopy of cherry trees, some with early blooms, stretch out in all directions under a cloudless blue sky. Shibata is a handsome man probably in his forties, formerly a secretary to Ikeda who now handles external affairs for the Gakkai in the United States, Australia, and New Zealand. Looking smart and dignified in his horn-rimmed glasses and well-tailored suit, he takes us on a tour of the garden, talking with me through Rie.

"Look here," Shibata says, gesturing toward a paved terrace. "This is a monument to President Makiguchi." A bust of him stands on a granite plinth with two large tablets with calligraphy on either side. "Monuments for each of the presidents have quotations from their work written in their own hand," he tells me. "The inscription under Makiguchi's statue reads 'stand alone spirit' or 'be or become independent,' so 'independent spirit' would be a good translation," he says as I lightly touch the angular characters blasted into stone.

"See, over there," he continues, gesturing across the lane to another terrace, plinth, bust, and tablets, "that one commemorates President Toda. His inscription reads 'Great Desire,' a reference to his longing to spread Buddhism, to further kosen-rufu, which means 'to declare, spread, and flow.'" People in the Gakkai speak often of kosen-rufu, a protean term I am coming to understand as encompassing the movement's many different activities, all of them understood as moving forward together toward an era of harmony and peace that Nichiren prophesied would unfold with the spread of his teachings.

"In the course of my interviews, I've developed an interest in Toda," I say to Shibata, keeping up my end of the conversation. "I think I might have liked him." A secular, earthly man, a teacher with a caustic sense of humor, Toda seems like someone I could relate to. But then he became a preacher of sorts, an evangelical, something I cannot imagine myself ever doing, in this lifetime or another.

"Further up the road, there is a third for President Ikeda," Shibata adds, "which reads 'Monument of the Twenty-First Century.'" A quick thought reflects an extreme in my cynical thinking—*"Monument of the century?" Is this monumental egotism on Ikeda's part?* But then Rie explains, still translating for Shibata. "In 1982, Mr. Ikeda asked SG members to write down their names and resolutions for the twenty-first century. Many millions sent in forms which were later buried there, where they will remain forever, a testimony to the Soka Gakkai's hopes for world peace."

I wince at the knee-jerk quality of my suspiciousness, beginning to weary of my reluctance to get a fix on Ikeda and thankful that Shibata and Rie cannot see what I am thinking.

As we stroll across the terrace, small birds making graceful swoops among the branches of the leafing trees, I cannot help but think of all the civic statuary I have ignored for years in the Boston Public Garden and in Central Park in New York City. *To peer into the monumental imaginations of other people,* I think, *is an enormous privilege. It is all laid out for you, like a table set for a feast.* Part of me is dying to take notes, but I cannot and do not care to violate the spirit of the occasion.

Shibata leads us to a small pond that swells in a quickly running stream, where gold, black, orange, and pink fish gather, sensing our footsteps and expecting to feed. Rob and the others stay well to the rear.

"Please," Shibata says, "feed the fish," gesturing toward a bucket of meal set within a niche on an arching footbridge. I relish the formality of the moment, archetypal rather than stereotypical in character, seeming to be transported to some quintessentially Japanese place with Shibata and Rie, an intelligent, elegant couple, standing beside me. *This was supposed to be a little trip,* I think, recalling how Rob had first pitched it to me, as koi thrash beneath the surface of the pond, darting for the pellets I cast to them. But it's as if I've stepped through a mirror to find a Japan that's just the way it's supposed to be but also a whole lot edgier, more political, and conflict-ridden than I'd imagined. It's like the United States in that regard, but moving to its own beat, a tempo I don't quite understand—a completely modern and familiar, yet totally foreign country.

Shibata lightly touches my shoulder and I turn to follow his lead up the lane to where an honor guard of young Gakkai members—men in ties and blazers, women in their pastel suits—await us, standing on either side of a small trail that opens into the hills and is covered with a long red carpet. They applaud my arrival with quiet courtesy. A young woman leads me to a newly planted tree marked with a placard bearing my wife's name in the form I'd suggested —Ann Seager Castle. It is also written in characters, so I wonder what she sounds like as a person with a name that is Japanese. No scrawny sapling wrapped in white tape, I note, guessing the tree to stand about forty feet tall.

The young woman hands me a small, gold-painted spade decorated with ribbon while gesturing toward a pile of freshly turned earth. I know to add a few scoops to the base of the tree, like the handfuls of dirt mourners cast into a grave at the end of a burial service. She then passes me a pail and ladle, and as I unsuccessfully attempt to choke back tears, I wet the soil, recalling the holy water I once sprinkled on my mother's coffin. I stand quietly for a moment, make the sign of the cross, and utter a prayer—the Our Father, Hail Mary, or Glory Be, I cannot now remember which—to express whatever faith it is that I have. But this is also a self-conscious act on my part, wanting to convey to these Buddhists that I too have a religion and that I know to take theirs seriously.

Once back in the car, Shibata and Rie having departed for their home, I say to Rob, who sits beside me, "I wonder how men's tears are regarded in Japanese culture." I hope I've not revealed something of myself that might be seen as weak. The two of us then ride in silence back to Tokyo, me pretending to nap most of the way, exhausted by Ann, the hundred daimoku, the pastel suits and pearls, and Ikeda's oratory, all fragments of experience and emotion wired up together inside me, made jagged by my need and desire to figure everything out, to make sense of Japan and its people and all things Japanese.

·   ·   ·

Toda was born in 1900 in a fishing village on the Sea of Japan, but was raised and educated on Hokkaido. In 1918 he began teaching at an elementary school in Yubari, a dreary inland coal-mining town. But he had long harbored a dream of becoming a successful businessman, so in 1920 he moved to Tokyo to explore the world of commerce while searching out his destiny.

In need of work, he applied for a teaching job and was hired by Makiguchi, then principal of Nishimachi Elementary School and in his late forties. The two men were very different—Makiguchi idealistic, scholarly, and stern; Toda more pragmatic and gregarious, a smoker who liked sake and whiskey, known to bounce an occasional check in the course of his business dealings. But the two took to each other quickly, with young Toda coming to view Makiguchi as the mentor he had long been seeking.

Within several years, Toda brought his interest in business and education together by publishing a best-selling mathematics textbook and by establishing a private school based on Makiguchi's theories. When Makiguchi turned to religion, Toda was skeptical, but followed him into Nichiren Shoshu out of a sense of respect and indebtedness. Like many businessmen, both Japanese and American, Toda tended to assess the efficacy of his religion in terms of his financial successes, so he understood his prosperity in terms of Makiguchi's ideas about creating value and benefits. While continuing to expand his business interests, he also began to edit Makiguchi's notes to prepare them for press and to use his ample resources to help bankroll the Soka Kyoiku Gakkai.

Toda's outlook on life shifted radically when he followed Makiguchi into prison, a choice he seems to have made as much out of regard for his mentor as in service to his own principled convictions. His imprisonment triggered what was essentially a conversion or, perhaps better, an awakening experience, which transformed his understanding of the Lotus Sutra and Nichiren's Buddhism and set him on course to becoming the leader of a mass social and religious movement.

Toda recalled his prison experience in bits and pieces in later speeches and writings and in an untranslated novel, *The Human Revolution*. Eventually his recollections became shaped into a paradigmatic story for the Gakkai in a semifictionalized history of the movement written by Ikeda, which he too titled *The Human Revolution*.[1] Ikeda's *Human Revolution* has been told and retold in comic books, animated cartoons, and a full-length feature film produced by a commercial Japanese studio in the '70s, all of which powerfully convey how Toda's prison experience in 1944 redirected the course of his life until his death in 1958.

Imagine Toda alone in a three-tatami-mat cell of his own with a small cache of Buddhist books, eating meager prison rations and enduring loneliness, anxiety, and sickness. At first, he can muster no interest in his books. He tries to give them away, but they keep coming back to him through curious circumstances. Eventually, he takes up the Lotus Sutra—out of boredom, perhaps, or a sense of desperation. He also begins to chant daimoku, maybe as a jailhouse coping strategy, and to visualize the gohonzon before him, likely unaware that such visualization techniques have an ancient history in Japan, China, and Tibet.

This disciplinary regime begins to pick up momentum, so Toda fashions *juzu*, rosary-like beads used when chanting daimoku, out of the cardboard caps of milk bottles strung on twine, now a most poignant item of his memorabilia. By the end of his two years in prison, he will have chanted daimoku two million times and have read and reread the Lotus Sutra and other scripture central to the philosophy and practice of Nichiren's Buddhism.

Toda's encounter with practice, the sutras, and himself finally resulted in a two-part transformation. The first part came as he struggled to conceive of the Buddha in modern terms, free of mythology and doctrine. Picture Toda as he is portrayed in literature and film, pacing his cell for long anguished days, wrapped in a tattered jacket for warmth, badly in need of a shave, deep in contemplation. He wrestles with a difficult passage in a sutra in which true Buddha is described by a method mystics call the *via negativa*, a way of grasping absolute reality by asserting what it is not. Toda knows the sutra's negations by heart—true Buddha is neither being nor nonbeing, itself nor another, square nor round; it is neither this nor that, neither past nor future. For days, he cannot grasp what this means, until suddenly he cries out in his cell "*Seimei* [life force]!" As he recalled a decade later, "It dawned on me, the Buddha is life-force. . . . I realized that life-force is the name of the Buddha, and that this is the fundamental force in the universe."[2] In making this conceptual move, Toda began to align Nichiren's Buddhism with a modern vitalistic philosophy that the Gakkai shares with other modern Japanese spiritual movements.[3]

A second transformation came several months later, when Toda realized he was a part of Shakyamuni's revelation on Eagle Peak. One imagines him the pragmatic businessman, mathematician, and secular educator once viewing the Lotus Sutra with dispassion, not deeply identified with it but respectful of its importance to his mentor. But in the course of this experience, Toda awakened to it with immediacy and fervor, just as Nichiren taught his disciples to do seven centuries earlier. He came to see that Eagle Peak is not simply a myth, metaphor, or place described in a book, but a dynamic reality, eternal and spiritual yet alive in the present. He came to understand himself as among the bodhisattvas arising from the earth with a mission to teach and preach awakening to suffering people.

The inner meaning of these experiences is graphically conveyed in a Gakkai anime for children. A creaking prison door slams shut and martial chords signal struggle while Toda stalks in his cell, pondering the negations. Finally the stone walls of his cell drop away to reveal stars and nebulae and Toda becomes one with the life of the universe, as a clear, joyful flute pipes, cicadas drone, crickets chirp, and birds sing. Then intense light streams through a prison window while strings, chimes, and triangles shimmer brilliantly as Toda, wide-eyed and awestruck, is transported to Eagle Peak to stand among a vast throng of bodhisattvas who arise from the earth. On his knees before a scintillating sun that signifies awakening, Toda fingers his juzu repeatedly, chanting "Nam-myoho-renge-kyo, Nam-myoho-renge-kyo, Nam-myoho-renge-kyo."

Toda's linkage of a modern, vitalistic concept of true Buddha as life force with the mission of bodhisattvas who arise from the earth anticipates the liberalism in Ikeda's Buddhist Humanism while restating the hybrid philosophy first forged by Makiguchi. But any upbeat sense of triumph that may have accompanied Toda's transformation was soon tested. Three months later, on January 8, 1945, he learned that Makiguchi was dead, having collapsed in his cell some fifty days earlier. That July, at the age of forty-five, he faced the chaos of a devastated Japan when he was released from Toyotama Prison in the closing days of the war, on the eve of the American occupation.

. . .

Rob and I eat once again in Akasaka-Mitsuke, an entertainment district near the hotel. The sidewalks are jammed with salarymen ready to drink after a twelve-hour workday and with hostesses who offer their services with a refreshing mix of frankness and dignity. We choose a small restaurant that serves red sauce and pasta Japan style, with a lightness lacking in most American treatments of Italian cuisine.

We order a few drinks, both of us needing to unpack the day's events. "I must wrestle with what to make of Ikeda's gestures—the hundred daimoku, the cherry tree," I begin, laying out the current blips on my radar. "No one who already distrusts the Gakkai will miss the opportunity to say, 'Ikeda got Seager in his pocket.'" But then I flip-flop. "On the other hand, most normal people would see it as an extremely gracious act made by a man who lives in a society that still values the grand gesture. That's not lost on me either."

Rob listens patiently, having heard such ruminations many times before. "You know," he replies after a few moments, "Ikeda does that kind of thing all the time: writes letters to members he's never met to encourage them, frets over the well-being of students. Last month he sent a case of juzu to a national meeting of gays and lesbians in Florida—just to lend his support, you know, in overcoming the obstacles they face as minorities."

From our brief encounter, I can see that Ikeda likes to connect with people, which is probably one reason he is so intense—that and the fact that he's a political-spiritual celebrity beloved by disciples and hated by enemies, a favorite target of the tabloid press, which pulls out his cult-leader reputation whenever Komeito faces a crucial election. Many American members have told me that Ikeda is the least Japanese person they've met, more spontaneous and gregarious; it's a line of thinking I shy away from because Ikeda, his wife, and his sons are, after all,

Japanese. That he made a special gesture in support of lesbians and gays for some reason does not surprise me. Despite formalities and courtesies, I often sense something "alternative" about the Gakkai, something that, for lack of a better word, feels very '60s to me. This instinctual response to the movement fosters a sense of affinity and trust, although I will only come to understand why on a subsequent trip to Japan.

After dinner, Rob and I wind our way through thinning crowds and stop at a Japanese version of a 7-Eleven to stockpile mineral water, diet Cokes, and vitamin C drinks. I buy a few bags of potato chips, knowing that later I'll want a familiar, comforting treat. Within half an hour I am hunkered down, ready to space out watching TV. But the BBC is off the air and all the shows are in Japanese and the chips are sugared, not salted. I try to read but the events of the day remain too much with me, so I just go to bed, leaving a music station running at low volume on the television.

Strings and flutes and the tinkle of temple bells soon envelop the room, creating a New Age mood, while images of robed priests performing rituals for reverent women in a darkened shrine roll across the screen. The camera cuts from time to time to scenes of waterfalls, ancient stonework, the rough texture of bark, a pebbled shoreline, cherry trees. I peek from under the covers to watch kimono-clad women doing a tea ceremony, a Shinto festival, a wedding scene in a splendid hall, a Western-style bride and groom standing before a white four-tiered cake.

I discern the show's intent as the camera repeatedly cuts to views of Mount Fuji shot from many different angles. Fuji from the east. Fuji from the west. Fuji from the air and from the floor of a valley. Fuji in spring rains, and snow-capped Fuji. It's a cultural treasure–civil religion video, I realize, a montage of Japan's national essence, like an old sign-off transmission in the U.S.—flags fluttering to the national anthem, fighter jets streaking over the Washington Monument, GIs raising the flag on Iwo Jima. Except this goes on and on: more robed men and reverent ladies . . . sparkling waters and temple groves . . . more views of Fuji.

Soon I'm thrashing in bed, the music tinkling in time to the flickering video, my thoughts starting to dart from Toda to kamikaze pilots and the A-bomb, to photos of modan gaaru in the Edo-Tokyo Museum, to Ikeda in the glare of Makiguchi Hall. The cadence of the music becomes fused to the rhythms of my Japanese vocabulary, which is limited to a few technical religious terms—*daimoku, gohonzon, kaidan; daimoku, gohonzon, kaidan*—as the bed starts to twirl.

Soon frazzled, I flip on the lights, silence the TV, and close the thick curtains at the window, having had enough things Japanese for one day. I slip into the bathroom to wash and brush my teeth again and to take two Excedrin PM, knowing I must have a half-decent sleep before taking on another SG day in Japan

. . .

On July 3, 1945, tubercular and asthmatic, Toda left prison to find his school and businesses destroyed by war. The Japan he encountered was grim, with hysterical plans for homeland defense barely masking widespread starvation and sickness. Broad swaths of Tokyo had been firebombed and, a month after his release, America's new atomic weapons leveled Hiroshima and Nagasaki. On August 15, the emperor announced Japan's surrender over the radio, the first time most Japanese citizens had ever heard his voice.

Immediately after the war, the Japanese displayed what John Dower, in his book *Embracing Defeat,* called the "*kyodatsu* condition," a widespread state of personal and collective disorientation and depression.[4] Originally a clinical psychological term, the phrase came into usage in the postwar era to describe a common social pathology rooted in years of war-weariness, sickness, and malnutrition, in a numbness that came with defeat, and in despair over postwar chaos and corruption. In retrospect, the rebuilding of Japan seems to have happened very quickly. But Dower observes that for the people who poured into Japan's cities in search of work and scoured ruins for food and shelter, "postwar recovery seemed agonizingly slow."[5] Their agony was deepened by the knowledge that privileged elites—bureaucrats, bankers, businessmen, the police—prospered in defeat even as they had in war.

The American occupation was a decisive event in Japan's history, which "forced Japanese in every walk of life to struggle, in exceptionally naked ways, with the most fundamental of life's issues," writes Dower.[6] Its opening was marked by a heady sense of new possibilities among both occupiers and occupied as Douglas MacArthur and his forces dismantled Japan's overseas empire and its domestic surveillance systems, attacked the great zaibatsu and secured rights for unions, broke the hold of feudal landlords in the countryside, and established equal rights for women.

The centerpiece of America's vision for the reconstruction of Japan was a new constitution designed to transform subjects of an emperor into fully modern citizens. It was written in English by MacArthur's staff, then translated into Japanese and submitted to the Diet, a process Kyoko Inoue, a professor at the University of Illinois, calls a "cross-linguistic, cross-cultural negotiation" fraught with "ambiguities" and "misunderstandings."[7]

One of MacArthur's goals was to demilitarize Japan, an end accomplished in Article Nine, in which Japan renounced war and offensive military force in perpetuity. This clause became the basis for Japan's so-called peace constitution and the charter document for the pacifist sentiments still widely held among the Japanese people.

Another goal was to dismantle State Shinto and secure religious freedom, a task that required subtle exchanges between Americans and Japanese in which, according to Inoue, "neither side really understood the ideas and concerns of the other."[8] MacArthur achieved this goal by affirming the emperor's status as a symbol of Japan while stripping him of his divinity, effectively ending his dual role as sacred Shinto priest and head of state. But MacArthur had sought an even deeper transformation, one more in the American grain, in which freedom of religion implied freedom of the individual conscience—an assumption that had been forged in the West during the Reformation and Enlightenment but that did not resonate with Japanese collectivism. As a result, Americans and Japanese tended to talk past each other on sensitive issues of church and state, a failure to connect that Inoue suggests may have actually contributed to the ultimate success of their negotiations.

The constitution did, however, create a new spiritual and political landscape in Japan. With established institutions discredited by their complicity with militarists and the traditional communal order giving way, new religious movements burgeoned, a development so conspicuous that one observer called the postwar years "the rush hour of the gods."[9] Large movements and numerous sects and cults, many no more than a handful of people, offered divine wisdom, faith healing, fellowship, and utopian visions of a peaceful, prosperous Japan to the impoverished, depressed, and dislocated. In this context, the new constitution became what David M. O'Brien called "a basis for dialogue and disagreement" as Shinto traditionalists, Marxists, Socialists, Christians, liberal secularists, and new religionists offered rival constructions for interpreting the nature and limits of rights and freedoms in a new Japan.[10]

Toda saw in this ferment a new opportunity for the Gakkai. For him, MacArthur was a modern-day Bonten (a helper of the Buddha in the

Lotus Sutra), and a *shoten zenjin*, a modern-day tutelary deity, who aided the dharma by bringing religious freedom to Japan.

But the heady hopes of the early days of the occupation soon waned, and a complex reaction set in. One indication of this "reverse course" came when the occupation began to ban strikes in the late '40s, fearing Communist agitators. The outbreak of conflict in Korea stoked Japan's economic recovery but dampened postwar idealism, as the nation became a key player in America's new Cold War alliance. Anticommunist witch hunts began and authorities grew wary of new religions as older ones reasserted their authority, even as Japan took on the public face of a thoroughly secular society. By 1955, big government, business, and labor held such power that the three are often referred to as the 55 System, a troika that remains at the center of Japan's establishment today.

During these years, Toda first attempted to revisit his prewar success in education and business by starting a correspondence school and various publishing concerns. These enterprises flourished briefly but soon collapsed, victims of scarce resources and an inflationary economy. He later opened a credit union, which brought him only legal entanglements and further indebtedness. Throughout this time, he also began to rebuild Soka Kyoiku Gakkai in small steps by visiting old members and former directors and by securing offices in the Kanda district in downtown Tokyo.

In the face of his financial reversals, Toda became convinced that his efforts to succeed in business again were misguided, so he refocused his attention on his prison experiences. Within a few years, he had begun to reshape the Soka Gakkai in ways that enabled ordinary people to address the postwar malaise. Toda's Buddhism was both a restatement of and an expansion upon Makiguchi's hybrid philosophy. He deepened its traditional aspects by an increased dependence on the Lotus Sutra, Nichiren's *Gosho*, and Nichiren Shoshu doctrine. He also strengthened its modernist elements by identifying the Buddha with the life force and by teaching Buddhism as a transformative force in culture and politics. These teachings had popular appeal, as evidenced by the Gakkai's rapid growth from a few thousand people in the late '40s to 70,000 families by 1953, 160,000 the following year, and 300,000 the next.[11]

The difference between Toda's intent in revitalizing the Gakkai and the Japanese public's perceptions of its goal and spirit was the source of much of the intense controversy that marks the movement's history. Toda saw the movement as a progressive force in building a new Japan in a postwar, mappo age, its spirit forged in Makiguchi's resistance to State Shinto and the two men's experience of repression and imprisonment. He understood the Gakkai's right to pursue this goal aggressively, moreover, as secured by the new constitution.

But Toda's, and later Ikeda's, critics often came to view things very differently. They saw violations of church-state separation in many of the Gakkai's initiatives. They feared, moreover, that they witnessed a resurgence of the prewar nationalism of Chigaku Tanaka, an ardent Buddhist visionary who promoted a lay-based Nichiren movement in support of Japan's militaristic expansion and its imperial system.[12]

Four related developments that were a source of the Gakkai's strength and contributed to its energy and success suggest the character of the movement under Toda. These also alarmed its critics, who grew increasingly wary as they watched the movement grow exponentially until Toda's death in 1958.

First, Toda made Nichiren's treatise *Rissho Ankoku Ron* ("On Establishing the Correct Teaching for the Peace of the Land") the platform of the Gakkai. Nichiren wrote it to admonish the state for its collusion with heretical religions and to persuade it to adopt his Buddhism as the only path to peace and harmony in Japan. By adopting it, Toda committed the Gakkai to a religion based on an exclusive claim to truth, a move that critics viewed as overzealous and intolerant. Toda's reliance on Nichiren, moreover, seemed to imply the expectation of state support for the Gakkai, which cast the movement's commitment to the new constitution in a questionable light.

Doubts about the Gakkai's commitment to the new constitutional freedoms increased when Toda called for the building of Nichiren's prophesied kaidan. Toda divorced his concept of the kaidan from prewar imperial ideology, intending it to be a symbol of the efficacy of Nichiren's Buddhism to empower people in the rebuilding of Japan. His critics' fears seemed justified, however, when Toda described it using the phrase *kokuritsu kaidan,* a term popularized by Chigaku Tanaka that meant "national kaidan" or more literally "an ordination platform established by the state."[13]

Toda's styling of Gakkai spirituality in terms of a "human revolution" was a third source of vitality and controversy. He borrowed the phrase from a 1947 address of Shigeru Nambara, president of Tokyo University, who saw a need for an inner transformation in the Japanese people if the social and political revolutions set in motion by the occupation were to succeed. In Gakkai circles, *human revolution* carries the meaning of becoming empowered by transforming one's karma through Buddhist practice, but in the postwar, Cold War years, this rhetoric underscored fears that Gakkai was a revolutionary force with the design of taking over Japan.

These concerns were focused and magnified by Toda's use of *shakubuku* as the engine of the Gakkai's growth. Shakubuku is written with the characters meaning "bend or break" and "subdue," a reference to a traditional Buddhist style of refuting errors through vigorous debate. Toda revived shakubuku as a strategy for propagation but used it to build a mass movement, creating what amounted to an evangelical form of Buddhism. Shakubuku came to define the ethos of the Gakkai, whose members understood propagation to be the chief method of fulfilling their bodhisattva vow to teach and preach. But the energy unleashed by Soka Gakkai's shakubuku campaigns and its success at recruiting new members drew alarmed criticism from both envious religious rivals and Communists, Socialists, and secularists hostile to strongly held religious convictions, particularly when they enter the public arena tied to politics.

Toda's intent was to build a movement that turned the poisons of postwar crises into spiritual and political medicine, which he accomplished by reinterpreting Makiguchi in a trial-and-error process. Much of the controversy this generated can, in retrospect, be traced to profound ambiguities in the postwar situation. The constitution, only recently adopted, had been written by Americans and more or less imposed on Japan by the occupation. Neither Toda nor his critics knew precisely what it implied or how it would be brought into play with the norms of Japanese civilization. Defeat, rapid reconstruction, and the Cold War, moreover, created a highly fluid, often volatile social situation. In this context, the Gakkai's well-coordinated and highly successful propagation campaigns could, quite understandably, spell danger, particularly in a society that, unlike the United States, had little experience with high-energy mass evangelization. Toda's theories and the Gakkai's activities both plowed new ground and probed the limits of unclear boundaries, so it is no great surprise that they elicited powerful emotions both for and against.

Another, quite different development was also of great significance for the subsequent history of the Gakkai. On August 14, 1947, Toda met Daisaku Ikeda, a literary young man from an ordinary family who, in ill health and confused by the tumult of the times, had set out on a philosophical quest. Ikeda went to a lecture given by Toda expecting to hear about the vitalistic philosophy of Henri Bergson, a well-known secular philosopher from France. He found Toda instead deep in an obscure discussion of Nichiren, the Lotus Sutra, and his Buddhist life-force philosophy, developing his strategies for the building of a new Japan.

. . .

The next morning, unexpectedly refreshed, I inhale a great hotel breakfast. Having thrashed half the night trying to connect the dots between Iwo Jima and Mount Fuji, I feel oddly purged. I'm leafing through a published collection of SG photos from the early days with what seem to be new eyes.

- Toda, thin as a rail, thick glasses over a small moustache, wearing pleated trousers and a sport shirt. Or in a dark suit bent over a podium at a Tokyo mass meeting, gently stroking a young girl's cheek, behind them tightly packed Japanese faces watching intently.

- Young Ikeda, shorter than Toda but fleshier even then, in an open-necked white shirt or casual jacket, hair slicked with Brylcreem or some Japanese pomade.

- The two at an athletic event or culture festival: Toda laughing, some kind of award ribbon tucked into the waistband of his pants; Ikeda holding a starting gun, wearing a baseball cap; barefoot boys in running togs in the background.

- Gakkai women in shirtwaist dresses, small pieces of jewelry on lapels. A few in kimono. All with mid-length hair parted to one side, often permed into neat curls.

They all look so ordinary and familiar, I think, *so '40s, so postwar, so PTA.* Any one of them could be an aunt or uncle on the Irish German side of my family—about the same age, young and just getting married, looking forward to moving on and up into life after a Depression childhood and the war. All of them, like my mother's family, eager for their new starts, wholly unaware of what it will mean to journey into the new global frontier of a postwar, Cold War world.

After a shower and shave, Rob and I are off to Shinanomachi, where I will conduct two important interviews. The first is with Yasu Kashiwabara, a woman in her eighties who knew Makiguchi well and was among the first to rejoin the Gakkai under Toda.[14] A schoolteacher and chief of the Women's Division, she was elected to the Upper House of the Diet in the campaigns begun by Toda in the '50s. In *The*

Human Revolution, Ikeda gave her the fictional name of Katsu Kiyohara.

A good-humored and determined woman, Kashiwabara is a Gakkai living treasure. She sits with her old scrapbooks before her on the conference room table, dressed in black slacks and a purple knit sweater. She tells me that her mind is not what it used to be, laughing at her need for these mementos to stimulate her memory. As we begin our conversation through Rie, I see that interviewing her is going to be tricky. When I ask her to recall the Toda years, I watch her as she leafs through her notes, recalling and storing up memories before she speaks. Then she starts right at the beginning—her first meeting with Makiguchi, moving then through the terror of the war years, to her hunting up Toda during the occupation. After a few, failed attempts to redirect her to what most concerns me, I see it is best simply to sit back and listen as her memories tumble out.

"Nobody came to us in the days after the war," she says, recalling the occupation. "It's not that the organization just naturally expanded. People didn't flock to Mr. Toda. We really had to struggle to communicate Buddhism to the Japanese people, and it was a very challenging time. *Difficult* does not describe what we went through! We just gave all we had in order to start this movement," she recalls.

"I lost all my friends. They all left when I started practicing Buddhism. There was all sorts of badmouthing going on around me. I got fired from my school, and I wasn't the only one. Other members who were teachers . . . well, most of them were dismissed," she complains, still agitated by her recollections of those times and the price she and others paid to be nonconformists in Japan. "In some families, parents disowned members. Brothers and sisters often severed any kind of family ties. So who would want to *come* to us? That's why, you know, this organization is so great. We didn't stand around waiting. We had to blaze the trail. People in those days said we were really aggressive, but we couldn't help it. We weren't criticizing individuals. We were attacking erroneous philosophy and religious teachings."

She pauses, a long chain of memories exhausted, which I take as an opening for me to attempt to redirect her associations "I understand you were originally drawn to Makiguchi as a teacher interested in educational reform. Can you tell me what it was like to take up Buddhism as a religion with Mr. Toda?"

She sits quietly for a few long moments, thinking so intently that I can almost watch her marshal her thoughts, then describes how Toda wedded shakubuku to life-force philosophy in his Buddhist evangelism.

"When I went to see Mr. Toda after his release from prison, I was not interested in religion," she begins. "So I asked him, 'Is this a good religion? Is it a bad religion? You say it's a correct teaching. What is that based on?' He attentively listened to my questions before answering me.

"'Who are you and what are you?' Mr. Toda asked me point-blank. So I thought to myself, *Yasu Kashiwabara,* but I remained silent, staring at him.

"'You are a spirit, are you not? But is that all you are? You are a body, your physical being is also there, isn't it?' he said.

"And I thought to myself, *Well, that's true.*

"'But what else is there?' he asked. 'You are a spirit and a body. But what else? What else?' He just wouldn't let up and kept saying, 'The body, the spirit. But what else?'" she recalls, making sharp gestures with both hands, which convey how Toda stirred her up.

"Finally he just said to me, 'You're alive. You are life. You are spirit, body, and life,'" she says. "'These three constitute a Buddha. The Buddha appears in this world in response to the environment. It has always existed and is unchanging, but something triggered it to manifest in you. The Buddha is not about meditating or about statues of the Buddha meditating. No matter whether you are sitting or standing or whatever, Buddha is compassionate wisdom in spirit, body, and life.'"

Kashiwabara pauses again, another run of memories complete, so I attempt to redirect her thoughts, curious about how Toda's philosophy became a source of controversy. "Critics sometimes expressed concern about the activities of Gakkai youth," I say. "Why was that?"

Kashiwabara's words create a snapshot of the early days when young women and men gathered together to chant daimoku in a member's small wood-frame house in one of Tokyo's dense neighborhoods, long before the Gakkai began to build community centers. Sometimes the house would overflow with people, all of them spirited, singing Gakkai songs, she says. Her memories awakened, she breaks into a few bars of "Doshi no uta" ("Song of Comrades"), whose spirit I can gauge from the lilting tone of her voice, though I do not understand the lyrics.

"So there would be all these people coming in and out," she says, "smoking cigarettes, and there's only one bathroom inside the small house. So there would be individuals who could not, well, you know . . ."—I wait through a delicate pause that is either Kashiwabara's or Rie's—"wait until they got home, so they might urinate in the street. And all the noise, coming from the songs, because we always sang our songs."

"And?" I say, wanting more. "Would neighbors complain?"

"Oh, yes! Some neighbors came screaming at us," she replies. "It wasn't just complaining."

"Did they ever call the police?"

"Sure! Sometimes."

"And what would Toda do in that situation?" I ask.

"Mr. Toda worried about it. He would give us guidance. He would himself go and apologize to the neighbors and say we're very sorry. We will not have this happen again. At his suggestion, we tried to create good, trustworthy friendships with neighbors around us, so they knew what was going on in that house, so we could get along."

Our conversation lasted for over two hours, with Kashiwabara crossing and recrossing the early years—her work evacuating children during the war, making long trips with Toda into the countryside to contact old members, often having to sleep in railway stations or at the side of the road. Finally it was clear she'd finished, her energy and memories tapped out. But after we exchanged good-byes, she left laughing, saying as she put on her sunglasses that she is too easily recognized in Shinanomachi. "Everyone has read *The Human Revolution* and wants to stop to talk with Katsu Kiyohara."

· · ·

After lunch we drive to the *Seikyo Shimbun* building, where I meet Einosuke Akiya, the current president of Soka Gakkai–Japan, who was also a disciple of Toda and knew Ikeda well in the early days.[15] Our car creeps up a narrow street in a corner of Shinanomachi through a neighborhood of apartment houses, offices, and a few walled compounds, suited men with walkie-talkies reporting our progress. We soon pull into a spacious drive in front of a seven-story building with a crowd of young people outside. They applaud enthusiastically as I step out of the van, photographers snapping pictures of my arrival. A man in a brown suit whom I take to be Akiya stands at the doorway extending his hand.

After cordial introductions, Akiya and I make our way to the elevator and ride up to a top-floor reception hall. He must be in his seventies, feels tall to me, and walks slowly, with a lanky gait. We speak through Rie, but I note a quiet, evenly paced bass resonance to his voice, quite different from Ikeda's gravelly, more rapid, almost spitfire manner of speaking. The reception hall is different as well: spacious and comfortable but woodier, more brown, rose, and green in tone, and airier, a cross between a corporate conference room and a library.

We are all shown to our chairs, which, as in Makiguchi Hall, are arranged around the center of the room in a large rectangle. Rob, a *Seikyo Shimbun* reporter, and a number of young men and women I take to be administrative aides sit on long couches. Akiya and I are in easy chairs next to each other, with Rie seated nearby. He and I exchange several polite volleys—"How good of you to come to see me," he says; "How pleased I am you had the time," I reply—before getting down to business.

"My concern today," I say, "is to hear about your experience in the Soka Gakkai and what light you can shed on Toda and his relationship with Ikeda."

Akiya begins to lay out the situation in 1951 when he was twenty-one, a senior on leave from Waseda University with chronic tuberculosis, as a young woman passes all of us cookies, juice, and coffee. He tells me of his postwar religious skepticism, shared with many in his generation—a reaction to the disastrous consequences of State Shinto and the formalism of Japan's traditional religions. He also recounts how he was engaged at the time in lengthy, heated debates with a cousin who shakubukued him, in an effort to persuade him to join the Soka Gakkai.

"My honest reaction was that he went insane, he'd gone crazy," Akiya tells me. "I felt I had a responsibility to save him! Once a week he visited me, however, and through continuous dialogue, I learned that the Buddhism he was talking about was not the one I was familiar with. It was not funeral Buddhism, a dead religion, a very ritualistic religion," he says, referring to Buddhism's close association with rites for the dead in Japan.

Akiya continues by recalling how he eventually attended one of Toda's lectures at the old headquarters. "I must admit that I did not really grasp or understand what he was trying to convey," he tells me, but he was impressed with Toda's passion, character, humor, and interest in youth. "I had never met this type of man before," he recalls. "It was a mind-boggling experience."

Akiya pauses to take a sip of coffee, which I take to mean that he is ready for me to pose another question. "I recall myself, in another time and place, how it was to be young and to talk with friends about issues," I say, thinking about the '60s, the war in Vietnam, and the student movement. "I wonder if you could tell me what was on your minds in those days?"

"We were young people who decided to practice a religion," he replies, "so the topic was, What then is religion for? Did we start this practice because we wanted to attain individual happiness? Or is there a purpose beyond that? If so, how can we contribute to that? We would discuss how Buddhism can contribute to other people's happiness because in Buddhism there's this concept of salvation for all of humankind. Now, this is a very large goal! So we would discuss what that meant to us, how we as individuals could put this into practice." Many discussions centered on the concept of kosen-rufu, he continues. "What is kosen-rufu? We believed that kosen-rufu could not just be a religious activity. The wisdom of Buddhism should be reflected in all realms of human endeavor, including culture, including education. Only by doing so will it have impact on human lives and society. The topic would therefore shift to, What is culture? Or what is ideal education for humanity? And so on."

The dynamic of our conversation—Akiya speaks; Rie translates; I reply; Rie translates for me—allows me plenty of time to organize thoughts and make observations. Akiya speaks softly and thoughtfully, making only occasional gestures, which strike me as courtly in their calm deliberateness. I find myself wondering about what he is like when he loses his temper, how he gets along with his wife, how large his family is.

"Were those discussions infused with debates about postwar Japan and democracy?" I ask, wanting to hear about Toda's take on religion and politics.

"Of course. Especially in the early days—1951, '52, to '55, right after the end of the war when we were experiencing the rapid reconstruction," he replies. "We saw a whole class of disenfranchised citizens with no voice in the political realm. Buddhism to us was confronting reality. It was natural to us, when thinking about the future of Japan, to think about voiceless people. We felt it was important for us to become active, responsible participants in politics." He talks of Toda's fears about venturing into the corrupt world of politics. "He was very pained to send his disciples into that world, like pushing them over the cliff. It was a great pain on his part."

Akiya goes on to describe Toda's efforts to educate youth in the Suiko-kai, a special leadership group within the much larger Youth Division. As Rie recounts his words to me, I find myself thinking about "conscious-raising" back in the '60s. Then an image from the auditorium at Soka University pops into my mind: Plato and Socrates striding together through the Academy in Athens, togas flowing, the two deep in philosophical conversation.

"The method President Toda used was to have us read great classic literature," he recalls, "and then to debate key human issues, social, political, and economic issues. For example, the Chinese classic *The Tale of Three Kingdoms* was one he used for study. It is set in classical China during the warring states period. So it was an opportunity to learn about strategy, to learn to think strategically, to think about the nature of human struggle, the nature of authority in society, and how struggles for power take shape. Those were the kinds of things he very strictly pounded into us. How should a young person view human society? Every time we studied with him, we felt that our worldview had been expanded greatly.

"Let me give you one example of how Mr. Toda would talk to us," he says, while gesturing to indicate that I should help myself to more cookies. "'In the old days, the focus was military. What's your military capacity, how many soldiers can you put on the field? In contemporary society, that comes down to money. How much money do you control? How much money do you have access to? This is a very blunt example of how the nature of power has shifted over time.' So Mr. Toda was very concrete, talking with us about the realities of human society."

As Rie translates this to me, I see a good opening to ask Akiya how he understands all the early controversies. "In *The Human Revolution*, Ikeda suggests that Toda occasionally had to rein in young men," I say, "who became too zealous in their debates with other Buddhists. Please talk a bit about that."

"Two things," he begins. "First, Mr. Toda would tell us to open our eyes to the reality of the religious world of Japan. 'Look at all these religions. They are extremely formal,' he would say. 'They no longer have the desire or the power to save people from their real suffering.' He encouraged us to debate and see how much more we knew than many priests. So we challenged priests. And we realized that they really had no knowledge of the sutras.

"Second, young people were often criticized for their heated discussions during shakubuku," he recalls. "But you have to understand that to introduce somebody to a new practice—if that person already has a belief system—you have to dialogue with them to change their view. It's like revolutionizing a person's worldview. We were not savvy communicators. All we felt was passion and conviction: 'I really want to talk about this. I want you to understand. I want you to start this practice.' You can imagine the reaction."

Throughout the interview, I closely watch the time, trying to pace our discussion to fit the allotted hour, so I take this opportunity to begin to wrap up the interview by asking him to talk about Toda and Ikeda's relationship.

"From the very beginning, I think Mr. Toda saw the qualities Mr. Ikeda possessed. One could tell because he was especially strict with President Ikeda. In those days, when Mr. Toda scolded us for something, all of us would stand behind Mr. Ikeda. He was our defense fortress," he recalls with a quiet, broad smile, "a breakwater that absorbed Toda's scolding. The kind of strong bond of mentor and disciple that had existed between Mr. Makiguchi and Mr. Toda was clearly apparent between them. It was very obvious and we all accepted it."

Akiya then develops his thoughts in a way that sheds light on the Gakkai's entire program by describing the mentor-disciple relationship, not in terms of demands and duties as many critics imagine it to be, but in terms of choice, freedom, and responsibility. "This is how I see the mentor-disciple relationship," he begins, "It's really the disciple's choice and decision to follow his mentor's vision. In response, it is the mentor's wish to raise and foster that disciple so that he can become a greater person than the mentor himself. His wish is to pull him up to where he is or even to surpass him. It is the right spirit of the disciple to earnestly absorb as much as possible from the mentor," he concludes. "As long as this spirit exists, the mentor-disciple relationship is established. How deep or how strong that bond is depends on that individual's spirit and attitude."

Our time together at an end, Akiya escorts me down to the front door of the building, where we part with several volleys of cordial words. As we drive off, Rob pokes me and tells me to wave good-bye, so I turn in my seat, back toward the building, to see Akiya standing alone on the curb, waving broadly, as we head back to the main street of Shinanomachi.

· · ·

The next day Rob and I fly back to the States, my bull-market foray into globalization over, my first Japan-Gakkai crash course at an end. For an hour, we celebrate the success of the trip with drinks, recalling episodes together, me frantically scribbling notes about visits with members, meals, impressions of Japan, and other things I fear I will otherwise forget.

Later, as the cabin grows quiet, I gaze at the towering clouds over the Pacific, recalling such vistas in old movies, the backdrop to buzz-bombers strafing battleships and dogfights between Americans and

Japanese. I take some satisfaction in knowing I have, at the very least, fleshed out my knowledge of Japan.

Much later, I crane my neck to see the snow-capped peaks of the Yukon far below me, out the window of a darkened cabin, Rob asleep in the seat beside me. *They are so much bigger than the Rockies,* I think. I absorb one last foreign vista before landing in the U.S., before returning to my life without Ann in the quiet hills of central New York.

A house where Gakkai members met for *zadankai* (discussion meeting); the paper lantern announces the meeting place in Yame City, Kyushu, around 1940. (The *Seikyo Shimbun.*)

Tsunesaburo Makiguchi (center) with participants in the first summer seminar of the Soka Kyoiku Gakkai at Shiraito waterfalls near Taisekiji, 1936. (The *Seikyo Shimbun.*)

A painting commemorating the meeting between young Daisaku Ikeda and Josei Toda at a public meeting in Ota Ward in 1947. (The *Seikyo Shimbun*.)

Covers of *Boys' Adventure,* later *Boys' Japan* magazine, one of Josei Toda's postwar business ventures, which was edited and managed by young Daisaku Ikeda. (The *Seikyo Shimbun*.)

Daisaku and Kaneko
Ikeda shortly after their
marriage in 1952.
(The *Seikyo Shimbun*.)

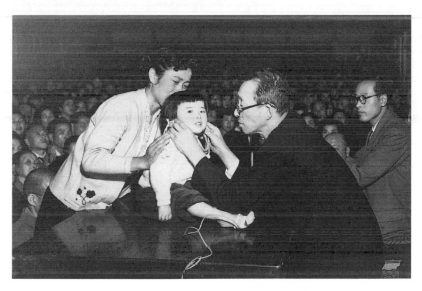

Josei Toda encourages a mother and her daughter, who suffers from encephalitis,
during a members' meeting at Taisekiji, October 5, 1957. (The *Seikyo Shimbun*.)

Scene outside Jozaiji, a Nichiren Shoshu temple in Tokyo, during the funeral of Josei Toda, 8 April 1958. (The *Seikyo Shimbun*.)

Josei Toda and Daisaku Ikeda at a Hokkaido athletic meet, 1957. (The *Seikyo Shimbun*.)

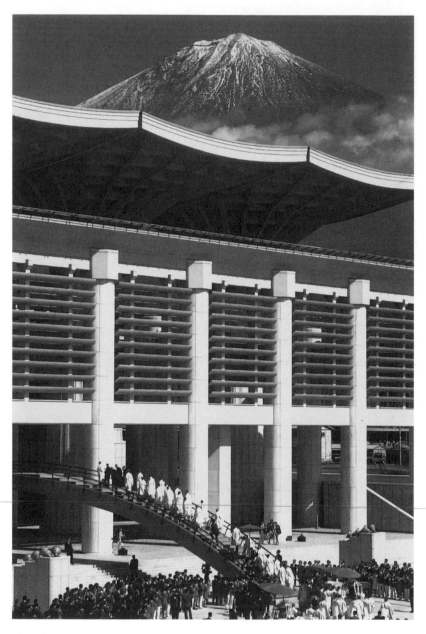

The Sho-Hondo, the Grand Main Temple, 1972, with Mount Fuji in the distance. The temple was built under the direction of Daisaku Ikeda and High Priest Nittatsu. (The *Seikyo Shimbun*.)

Historian Arnold Toynbee and his wife with Daisaku and Kaneko Ikeda in the Toynbees' living room in England, 1972. (The *Seikyo Shimbun*.)

Daisaku Ikeda (right center) with Austregésilo de Athayde (left center), a noted civil rights advocate, at the Brazilian Academy of Letters in Rio de Janeiro, 1993. (The *Seikyo Shimbun*.)

A Soka Gakkai meeting in Los Angeles during the '60s, the *Hippy to Happy* era, when L.A.-style street *shakubuku* was highly successful in recruiting new members. (Photographer: Gregory Nakasuji, SGI-USA. Reprinted with permission from SGI-USA.)

CHAPTER 4

Rising Star

Toda's life as a businessman and educator, his imprisonment, and his firsthand knowledge of war gave him a deep understanding of perils and opportunities in Japan. These experiences also contributed to his personal style—a mix of hard-nosed realism and visionary idealism shot through with earthy humor—which served him well as a postwar religious leader.

"He was a hard-sell pitchman for his faith—frank, vigorous, often rude, talkative, fond of tobacco and alcohol in quantity, impulsive, and activistic," wrote James White, an American sociologist, in his examination of the Gakkai circa 1965. He "could beat down, win over, and inspire his adversaries much in the tradition of his predecessor Nichiren."[1] There was also "a very tender side of Toda," adds Daniel Metraux, a scholar whose work has done much to dispel the pall cast over the Gakkai by its rivals, enemies, and critics. "His own familiarity with the postwar suffering of the Japanese, his genuine ability to counsel the many miserable people who came to his door, and his hard work and organizational abilities guaranteed the success of his group. When he died in 1958, Toda had become a nationally known figure whose funeral was attended by many of Japan's ruling elite."[2]

Toda's combination of vision and deep, yet irreverent, conviction appealed to Ikeda and other young people who came of age during these years and needed a straight-talking teacher and leader. "His voice was hoarse but he gave the impression of being completely at ease," Ikeda recalls, writing of his first encounter with Toda in 1947. "At first, I couldn't grasp what he was talking about, something about

Buddhism. . . . The room was filled with people in shabby clothes, but there was energy and excitement in the air. Mr. Toda was unlike anyone I had ever met. He spoke in simple, almost rough language, yet radiated warmth. . . . When I learned that he had spent two years in jail for opposing Japan's war of aggression, remaining true to his beliefs through everything, I knew this was someone in whom I could put complete trust."[3]

The fit between Toda and a new generation enabled the Gakkai to grow into a dynamic force, and much of its success can be attributed to the collaborative efforts of the ailing Toda and the youthful, energetic Ikeda. A strategic thinker by instinct, Toda adopted a military style that critics read as evidence of the Gakkai's militancy—Toda the general in command, Ikeda his young lieutenant. But within the Gakkai, it was more the case that Toda was president, teacher, and leader and Ikeda his right-hand man, the rising star, the disciple who was singularly adept at realizing his mentor's vision.

.   .   .

No high-energy Gakkai people, no fascinating interviewees, no chatty Shinjuku dinners with Rob break my days after returning from Tokyo to Deansboro, the hamlet where I live, which I fondly refer to as a burg outside another burg. Disoriented by my jump from Tokyo's zip to the languid pace of rural New York, I spend a few days sleeping as I begin to process my first Asian journey. Back home, I'm confronted again by Ann's startling absence and often feel newly harrowed by her death. But I'm also aware of being suffused with a quiet newness, a satisfaction that seems related to having become a globalized person, having stretched myself by rising to the occasion of doing real-life, in-the-trenches academic work in the East.

As I reacclimate myself to village life alone—waking to the flat clang of the bell of the Living Waters church, reading on warm, golden mornings, wasting afternoons in the small mall ten miles away or with a stint at the gym—I explore the root causes of all the flip-flopping I did in Japan.

From my stable Deansboro perch, I see how the Gakkai, Ikeda—all things Japanese, really—became a living Rorschach test that I'd gazed at for more than a week, its kaleidoscopic modern–East Asian patterns amenable to many interpretations, all inevitably colored by my emotional needs. Still on unsure footing since losing Ann, deaf and dumb in a foreign language, probing a sociohistorical reality seemingly familiar yet alien, I'd alternately let fears of crafty Japanese, inculcated during a postwar childhood, and romantic, '60s-era yearnings for Asian spiritualities get the better of me.

But I also allow that I'd had to field hard issues like the fact that the trip was funded by the Boston Research Center, a Gakkai affiliate in the United States. That Gakkai money was to pay for Gakkai research was something I'd dealt with before leaving, knowing well from graduate school how Protestants tend to fund research on Protestants, Catholics on Catholics, Jews on Jews, and so on. What I hadn't factored in was how a latent Japanophobia might intersect with money to have me homing in on manipulation issues.

More subtle but equally unexpected, money also brought to the surface a "good boy" syndrome, in which my sense of autonomy came into conflict with an instinctual eagerness to please, the result being an internalized conflict of interests. That no one in Japan had in any way pressured me is both a fact and a revelation, although there were, of course, the hundred daimoku for Ann and her cherry tree.

As I ponder all this, it becomes clear that my interpretive quandaries wheel around what I make of Toda and Ikeda, an evaluation made difficult by their enemies, whose often wildly exaggerated blasts are easily understood to be politically motivated. Quite different is what to make of Ikeda in light of how he is regarded by many of his disciples, both in Japan and overseas. To those outside the movement, members often seem to hold Ikeda in inflated esteem, loving him too much, quoting him too often, imputing to him a degree of genius not readily apparent to dispassionate observers. All this has led to charges that the Gakkai's Buddhism is "Ikedaism," its institutions controlling, its members prone to a spiritual groupthink based on his ideas.

Fresh from wrestling with myself and with the Gakkai in Japan, I'm eager to burrow back into research as soon as I get over jet lag. I sense that I'm ready to look at the movement's history of controversy in a somewhat new light.

Soon, I'm devoting my days to the academic literature on the movement and am intrigued to see a meaningful pattern emerge. Newer scholarship, such as *Global Citizens: The Soka Gakkai Buddhist Movement in the World* or "The Soka Gakkai: Buddhism and the Creation of a Harmonious and Peaceful Society" praises the movement for its progressive values and its members' sense of civic duty.[4] Older articles and books, by contrast, are consistently preoccupied with a varied array of virulent charges. The fact that these two literatures are not in dialogue with each other creates a fractured view of the Soka Gakkai, a view quite like my own when I'm flip-flopping.

My understanding of how the Gakkai's controversial reputation went international begins to take shape as I see how an earlier generation of Cold War scholars, mostly Americans, were driven by concern for the future of Japan and, more particularly, for the rapidly expanding U.S. interests in the Pacific. Most were alarmed by the success of the Gakkai's charismatic leaders at forging a highly cohesive movement. Many expressed wariness about the Gakkai's grassroots character, fearing that underclass Japaneseness was fertile ground for reactionary extremism. Others viewed the Gakkai's aspiration to proselytize on the Asian mainland as a replay of Japan's prewar Asian co-prosperity sphere or, alternatively, as an overture to Communist China. Some reiterated charges made by Japan's Socialists that the Gakkai was a "time bomb" in Japanese society.[5] Commentators rarely accused the Gakkai directly of sedition or revolutionary activities, but their frequently stated concerns helped to create its reputation as a religious and political threat to a stable, America-friendly, free-market democracy in Japan.

Two book-length assessments of the postwar movement, both of them thoughtful and balanced, thoroughly cover this ground.[6] The more exhaustive of the two, *The Sokagakkai and Mass Society* by sociologist James White, is a study framed in terms of the threat posed to the democratic process by postwar-era mass alienation. Writing at a time when memories of the rise of fascism in Europe were fresh and a premium had been placed on the stability of Japan, White examines the motives of the movement's members and analyzes its structure and ideology. Writing also at a time when Ikeda was just coming into his own as a mature leader, White draws conclusions that, while measured, cautious, and qualified, essentially cleared the movement of critics' most significant charges.

A more ominous picture was sometimes drawn by Western journalists who, according to Takesato Watanabe, a communications studies professor at Doshisha University, tend to cater to "latent anti-Japanese sentiments," their writing often "the culmination of stereotypical notions about the 'alien' nature of Japan and Japanese religion."[7]

Such was the case in the ominous portrait drawn in a brief article in the popular photojournalism magazine *Look* in 1963.[8] *Look* noted the failure of established religions to aid ordinary Japanese in the postwar crisis and cited the Gakkai's "near miraculous pole vault into national prominence." But it dismissed Ikeda, then thirty-five, as "energetic, genial, and glib," in particular criticizing him for his poor grasp of Christianity. Much of the article consists of testimonies by Gakkai rivals and old-line scholars, who together characterized the movement as superficial, pathologically intolerant, and highly materialistic. Makiguchi is not principled but "pugnacious"; strong convictions are "fanatical egotism." Daimoku is described as a "hypnotic drone" said to mean "I am the Supreme Power." The main point to be taken—that neither the Japanese nor Ikeda are entirely to be trusted—is made clear in the quote framing the article: "Japanese people either want to be a leader or want to be led. Soka Gakkai guarantees fulfillment for both the shepherd and the sheep . . . or a Hitler and the hordes."

A more balanced, yet wary, take on the Gakkai appeared in the *New York Times Magazine* in a 1965 article, "Soka Gakkai Brings 'Absolute Happiness,'" one that implicitly tied concern about the Gakkai to the rapidly escalating Vietnam conflict.[9] Half a dozen photos—of a mass political rally, chanting throngs, a pilgrimage to Taisekiji—underscore a concern for "the political implications that this [movement] may have for American policy," ones "potentially more important than the anti-Western neutralism propagated by the saffron-robed monks of South Vietnam." The *Times* intelligently handled Makiguchi, the Gakkai's ability to address the malaise of the postwar years, and its ongoing electoral successes. It noted political bywords then current in the movement such as "neo-socialism," "a third culture" neither capitalist nor socialist, "global nationalism," and "Buddhist democracy." Describing the Gakkai as a "militant society" of lay Buddhists whose most overzealous members have occasionally become violent, the *Times* also dismissed charges that the Gakkai was fascist or even right wing. Its main concern was that should the Gakkai's presence in the Diet grow, it might "favor a more independent and neutralist course for the United States's principal ally in the Far East."

In off hours, I try to fill out the big picture of modern Japan by reading history and literature from Fujitani's *Splendid Monarchy* to the novels of Kenzaburo Oe. I also inhale Japanese videos, always working to educate my instincts. I cry over *Grave of the Fireflies,* an animated film about children made parentless by the war who eventually die of starvation. I puzzle over Akira Kurosawa's *Dodes'ka-Den,* a fantasy about Nichiren Buddhists in postwar Tokyo whose anguished poverty gives rise to hope for a utopian future. I see my parents in Yasujiro Ozu's *Tokyo Story,* a look at the generation gap between urban postwar children and their provincial parents.

It is not just the story I follow in each but details that speak of sameness and difference to me—Tokyo apartment buildings with tricycles and kids in the halls that recall Chicago tenements; noodle shops with counters and stools like diners in Boston; an old-fashioned grandmother much like my own but clad in a kimono, alarmed by the brazenness of her daughter. I learn to love sniffing out Japan-bashing in Hollywood movies such as *Rising Sun*, which, as late as 1993, still exploited widespread fears of a Japanese takeover of the U.S. economy.

I see it as a sign, a good one I think, when I begin to dream in Japanese, long episodes from which I awake startled not to understand my own dream activity, but pleased that some creative psychic process may be under way. I take them to be saying that I've begun to crawl out of my American skin a bit, to go a bit deeper than the dichotomy of similarity and difference into the shared human condition of our globalizing modernity.

One afternoon a brown UPS van delivers all the material I'd collected in Japan—books, flyers, videos, brochures, and articles. In a satin-lined box, I find a gold medallion I received at the leaders' meeting in Makiguchi Hall, an award for my work in the humanities presented to me by Akiya. "The Japanese Socrates!" I exclaim, running my fingers over his Attic profile, happy to recall Hugo, Leonardo, Whitman, and the rest of the crew at Soka University. And the gifts—Waterman pens, etched-glass plates, a pocket watch, fine-arts books, lapel pins.

Memories tinged with nostalgia sweep over me as I recall stepping in and out of shoes, the little bows made in greeting, the civilized tradition of gift giving and receiving. As I sift through boxes, the oranges and grapefruits set before the gohonzon, my conversations with Rie, Akiya's courtly manner when offering me cookies, and Ann's cherry tree all come rushing back. Right here in Deansboro! The sparkle of the spirit of SG-Japan!

. . .

I spend one afternoon flipping through a fat file of ephemera: matchbooks, menus, notes scribbled on trains, snapshots processed in the hotel, a Komeito flyer handed to me on a street in Ota Ward by a man who did not know I was there to explore Ikeda's old haunts. I recall that my first glimpse of Ota—today one of Tokyo's twenty-three wards, with a population of some six hundred thousand—reminded me of Lynn, Massachusetts, an old industrial city north of Boston: decent and

solid, but scrappy. Few visual cues suggested the pastoral, coastal land-
scapes Ikeda evokes in his recollections of his childhood—rice paddies
and pomegranate trees, geishas in summer pavilions frequented by the
wealthy, bamboo frames called *hibi* used in the cultivation of seaweed
bobbing offshore in the shallows, kites flying over the beach at
Morigasaki. "How different the area of Tokyo where my home was situated looks today!" Ikeda writes in *Glass Children*, an engaging collection of brief reflective essays. "Now an express highway has been built
through the area, the monorail passes through it on its way to the airport, and the new super-express train runs close by."[10]

The communities that now comprise Ota Ward began to industrialize
in the '30s, when Ikeda was still a child, and they are now part of the
Keihin Industrial Zone. By the '40s, they had become enough of a man-
ufacturing powerhouse that they were repeatedly pummeled by
American bombs, leaving little after the war but scorched earth and
rubble-strewn streets. My snapshots capture an Ota that has the look of
having been built in the '60s—family-owned microfactories, midsize
industrial complexes, commercial storefronts with roll-down steel doors,
low-rise concrete apartment buildings. Since the war, so much of Tokyo
Bay has been filled that Ota hardly hints that it borders on the sea.

Ikeda spent almost forty years, from his birth in 1928 to 1966, when
he and his family moved to Shinanomachi, in various towns in Ota
Ward: Iriarai, where he was born; Kojiya, where he delivered newspa-
pers. Later, after Pearl Harbor, at the age of fourteen, he milled parts
for warships in the Niigata Steelworks in Kamata, including one-man
submarines, "human torpedoes," the naval equivalent of the planes
flown by kamikaze pilots in the desperate closing years of the war. Like
many in his generation, Ikeda sees his antiwar sentiments as having
roots in a childhood spent in the shadow of militarism—marching with
oak staves in grade school; factory work under the gaze of soldiers; the
conscription of his eldest brother, Kiichi, who would die in Burma, and
then the drafting of his three other older brothers. When Ikeda himself
thought to enlist when he was about sixteen, Kiichi counseled him not
to and his father forbade him.

Toward the end of the war, the Ikeda family lived with an aunt in
nearby Magome. They'd been forcibly evacuated from their house by
the government, which tore it down to prevent the spread of fires from
incendiary bombs. But the aunt's house received a direct hit soon after
they moved in, destroying all the family's possessions and leaving them
to live for a time in a tin-roofed, makeshift shelter. "These cherry trees

have survived the ravages of war; / The sky is pure blue, a tumult of falling petals," Ikeda wrote about this time, an early example of the verse he would write for the rest of his life. "Against the backdrop of a world in ruins, / People in their misery see no blossoms."[11]

After the war, the family lived in Morigasaki, which is right on the coast, while Ikeda attended a commercial high school. But establishing his independence, he soon moved to nearby Araijuku to live alone in a single room. When he and Kaneko married in 1952, with Toda acting as go-between with their parents, the two continued to live in the area. They then moved to nearby Kobayashicho to be closer to Kaneko's family; during this time Ikeda spent long days at headquarters, more than an hour north by train in central Tokyo, or in Osaka or Hokkaido, always on the run, busy leading the Youth Division and directing shakubuku campaigns.

Ikeda's fondest childhood memories are tied to an earlier Ota and the sea, when his parents cultivated, harvested, and processed laver or nori, an edible seaweed used as the thin, green wrapping on rolled sushi. His mother's people were Ota farmers, but his father's family had been in laver since the Tokugawa period, achieving some prosperity with operations in Ota and Chiba, east across the Bay of Tokyo, and even some far to the north in Hokkaido. But seaweed cultivation suffered after the Kanto earthquake of 1923, when the level of the bay dropped two feet, making aquaculture difficult. So in his recollections of his childhood days, Ikeda conveys a sense of a large, hardworking, and happy family—seven sons and one daughter—with fortunes in decline, but with daily and seasonal schedules that remained tied to the sea.

These good early years, however, seemed remote to Ikeda in the wake of the war, when he was confused, deeply skeptical, and searching for some meaning in life—a young man much like those described to me by President Akiya. "When the war ended," he writes, "I found myself in the same situation as many of my contemporaries. I could no longer believe in anything. . . . Confronted with the ruin of our adolescence, we reflected in anguish on those bygone days. But not a shred of the past remained. All that remained for me was the tragic experience itself."[12] It was also about this time that Ikeda, always an avid reader with an interest in literature and philosophy, searched out a lecture on the French life-force philosopher Henri Bergson, only to discover Toda and the Lotus Sutra. This too happened in Ota.

A sense of Ikeda's manner and mood in 1949 and 1950 is revealed in his diary, which has been published in a number of languages and is now considered inspirational reading. In its first pages, one sees him at twenty-two during his first year of living apart from his family, making lists to guide his self-improvement—"1. Study Buddhism. 2. Cut down on expenses. 3. Live productively"; "1. Take care of my health. 2. Study hard. 3. Live productively"; "Effort . . . Patience . . . Confidence . . . Conviction . . . Faith"—while enduring a cold room, worrying about his headaches and losing weight, and fretting over the conflict in Korea.[13] Much of his life revolved around his new religion: attending group meetings, chanting, going on pilgrimage to Taisekiji, attempting to propagate Buddhism to a struggling bureaucrat or stray artist. But more of the diary is devoted to Toda and his ailing businesses about the time the two began to forge their mentor-disciple relationship:

> Thursday. June 16 [1949]. Rain. Scolded by Mr. Toda. Agonizing. All my fault. Must reflect on myself. I believe in Mr. Toda.
> Tuesday. May 16 [1950]. Cloudy. Paid my rent. Mr. Toda is facing terrible battles. He is called upon both to attack and defend. I must resolve to stand up soon. The time has come when a son of the revolution must arise!
> Tuesday. August 22 [1950]. Clear. Our company has decided to suspend operations. Exchanged parting cups with Mr. Toda. . . . I felt as though my heart would break. How mortifying! How tragic! I, however, will advance with Mr. Toda toward our next effort. Nothing else matters. Forward. Eternally forward.
> Saturday. October 21 [1950]. Light rain. Mr. Josei Toda spoke to me, entrusting to me in detail various matters for the future. His will reverberates in my heart.[14]

Through all this, Ikeda reminds himself to study Buddhism diligently but "to study other subjects too," particularly literature—Goethe; Schiller; Chogyu Takayama, a novelist who embraced both Nichiren and Nietzsche. He reads Tolstoy's *Diaries;* Whitman's *Leaves of Grass; A Solitary Cell* by Takiji Kobayashi, a Taisho leftist who died during a police interrogation; Pascal's *Pensées;* and essays of Francis Bacon. He also frequents movies, often alone, seeing *Listen, the Waves* at the Globe, *Les Misérables* in Shimbashi, and *The Babe Ruth Story* in Omori. He sees *Wuthering Heights* with friends whom he treats to *chirashi-zushi,* a vinegared rice treat. He later reflects that inviting people out is fine, but it is a far better gesture of friendship to convince them to take up the practice of true Buddhism.

Each page bristles with a literate effervescence consistent with Ikeda in later years: "Youth amid the storm: profound, remote, mysterious. Youth, like the surging strains of Beethoven. Youth, brimming with poetry as wildly impassioned as Dante's." Some of this might be attributable to later editing, but his reflections on *Boys' Japan,* one of Toda's ailing publications, sound like those of a romantic young man and surely must be pure and early Ikeda. "Boys' Japan—what a broad and powerful phrase! Boys growing toward the future, motions lighthearted as spring. Eyes clear as autumn skies. . . . Boys of Japan! Boys of the whole world! Each of you, be forever cheerful and courageous, like a messenger of heaven."[15]

Our visit to Ota was led by Nanae Kimura, a young woman raised in the area who knows it well and is now editor of an English-language newsletter in an office in Shinanomachi. Rob, Rie, and I looked out from the bus as Nanae narrated, her remarks underscoring how things had changed since Ikeda's childhood. Pointing out a microfactory or freeway interchange, she would say, "Just about here was the Magome house of President Ikeda's aunt, where the family moved after they were evacuated," or "Up that street is where the building the Ikedas lived in after they married used to be." A few buildings still exist that suggest the old days—a public bathhouse Ikeda used when he lived in Morigasaki with his family; the Ikeda Supermarket, a local operation run by a brother, cousin, or uncle, I cannot recall which.

Ota has become a destination of sorts for Gakkai members, who come to visit sites now fabled only because of their prominence in Ikeda's writings, among them the beach where he took solitary walks among pine groves. Ikeda wrote "Morigasaki Beach" in 1947, but the poem was eventually set to music and became a popular movement song. It recounts a youthful exchange, poignant with spiritual yearning, between Ikeda and a friend who worked with him at Niigata Steelworks. In it Ikeda wonders aloud, in the company of this friend who had become Christian, about what his own spiritual path will be. "I wish you all luck, my friend!" he writes; "Next time we meet—/when will it be? Wordless we depart/upon our separate journeys/silver waves sway gently/Morigasaki."[16]

Following Nanae's lead, Rob, Rie, and I had to scramble over several embankments of fill before we arrived at the beach, where it was still quiet and contemplative in the hazy sun. But as I recall it, the beach is now more a strand of stones trucked in to front the fill, and it opens onto a view of manmade islands, an engineered landscape like the buttressed banks of all the rivers that flow through Ota to the shore.

The Miyake house, a small, old-style residence on a narrow leafy street, is where Toda and Ikeda first met in 1947. It is another fabled

Ota site that, like many homes in Japan, has remained for generations within the same family. Mr. Miyake, a small man perhaps in his seventies, greeted us at the door and fell quickly into his role as tour guide.

"So, Doctor, this is the place where fifty-three years ago President Toda and the young President Ikeda met for the first time, just here," he said, pointing out the exact spot. "From here a great revolution started. This is President Toda," he continued, gesturing at one of many photos that hung on the living room wall. "And this is President Ikeda, nineteen years old. The discussion meeting where they met spanned all three rooms. President Ikeda came through that door and down that passage," he said, showing me the precise layout of the first encounter between Toda and Ikeda in a scale model of the house as it was in 1947.

I recall being enthralled by the rich memorabilia—an oil painting of that first discussion meeting, another of Ikeda as a young man on Morigasaki beach, collections of old badges and certificates given to those who passed exams on the Lotus Sutra—and intrigued by Miyake himself. At the time, I had yet to meet rank-and-file members from the old days, so my take on the Gakkai was informed by younger people, professionals in the movement, who had come of age taking Ikeda's Buddhist Humanism for granted. But Miyake was a different breed, a person whose thought processes revealed an older Gakkai worldview and mentality.

"This lintel has been preserved from the house as it was at the time of their meeting," he said, pointing with pride to a darkened beam set within the ceiling. Gesturing toward a recess in the floor, he continued, "Down there are floorboards from that time too. When we were redoing the house, we pulled up the floors and saw that the wood came from Sado in Niigata Prefecture—Sado Island to which Nichiren was exiled by authorities in Kamakura, where he wrote important letters to his disciples. So President Toda and President Ikeda were actually standing on a pine tree from Sado Island when they had their first meeting."

Miyake went on to explain how the karma of the house played a role in the historic meeting. His mother, he said, attended a meeting in 1942 where she heard Makiguchi say that faith can spare people from disaster. So in 1945, when the neighborhood was evacuated, she remained in the house to prove the power of her faith. As Miyake told it, three incendiary bombs fell nearby that his mother—precisely how was never clear—kept away from the house. "Everyplace else, the whole neighborhood was burned out. From here over, for the next two kilometers, all the way to Kamata Station, there wasn't a house in sight, and there wasn't another one for the next two kilometers off in the opposite direction either."

For Miyake, the religious meaning of the story was perfectly clear: the law of karma had worked through Makiguchi, his mother, and her house to play its role in bringing Toda and Ikeda together. "This house was not burned. That was the protection and benefit of the gohonzon. I find it very mystic that the house survived because of the guidance of President Makiguchi. And then it was at this very house that President Toda and President Ikeda met each other. I feel a very profound mystical connection in this."

In the bus a few minutes later, I struck up a conversation about what to make of Miyake's story, wanting to gauge the range of religious attitudes current in the Gakkai today. Nanae made a few remarks to the effect that the house certainly had historic meaning since it was the place where President Toda and Mr. Ikeda met. But Rie saw in Miyake's remarks a mentality expressive of a traditional, magical worldview found among older pioneers, one that fell out of favor in a later generation and is quite alien to her own. Rob held his cards close, but he appeared to enjoy himself immensely.

• • •

Ikeda formally joined the Soka Gakkai in August 1947 in a ceremony at a Nichiren Shoshu temple in Tokyo. "The trip from Ota Ward to the temple . . . seemed extremely long and tough, suffering as I was from tuberculosis and pleurisy," he recalled recently. "The chanting and sutra recitation during the gohonzon-conferral ceremony seemed to go on forever. Not being used to sitting on my knees for extended periods, my legs went numb."[17] Soon after, Ikeda began to take charge of practical matters for Toda ranging from editorial assignments to cleaning up financial messes—much the same role Toda had played for Makiguchi. To take on this work, Ikeda dropped out of school, so Toda took charge of his education, while devoting himself full-time to rebuilding the Gakkai.

Soon the two forged a mentor-disciple relationship that was also an intimate friendship. "Mr. Ikeda was often summoned to President Toda's office," Yasu Kashiwabara recalled. "People watching their interactions could see that there was some special bond between them, just in the way that they talked together."[18] Einosuke Akiya described how "they had an extraordinarily profound rapport from the beginning," which he characterized as "a rhythm of breathing together."[19] In May 1951, Toda assumed the presidency, vowing to increase membership from a few thousand to 750,000 families. To achieve this goal, he launched the *Shakubuku Dai-Koshin* (Great Propagation Drive) in July. In November, he published the *Shakubuku Kyoten (Propagation Handbook)*, a how-to manual containing tactical strategies and doctrinal arguments for use in debates against rival religions and sects.

Ikeda had an insider's view as Toda created a nationwide movement united by "the vertical line," a chain of communication that linked Tokyo headquarters to the grassroots through an ever-evolving organization of districts, chapters, units, and groups. He assisted Toda in founding *Seikyo Shimbun,* the "sacred teachings newspaper," to disseminate campaign plans and Buddhist study materials. He was privy to Toda's thoughts as the president constantly tinkered with the structure of the organization, creating new departments and divisions and revitalizing old ones. The Study Department became central to the new organization by providing systematic courses and graduated exams on doctrine and the Lotus Sutra. The Youth Division cultivated new leaders by allowing young men and women a high degree of autonomy in a society that privileged senior men. Similar ends were achieved in the Women's Division where women, whose rights had recently been guaranteed by the new constitution, developed their own initiatives.

A charter member of the Youth Division, Ikeda became Toda's point man in shakubuku campaigns while in his early twenties and by 1954 was chief of staff of the Youth Division, responsible for leadership development among young men and women. Under his direction, the Youth Division led campaigns so successful that James White, the wary but ultimately sympathetic observer, called them Toda's "shock troops."[20] The Gakkai, however, attributes Ikeda's success to his insistence that piety, practice, and purity of intention take precedence over recruitment. A model leader, he attended to members' personal struggles and offered encouragement in the *zadankai,* small face-to-face meetings that functioned much like consciousness-raising groups. His heartfelt charisma and personalized style were effective in building the movement and later became a hallmark of his presidency when he moderated and, to a significant degree, secularized the spirit of the Gakkai.

But in the '50s, Ikeda learned from Toda a spirituality with political implications that were often coded in literalistic religious language that Winston Davis suggests roughly approximated that of fundamentalists in the West.[21] This approach enabled Toda to address successfully the

Gakkai's main constituency—working-class men and women, small-business owners, shopkeepers, and housewives. Often traditional in background and instinct, these people had been displaced by war and rapid social change. They were also neglected by big government, unions, and business and plagued by the kyodatsu condition. To these people the Gakkai gave meaning, motive, and community, creating what White called a "psychic haven" for people whose traditional kinship groups and regional associations had largely disintegrated.[22]

Toda taught people who were accustomed to playing passive roles in the rituals of the temple, but he recast their received knowledge in a way that shifted the focus from priests to the people. Members learned not to hire priests to chant, as had long been customary, but to chant for themselves, a change they found both disarming and empowering. The basic practice regime Toda prescribed was as rigorous as that of priests—faith in the power of the gohonzon and the practice of gongyo, twice-daily chanting of daimoku, and the recitation of parts of the Lotus Sutra. His insistence on courses and exams rounded out a program of faith, practice, and study to create an informed laity that, while taken for granted today, was innovative, even radical at the time.

Toda's identification of Buddha with life force also gave a radical cast to the spirituality he was teaching. Susumu Shimazono, a University of Tokyo historian of religion, called Toda's reworking of Nichiren Shoshu doctrine "reality-transformative."[23] To realize Buddha nature was to change one's karma, to take charge of one's destiny in the harsh postwar world. In Makiguchi's terms, to awaken Buddha nature was to seek happiness and to create value in the form of benefits; Toda taught, moreover, that these benefits could be both spiritual and material. At his urging, Gakkai members learned to chant for vitality, courage, and mental and physical health; adequate food and housing; a decent job; a good spouse and a happy family. This emphasis on benefits has been viewed with great suspicion by some Gakkai critics in the West. But Ian Reader and George J. Tanabe Jr. argue that "the promise of this-worldly benefits is an intrinsic element within Japanese religion in general," is in fact "typical" of Japanese religions, whether traditional or innovative.[24]

Furthermore, Toda taught that personal awakening was intimately tied to social transformation and a compassionate concern for others, a modernist interpretation of the mission of the bodhisattva. Shimazono writes that at the core of Toda's Buddhism was the "aspiration to transform the self and life around oneself, and the belief that these efforts have to do with salvation."[25] This reality-transformative Buddhism was the driving force behind Toda's shakubuku campaigns, which carried within them a revolutionary thrust insofar as private aspirations became social, and personal needs implicitly political.

Still, this radical thrust remained couched in conventional religious language, a traditionalism underscored by Toda's strengthening the movement's ties with Nichiren Shoshu. New members received their gohonzons only from priests and were encouraged by Toda to go on *tozan*, pilgrimage to Taisekiji, which remained a central element in Gakkai piety until the excommunication. Members took on building campaigns, adding many temples to Nichiren Shoshu and modernizing Taisekiji's facilities to handle the growing crowds who flocked there to chant before the dai-gohonzon. Toda himself developed solid working relations with a succession of high priests, who understood the imperatives of the postwar years, supported lay initiatives, and benefited from the Gakkai's propagation activities. He took the tradition's intellectual heritage seriously, collaborating with Hori Nichiko, a scholar and retired high priest, on a collection of Nichiren's writings.

Young Ikeda was in the thick of all this, heading up shakubuku campaigns and rallying Gakkai forces in support of its candidates. In *The Human Revolution,* he affectionately recalls these years in sketches of key events from debates with rival sects, which Gakkai youth took delight in as if they were competitive games, to pitched struggles between Gakkai miners and Tanro, the coal miners union. In these incidents, Ikeda portrays members as overcoming obstacles in defense of truth, as struggling to realize kosen-rufu while becoming citizens empowered to pursue personal and collective happiness in Japan's new participatory democracy. In his view, the Gakkai both manifested and defended religious freedom. But controversy grew with each political success—some fifty victories, mainly in ward assemblies in Tokyo, in 1955; in 1956 three members elected to the Upper House of the Diet.

Ikeda recalls the "Osaka incident"—actually a sequence of events over a number of years—as a pivotal moment in Gakkai history. It began with Toda's decision to run Giichiro Shiraki, a Gakkai member and popular baseball player, for office in the politically important Osaka-Kansai region in 1956. With some thirty thousand Gakkai households, the movement was weak, and Toda calculated that Shiraki needed two hundred thousand votes to win. To achieve this goal, Toda sent Ikeda to Osaka to lead shakubuku campaigns to increase membership and thus the number of Gakkai-affiliated voters. Ikeda performed this task brilliantly, leading Shiraki to victory.

In Osaka, Ikeda secured his reputation for bold leadership by creating a populist spirituality that was a rich mix of culture, politics, and religion. He showcased this new style of activism in a celebration held in the Osaka baseball stadium that became a model for Gakkai culture festivals, now held around the world. On Shakyamuni's birthday, amid brass bands, choral groups, flags, banners, and gymnastic displays, Ikeda spoke before some twenty thousand members in gusting winds and a downpour of rain. "President Toda always tells us that we must return in spirit to the days when Nichiren was alive and must try to imbue ourselves with his faith," he proclaimed. Speaking of the ongoing efforts in Kansai, he continued, saying that this "campaign is totally different from ordinary political activity because it is part of our work for the universal propagation of true Buddhism. . . . While cultural in nature, [it] is religious too since it is part of our drive toward kosen-rufu, part of our work for the salvation of the suffering people of the world."[26]

But the following year, during a second and ultimately unsuccessful Osaka campaign, Ikeda also felt the weight of his critics, when he was arrested on charges of election fraud. A few undisputed facts stand at the center of a much larger controversy. A Kyoto member was charged with door-to-door canvassing in the 1956 campaign, others with distributing cigarette packs bearing the name of the Gakkai's candidate in 1957—both illegal activities. Ikeda himself was acquitted of all charges in a trial that dragged on until 1962, but not before he had been imprisoned, interrogated, and marched in handcuffs through the streets of Osaka. Gakkai members were outraged by the response of authorities and the press, which they saw as heavy-handed and politically motivated, and the Youth Division staged spirited demonstrations in downtown Osaka.

The Osaka incident made Ikeda a public figure, even as it fixed the controversial image of the Gakkai in the public's mind. Takesato Watanabe, the media professor at Doshisha University, writes that it was during these years that the movement came to be stigmatized by the press as a "frightening religion" of the poor and the sick, a strategy meant to neutralize its criticism of the establishment.[27] The incident also forced the Gakkai into a defensive posture toward the rest of Japan. Ikeda would begin to correct this problem in 1970, in the course of another, larger crisis that became one of the most important turning points in his long presidency.

• • •

As months pass, the Japan-Gakkai sparkle dims, but immersion in research buys me time to square off with Ann's death; work compensates, at least in part, for my spending far too many hours alone. I start to look back on the drama of grief after Ann's death as profoundly religious, its sharp edges and dull thuds always having me poised at the brink of life and death. But I lost that religion months ago, and friends now tenderly suggest that it's time for me to think about getting a new wife, a girlfriend, a boyfriend, a dog, a canary, someone or something living, to mark a start on a new life. A force drives me, however, to confront issues of faith rather than to date—my profession; Catholicism; the law of karma, maybe; or the Gakkai, a cause under my skin working to an unknown effect.

Between writing, going to the gym, and watching TV, I dip into the Gakkai's esoteric side, an aspect of religion I normally keep at arm's length. From time to time, I chant "Nam-myoho-renge-kyo, Nam-myoho-renge-kyo, Nam-myoho-renge-kyo" to experiment with technique, working with MP3 files I download from an SGI site on the Web. But I don't try in any special way to get chanting to "work" for me, preferring to style it as research and healthful recreation instead, like doing some yoga.

I soon delve into *ichinen sanzen*, an ancient doctrine used by Gakkai members to describe what they call the "life condition." A theory of daunting complexity, the gist of it holds that there are ten realms ranging from despair, anger, and craving to love and rapture—the so-called ten worlds or life conditions. These are always present, but one or another dominates from moment to moment in response to prompts from the external environment, which accounts for how a person can move from despair to hope when the sun moves out from behind a cloud or from love to rage upon reading a Dear John letter. The theory also posits that these transitory, unstable, and ultimately illusory emotions can be suffused with, illumined by, and in some sense redeemed by the awakening of Buddha nature.

All this research will eventually work its way into the book, I am sure, but I value it most as creative play that, without my quite intending it, becomes a part of the newness I am cultivating. Whenever I chant, I let the big issues crash over me—loneliness; the specter of aging alone; the obsessive pondering of life and its meaning that seems to come with my professional responsibilities. On bad days, I nearly drown. But on good ones, such anxieties are waves that, however raging and fierce, can't swamp a budding sense of inner poise that borders on serenity. Amazed by the outrageous simplicity of the Gakkai's faith that people actually deserve happiness, I embrace the conceit that I am enacting a human revolution of my own, right here in Deansboro. I take to shakubukuing myself to bolster my courage. Like taking my psychic temperature, I keep a close eye on the shifting terrain of my life condition.

By fall, however, jitters in the market, followed by its full-blown collapse, put a new, bold, and frankly scary face on the meaning of globalization. I'm surprised at the perverse pleasure I take in the bull market going bear, despite blows to my modest portfolio. As a religionist, I never trusted dot-com mania, seeing in it a familiar American excess of enthusiasm for the next great age of man, always part utopia and part scam, coming down the road. Now too much glee on the part of entrepreneurial heavyweights is, predictably, giving way to hand wringing and born-again remorse.

It's good to be reminded that there are solid grounds for cynicism, I think, and it consoles me, during those bouts of hard-edged grief that still arise unexpectedly, to know that the rest of the world is not as rich, glossy, and sassy as we all thought we would be. But the panic and dread that exude from commentators begin to intrude on my own life condition, threatening to give a desperate tinge to my sense of new possibilities. "No fear, it's only life on earth; no fear, it's only life on earth; no fear, it's only life on earth," I take to chanting frequently, each syllable seeming to center me a bit in both my aloneness and my God. Soon I've made it my own cobbled-together daimoku, my custom-built Jesus prayer, a tough winter's calming, grounding mantra.

By spring, I seem to have righted myself again by embracing my widowerhood, my wounded 401(k), and the empty, open road ahead. Apparently a man of no great, booming faith, I seem neither to need nor to receive blazing conversions or dramatic awakenings. It is enough to enjoy this life connection to the Buddha that circumstances gave me and this new readiness to live, small movements of the soul that Ann would most certainly call grace.

And as if this acceptance were itself a good cause calling forth a very good effect, Rob phones to ask if I want to look at Gakkai operations in Singapore and Brazil, maybe, and whether I'm ready to make a second trip to Japan.

. . .

During his short presidency, Toda built the Gakkai into the largest, most influential of Japan's new religious movements and fashioned a

highly dynamic expression of modernist Buddhism on the legacy
bequeathed to him by Makiguchi. During the final year of his life, as
the Cold War deepened, he placed increasing emphasis on peace and on
the importance of the role of youth in the future. Ikeda would underscore these emphases in his own presidency, one tribute among many to
the work of his mentor.

In September 1957, seven months before his death, Toda offered
Gakkai youth some final guidance at a culture festival in Yokohama, as
the nuclear arms race began to heat up after the first successful Soviet
test of an intercontinental ballistic missile. "We, the citizens of the
world, have an inviolable right to live," he proclaimed, a call that resonated both with his identification of Buddha as life force and with the
fact that the Japanese alone truly grasp the horror America unleashed at
Hiroshima and Nagasaki. "Anyone who tries to jeopardize that right
[by the use of nuclear weapons] is a devil incarnate, a fiend, a monster,"
such deliberately provocative rhetoric a hallmark of Toda's style. "I pro-
pose that humankind apply, in every case, the death penalty to anyone
responsible for using nuclear weapons, even if that person is on the win-
ning side. . . . I believe it is the mission of every member of the Youth
Division in Japan to disseminate this idea throughout the globe."[28]

In March the following year, his health worsening, Toda made his
final pilgrimage to Taisekiji. It was a festive occasion as some seven thousand pilgrims gathered to celebrate the dedication of the Grand Lecture
Hall, one of the building projects for Nichiren Shoshu undertaken by
the Gakkai. Toda was so sick and weak that Youth Division members
built him a palanquin and carried him around the temple grounds to
enable him to survey the proceedings. Toda's one disappointment was
that although Nobusuke Kishi, Japan's prime minister, had been scheduled to attend—a confirmation of the Gakkai's political prominence—
he canceled at the last minute, sending his wife and family instead.

That day, however, March 16, became important in Gakkai history
when Toda, frail and pale, sitting upon his palanquin with snow-capped
Fuji in the distance, formally transmitted his vision to the Youth
Division. "Prosperity and happiness for individuals and the entire
nation can only be achieved if we make the True Law the foundation
for our thoughts and actions," he told them. "And this is only possible
if we accomplish kosen-rufu. That is our mission. I now bequeath that
mission, and the future, to you."[29]

In *The Human Revolution*, Ikeda recalls how Toda's thoughts at that
time turned to his imminent death. He would reside for a time with

Nichiren on Eagle Peak, he said, but reincarnate in seven days, maybe on Earth, perhaps on another planet, to continue his work for kosen-rufu. As the pilgrimage drew to a close, young members sat at Toda's bedside in his lodging on the temple grounds, cheering him by singing his favorite Gakkai songs.

Toda soon returned to Tokyo, where he died on April 2, 1958. The family funeral was held at his home, but afterward his coffin was carried past weeping, chanting crowds to Jozaiji, a temple in the Ikebukuro district, for services led by Nichijun, the high priest of Nichiren Shoshu, during which 120,000 people lined up to offer incense in his memory. Later that week, Nichijun posthumously appointed him *sokoto*, the head of all Nichiren Shoshu lay organizations.

On April 20, two hundred thousand people gathered for Toda's public funeral. After Nichijun led the assembly in reciting the Lotus Sutra, the Gakkai brass band played and all sang together "A Star Falls in the Autumn Wind on Wuchang Plain." It was a Toda favorite, inspired by the Chinese classics he loved to read with young people to teach them to think strategically about society, authority, and freedom. One understands its forlorn mood even without catching the references or knowing the melody:

> The autumn wind, with deepening sorrow,
> Blows from Mount Ch'i
> Gloomy clouds gather over the battleground
> of Wuchang Plain.
> The world's troubles, like raging swells on stormy seas,
> Have yet to be quelled
> And the people suffer, while heaven weeps.[30]

Ikeda felt not only a grievous personal loss but a powerful marshaling within him of energies he would need to continue to realize Toda's vision. "My beloved mentor is gone," he wrote the week of Toda's death. "Standing in the vanguard of the disciples / who have emerged from the earth, / I advance again today / like a surging wave."[31]

He reflected on Toda's conviction that Gakkai history was structured in sevens—seven years from its founding by Makiguchi in 1930 to his assuming the presidency in 1937, seven more to Makiguchi's death in prison; seven years from Toda's becoming president to his death in 1958. Ikeda vowed to realize Toda's hope that Gakkai membership would soar to three million, setting a target of 1965, seven years in the future, and then to double it again by 1972. He also vowed that by 1972 the Gakkai would build a new grand main temple at Taisekiji, thus fulfilling Nichiren's prophecy about the establishment of the kaidan, the third of his three secret laws.

Meanwhile, the press speculated on the fate of the Soka Gakkai without Toda at the helm, betting that everything would soon fall apart. For the next two years, Ikeda resisted taking up the presidency, either deferring to others or vacillating himself. He finally assumed office on May 3, 1960, at the age of thirty-two, a very unusual development in Japan where much was still made of age and seniority. He then surprised everyone with an unexpected move by making an overseas journey, his first stop Hawaii, followed by Brazil and the United States, where he set the global kosen-rufu movement in motion.

CHAPTER 5

Sea Change

The first half of Ikeda's presidency was marked by continuity and change as Japan grew into its role as Asia's economic powerhouse and America's Cold War ally. During the first decade, Ikeda continued to cultivate youth, encourage political activism, and promote the movement's growth with shakubuku campaigns, membership jumping to three million in 1962 and then to more than seven million families by 1970. As Japan's boom stabilized, however, he began to innovate in ways that altered the tenor of the movement and reshaped it for more prosperous times. "The tensions and widespread dislocations of the Occupation and early post-Occupation years were giving way," James White wrote, "to increasing social stability, economic affluence, and expanding popular perspectives." In this context, Ikeda's new "tactics and strategies . . . proved admirably successful."[1]

Some of Ikeda's innovations were linked to laying the foundations for organizations overseas, the goal of his journey to the Americas, the Asian mainland, and Europe in 1960 and '61, when the Soka Gakkai began to move onto the global scene. More fundamental innovations took place in Japan as Ikeda reshaped the movement in ways that allowed the energy unleashed by practice, which during the Toda years had been largely plowed back into propagation, to be channeled into education, the peace movement, and relief work; and into theater, dance, music, and art.

A signal moment in this sea change came in 1970 amid new controversies, when Ikeda urged members to reaffirm the fundamentals of their faith while cultivating a new and more liberal spirit of openness. Around this time, he also began to cast about for contemporary language

freed from doctrine to express Nichiren Buddhism in terms suited to a
new generation. By the mid-'70s, he was teaching with some consistency
and confidence about Nichiren and the Lotus Sutra in terms of Buddhist
Humanism and its three pillars of peace, culture, and education, renew-
ing in the process the secular emphasis of Makiguchi's original liberal-
arts pedagogy.

·   ·   ·

This time around in Japan, my hotel room is more workshop than
refuge and cocoon. During the day, the Gakkai keeps me busy—
interviewing Korean, Burakumin, and other minority members; getting
briefs on the shape of the movement in Africa, Asia, and Europe. At
night, I sleep poorly again and must cope with jet lag, but I'm getting
lots of reading and some writing done because suspicion isn't eating
me. I seem not to need to fly to thoughts of Ann for protection. I'm
not obsessing about communists and fascists. Nor do I flip-flop.

This time around I also see my role as a scholar quite differently. On
the first trip over, I feared being jobbed in to legitimate the Gakkai and
was constantly on guard for signs of manipulation. This time I think of
myself more as a consultant, like a Harvard scholar hired to reflect on
Presbyterian church history; an academic researching values for a foundation like Ford, Pew, or Lilly; a trained professional free to do my own
thinking while mirroring the Gakkai back to itself in critical terms.

I've also begun to develop my thesis further. I see the Gakkai now
not only as an expression of East Asian religious liberalism and Buddhist
modernism, but as a grassroots epitome of Japan's modern history.
Makiguchi is the critical and cosmopolitan thrust of the Meiji
Restoration; Toda, the hope and energy of postwar occupation and
reconstruction; Ikeda the global success story of Japan's postwar social
and economic miracle. Far from being the anomaly, the aberration, the
perverse distortion that its enemies and critics would have it be, the
Gakkai seems to represent much of what is quintessentially modern and
Japanese—diligence, activism, energy, idealism, individualism within a
strong group orientation, and a great success—a modernist humanist
movement for Japan's globalizing century.

·   ·   ·

On October 2, 1960, only five months into his presidency, Ikeda and a
small party that included Einosuke Akiya, then Youth Division chief,

and Yasu Kashiwabara, chief of the Women's Division, flew out of the old Haneda airport south of Tokyo, over the rooftops of Ota and Morigasaki beach, Ikeda's boyhood haunts. It was precisely seven hundred years—another seven at work in Gakkai history—since Nichiren had written his *Rissho Ankoku Ron,* a fact Ikeda recalls in his account of the early years of his presidency, *The New Human Revolution.* This timing suggested to him that the law of karma was at work in this journey to Honolulu, San Francisco, Seattle, Chicago, Toronto, Washington, and New York, then on to São Paulo, Brazil, with a return to Tokyo via Los Angeles.

Overseas travel was then rarely undertaken by ordinary Japanese, but this trip was all the more extraordinary because it was a Buddhist mission to the West, the symbolic import of which was not lost on Ikeda. Over the Pacific, he reflected on how Toda had viewed MacArthur as an American Bonten, the Buddha's divine helper in the Lotus Sutra, bringing religious freedom to Japan. In fulfilling Toda's dream to bring the kosen-rufu movement to the States, Ikeda understood himself as returning the favor. Standing on San Francisco's Telegraph Hill, Ikeda saw a parallel between Columbus and his own mission to set kosen-rufu in motion in America: "We have now made the first footprint on this continent as did Christopher Columbus."[2] Later, recalling his first glimpse of Manhattan, he wrote that "the compassionate light of Buddhism" was "about to illuminate the skyscrapers of the United States' largest city."[3]

In the months before their departure, Ikeda created one of his numerous institutional innovations, Soka Gakkai's Overseas Affairs Section, anticipating the growth of the organization around the world. Thanks to the success of the trip, he upgraded it into a full-fledged division before returning home to Japan. Before leaving, he also saw to the publication of an English-language book about the Gakkai and Nichiren Shoshu, the creation of a slide show about the Japanese movement, and the formation of translation teams to facilitate future communication between Japan and the English-speaking world.

Before his departure, overseas section staff also contacted Japanese members abroad to encourage them to greet Ikeda and his party on their arrival. So as he moved from city to city, Ikeda found small clutches of people awaiting him, singing Gakkai songs in the airport or in a hotel lobby—"Today and tomorrow, / as the march for propagation advances, / our ardor surges."[4] Some familiar faces might appear from the old days in Japan, which would occasion rounds of happy greetings.

But most were new, primarily postwar immigrants, some of whom drove to San Francisco or Seattle from Nevada or Montana to meet their new teacher. Ikeda usually found a few Caucasians and African Americans, military spouses of Japanese women, among the greeters.

Ikeda's face-to-face leadership style played a crucial role in creating new and warm bonds among members, who would engage in discussions about Japan and America and often share Japanese meals. At each stop, Ikeda distributed gifts of *fukusa,* squares of cloth used for wrapping special items like prayer beads, each printed with the characters meaning "joy" inscribed in his hand. In the course of zadankai, Ikeda would teach basic philosophy and doctrine; everyone would view the slide show and, of course, chant daimoku and recite the Lotus Sutra together.

Ikeda spent much of his time listening to stories of Japanese members about sickness and loneliness, their disappointment at what they'd found in the New World, or difficulties in their marriages to American men. He offered words of encouragement to each, while urging them to strengthen practice to change their karma, and to overcome obstacles to experiencing genuine happiness and freedom. He might urge a woman homesick for her parents and siblings in Japan to focus on bringing joy to her new family in Seattle or Chicago, or tell a farmer in Brazil, devastated by the loss of a harvest, to practice daimoku diligently, but also to consult experts about soil, water, and climate before sowing another crop.

Throughout the trip, Ikeda instructed members to adapt their life and practice to their new surroundings according to the principle of *zuiho-bini,* an ancient concept in Buddhism about the necessity of adapting the essence of the dharma to new circumstances. So Ikeda encouraged members, mostly women in the United States, to shed incidental Japanese ways such as dress and hairstyle, to trust American society, and to cease worrying about sending their children to Christian schools. He urged them to be good citizens and neighbors, to learn to drive cars, and to master English, seeing these not only as practical ways for them to overcome isolation but also as rudimentary steps in their adaptation of Buddhism to the Western Hemisphere and as aids in their taking up the mission of shakubukuing the Americas.

By the time Ikeda's party returned to Japan in late October, much had been accomplished—chapters formed in Brazil and Los Angeles, and districts in Hawaii, Seattle, and other cities, six in Southern California alone. In each city, Ikeda selected a Japanese woman or man as leader who later

contacted lapsed members and sought new ones, either through networks of family and friends or through door-to-door canvassing. These
early, modest shakubuku activities positioned the Gakkai to gain many
new members less than a decade later, when a vogue for Asian religions
swept the United States and the rest of the Western world.

Once back in Japan, Ikeda planned trips to the Asian mainland and
to Western Europe for the following year. These resembled the
American trip insofar as their goal was to inaugurate the global kosen-
rufu movement. But mass migration from Japan had not already begun
to spread the Gakkai to these continents, so Ikeda and his parties
expected and discovered fewer members. They did, however, contact
some—a dozen or so in Hong Kong, a few Japanese businessmen in
Europe, a young cook in the Japanese embassy in Ceylon. They were
surprised to discover that their waitress in a Rangoon restaurant was
Soka Gakkai.

The Asian trip to Hong Kong, Sri Lanka, India, Burma, Thailand,
and Cambodia was the more symbolic of the two, which was reflected
in Ikeda's traveling with Nittatsu, then high priest of Nichiren Shoshu.
Both men saw the journey as a fulfillment of Nichiren's prophecy that
his Buddhism would one day surge from Japan back to India, and they
saw themselves as carrying the banner for Nichiren's Buddhism of the
Latter Day of the Law, the dharma for the age of mappo. This symbolic
aspect of the trip centered on their visit to Bodhgaya, the place where
Shakyamuni attained enlightenment and long a major pilgrimage site
for Buddhists from around the world, comparable in stature to
Bethlehem or Jerusalem for Christians. There the two men buried
tokens of their faith and conviction—a copy of Nichiren's letter "On
the Three Great Secret Laws" inscribed by Nittatsu; a granite plaque
engraved with the phrase Kosen-rufu in Asia, inscribed in Ikeda's hand;
a teacup fired from clay dug out of the ground at Taisekiji.

Ikeda began to write *The New Human Revolution* only in the early
'90s, so his accounts of these first trips are replete with allusions that
reflect his fully developed ideas about Buddhist Humanism. As much a
sacred history as his earlier account of the Makiguchi and Toda eras, it
reads very differently, less a heroic saga of resistance against militarism
or of movement-building among the dispossessed than a primer on the
Buddhist internationalism he teaches under the rubrics of peace, culture, and education. In reading it, one begins to see how Ikeda's long-
standing passion for literature, culture, and art gained expression in his
role as a spiritual teacher of modernist Buddhism.

One can also begin to see clearly why icons of Western culture—
Socrates, Hugo, Whitman, and so on—make their appearance on the
campus of Soka University. Throughout *The New Human Revolution*,
Ikeda uses his travels to educate readers about great contributors to
modern humanism. When in Germany, he alludes to the poet Heinrich
Heine; in France, the reader catches a glimpse of Victor Hugo; in India,
Ikeda sketches in the life and work of Tagore, Gandhi, and Nehru. In
New York City, Ikeda recalls the exuberant poetry of Walt Whitman,
whose expansive poetic style he often seems to emulate.

He brings his readers, mostly Japanese Gakkai members, up to speed
on contemporary overseas issues—a racist gesture observed in a park in
Chicago, for instance, elicits his thoughts about Lincoln, the
Emancipation Proclamation, the civil rights movement, and the principled defiance of Rosa Parks. He offers readers some basic religious history in his discussions of Shakyamuni while in Bodhgaya and of Jesus
while touring Rome. An alert reader discovers that Ikeda, in paying
homage to Makiguchi, has boned up on his pioneering education the-
orists—his references to pedagogues N. F. S. Grundtvig while in
Copenhagen and Johann Pestalozzi in Zurich are far too esoteric to
reflect the interest of a casual tourist.

This didacticism aside, humorous stories about these trips, still
enjoyed in Gakkai circles, serve as reminders of what an exhilarating
experience it was for Ikeda and his company to travel, after long decades
of isolation, war, and the rebuilding of Japan. Yumiko Hachiya, who as
a young aide helped prepare for the American trip, laughingly recalled
for me how she'd seen photographs of American men wearing broad-
brimmed hats, so she bought some for Ikeda and the other men in the
party who traveled to the United States. Upon his return, Ikeda
reported that few men in America wore hats.[5] Despite careful planning,
they all failed to factor the International Dateline into their flight
arrangements, so Ikeda arrived in Honolulu a day earlier than expected,
and there was no formal welcoming party at the airport to greet him.
"It was a question of groping along, feeling our way as we went, a real
eye-opener," Akiya told me, recalling his own experience on these trips.
"My overall impression was that Japan was not located on the main
street of the world but in a back alley."[6]

Such insight into Japan's parochialism sheds light on Ikeda's frequent
criticism of Japan's insularity and helps to account for why internationalism would become a hallmark of his presidency. Such anecdotes also help
an attentive reader to see past the didactic intent of *The New Human*

Revolution to recapture a bit of a thirty-three-year-old Ikeda on his first journeys away from home—a classic pilgrim inasmuch as his devout interest in learning is shot through with curiosity and pleasure-taking.

A secondary purpose of these trips was to scout materials for a new construction project at Taisekiji, another of the Gakkai's efforts to rejuvenate Nichiren Shoshu. So the reader catches brief glimpses of Ikeda shopping—for carpets in Zurich, chandeliers in Vienna, decorative ceramics in Copenhagen. One sees him wading into the Danube and Ganges to collect stones for the foundation of the new building and honing his architectural tastes on the Mall in Washington, in south Asian temples, and in Vatican City. But Ikeda and his companions also visit Niagara Falls, the Taj Mahal, Buckingham Palace, Versailles, the Roman Forum and catacombs, and other conventional tourist destinations, each experienced as an upbeat object lesson in global humanism but also as occasions for fun, both exciting and invigorating.

Ikeda recognizes the tragic dimension of life as well, however—especially in Asia, where he often reflects on the cruelty of Japan's wartime occupation and ponders the death of his brother Kiichi, a highly personal source of his wariness about the spirit of Japan. He chants daimoku for Kiichi and Japan's war dead in a Japanese cemetery in Burma, for Americans who died in the Pacific theater at the National Cemetery, and for all the dead on the cremation ghats on the banks of the Ganges. But still, Eagle Peak, which the party drives past as sunset approaches after their visit to Bodhgaya, becomes a photo opportunity for Ikeda and Nittatsu. One reads of them standing together on a patio at a nearby hot springs, taking snapshots, wondering whether Shakyamuni himself bathed there, chatting about philosophy, and laughing together about Toda's wish to celebrate a water festival after the discovery of a spring on the grounds of Taisekiji.

These early trips signaled Ikeda's intention to realize Toda's dream for Nichiren's Buddhism to become a universal religion at work around the globe. But they also suggest much about a young Ikeda as he began to shape his own presidency. Upbeat and optimistic, curious and relentlessly devoted to self-education, pious but eager to be immersed in the thick of things, Ikeda made a point of propelling himself beyond the narrow horizons of the island world of Japan as his first step in taking up the reins of the Gakkai. This trajectory reflects his long-standing interests in art and culture and points to how Ikeda's passions resonated with those of the early Makiguchi, a philosopher, scholar, and geographer, and a man he never met but through his own mentor. Ikeda seems to have understood from the outset that part of his own role as mentor would be to model cosmopolitan spirituality for ordinary Japanese folks like himself, who'd lifted themselves up by faith and practice through the long, bitter years of war and desolation.

• • •

On the domestic front, Ikeda devoted much of his first decade as president to increasing the Gakkai's size through Toda-style shakubuku campaigns. During his second decade at the helm, however, the unique character of his presidency began to emerge as he retuned the legacy bequeathed to him in response to radically changing circumstances.

Three developments contributed to a sea change in the spiritual tone of the Gakkai. The first was tied to Japan's economy, which, having boomed for twenty years, began to stabilize at a level of prosperity barely dreamed of in the crisis years of the postwar era. "The period of the Soka Gakkai's most rapid growth was from 1951 to 1970, which happened to coincide with a period of rapid development of the Japanese economy," writes Hiroshi Aruga, a political scientist and emeritus professor at Tokyo University. "It was not until the 1970s that the prospect of continued growth began to wane, and with the first oil shock of 1973, the Japanese economy entered a new phase. The growth of the Soka Gakkai proceeded as if following the pace of the economy."[7]

Domestic Cold War cultural politics also contributed to this shift in ways that helped me to account for why, on my first trip to Japan, I'd instinctually sensed something very '60s about the Soka Gakkai. Early in that decade the *zengakuren*—the fiercely factional, often very radical Japanese student movement—began to influence the ideals of a new Gakkai generation raised in prosperity. Between 1960 and 1970, nationwide protests over the Japan U.S. Security Treaty raged, which broadened into demands for university reform, minority rights, and an end to the Vietnam War and opened up Japan's version of the '60s generation gap. One 1969 sourcebook for activists suggests the degree to which Gakkai students stood in the thick of it. Their Shingakudo (New Student League) is described as a "structural reform group" representing "270,000 members in 315 universities," its helmets "white in color with the characters for Shingakudo in red on the front." Moderate when compared to anarchists and the Red Brigade, the league was nevertheless "anti-war, "anti-dictatorship," and in "opposition to the government" with long-term plans to mobilize "ordinary people and students on a wide scale," thus making it a "natural rival" of the Japan Communist Party.[8]

Ikeda's response to young people's interests and needs accounts for much in the altered tone of the Gakkai. Under his guidance, students began to pry Toda's progressive ideals loose from their moorings in literalistic religious language in an effort to make Nichiren's Buddhism speak in a more contemporary voice.

"President Ikeda felt the need to create a movement so that student activists within the Gakkai could express their feelings and sentiments. That's why Shingakudo was created," Toru Shiotsu, a law professor at Soka University, notes as he reminisces about those years. "I recall talking to Mr. Ikeda with other students and his saying that times change, social values change. What is important is for young people to have an understanding of what justice is, what it is not, and to take action based on that distinction. That is humanism.

"Mr. Ikeda's style was to give freedom to young people to express themselves," Shiotsu continues, while I try to picture him, now stylishly professorial in suit, sweater vest, and tie, manning the barricades in his red-and-white Shingakudo helmet. "We were straightforward in sharing our thoughts with him and, in one sense, I'm embarrassed about what I used to say to him. We'd go to headquarters and have meetings with all these top leaders in their navy blue suits. We'd be in T-shirts and jeans, criticizing their authoritarianism, telling them to think critically about their own attitudes. The big transition that took place in the Soka Gakkai in 1970—it is all thanks to the fact that President Ikeda used young people as a resource. Many became part of the administration. Their input was reflected in big changes in the Soka Gakkai around that time."[9]

Minoru Harada, now secretary general of the Gakkai, seconds Shiotsu's observations. Once a protestor at Tokyo University, Harada recalls Ikeda responding to students' disillusionment with radicalism by teaching them that inner revolution is the only path to lasting social change. Teaching from Nichiren's *Gosho*, Ikeda urged students to make kosen-rufu a movement for constructive engagement, charging them to apply Buddhism to the concerns of their own generation. "He gathered representatives of the Student Division to talk to us directly," Harada says, referring to leadership seminars Ikeda taught during those years. "He emphasized discarding archaic concepts as hindrances for modern people, teaching us that our mission was to propagate Buddhism in new ways."[10]

The "free speech issue" was a third and decisive development that contributed to this shift. In many respects the culmination of controversies over the goal and intent of the Gakkai since its revitalization by Toda, this incident circled around unresolved constitutional issues in postwar Japan. It also occurred while the Gakkai was reaching a new plateau of influence and wealth under Ikeda's leadership, which made it an attractive target for what amounted to a conspiracy theory advanced in the 1969 book *I Denounce Soka Gakkai,* written by commentator Hirotatsu Fujiwara. The issue ultimately broke, however, as a result of a misstep by leaders of the Gakkai's new political organization, the Komeito or "clean government" party.

The convoluted story begins in 1965 when a committee led by Ikeda met to formulate plans to build the Sho-Hondo, a "grand main temple" to house the dai-gohonzon. This project was intended to fulfill Toda's dream of establishing the prophesied kaidan, Nichiren's third secret law. Ikeda's remarks before the committee reflect both his love of history and art and the grandeur of his vision. "The majestic temples of Thebes in Egypt, the Parthenon in Greece, and Angkor Wat in Cambodia have, with the lapse of time, declined and today are in ruins," he proclaimed. "The Sho-Hondo, the new hall of practice for world peace," will be "an immortal edifice to eternity beyond the ten thousand years of the age of mappo."[11]

Public concern over the Sho-Hondo reflected an understanding of the kaidan rooted in medieval doctrine, precisely the kind of archaism Ikeda was urging Gakkai students to abandon. The crux of the matter was that Toda, and after him Ikeda, had used the phrase *kokuritsu kaidan,* a state-built or national hall of worship, to describe the new sanctuary at Taisekiji. This raised the charge that the Gakkai intended to violate church-state separation, an accusation that led both High Priest Nittatsu and Ikeda to retailor the concept to suit the ethos of Japan's modern democracy, with its constitutional guarantees of religious freedom. The controversy, nevertheless, persisted.[12]

Making constitutional issues go away at this point was difficult because the Gakkai, by the mid-'60s, had begun to cut a very high public profile. In 1964, Ikeda startled both members and the Japanese public by announcing the foundation of the Komeito party. The next year he launched a Sho-Hondo funding campaign that raised more than thirty-five billion yen—ten times the target amount, about one hundred million 1969 dollars—the bulk of it donated by Gakkai members in only four days. In 1967, on the heels of the Tokyo Olympics, sixty-two thousand Gakkai members mounted an immense culture festival in Tokyo National Stadium, the site of the games. That same year the Komeito party fielded thirty-two candidates for seats in the influential Lower House of the Diet, twenty-five of whom went on to victory. In 1969, Komeito became Japan's third largest political party.

Thus by 1970 many people had reasons for admiring, fearing, envying, and competing with the Soka Gakkai, among them Fujiwara, a conservative political commentator and professor who had used his academic credentials to become a media personality with a reputation for inflammatory rhetoric. Henry Scott-Stokes, an old Japan hand, called him a "rebarbative hack," but Fujiwara styled himself a champion of the constitution, a great defender of free speech, and a watchdog on guard against resurgent totalitarianism.[13]

In *I Denounce Soka Gakkai,* Fujiwara raised constitutional questions about the relation of religion to politics that cried out for clarification. But these became obscured by the often circular, deliberately incendiary quality of his arguments in which he skewed recent events and reiterated old charges to outline a Gakkai plot to take over Japan. Hostile to religion, he painted Ikeda as a cult leader skillfully manipulating his disciples, whom Fujiwara called dupes in a spiritual shell game and the dregs of Japan's democracy. He saw Ikeda and Nittatsu's attempt to update the concept of the kaidan as an "opportunistic tactic" with "a clear parallel in the shifting policies and diplomacy by which the Nazis came to power in Germany." The dancers and gymnasts in the Tokyo culture festival displayed the "weird charisma" of "fanatic super-nationalists." Much of the book consists of oblique attacks on Ikeda who, Fujiwara suggested, coveted the symbolic role of the emperor. But his most sustained effort was to discredit the Buddhist politics of Komeito, whose "filthy" relations with religion led him to characterize it as "the sinful, bastard child of Soka Gakkai."[14]

The ensuing controversy, however, resulted from a serious mistake on the part of Gakkai members in the Komeito party, not Fujiwara's diatribe. Knowing the book was timed to influence a 1969 election, several party leaders approached Fujiwara in private and asked him to correct inaccuracies. Fujiwara refused, so they attempted to persuade him to delay its publication, an overture he captured on tape and reported to the press. At that point, the free speech issue erupted, fanned into flame by the Gakkai's chief political rival, the Japan Communist Party, and resulted in impassioned debates about Ikeda and the Soka Gakkai on the floor of the Diet.

In his study of constitutional issues in Japan, Lawrence Ward Beer, an American scholar, described this episode as a "constructive explosion" that "slightly heightened awareness of freedom and its problems" in Japanese society.[15] Ikeda, however, took the issue seriously and made it the starting point for a process of critical self-examination that resulted in his once again re-creating the Gakkai.

Ikeda set this process in motion with a speech in May 1970 at the thirty-third general meeting of the Soka Gakkai, held at Nihon University. Speaking before some two hundred Nichiren Shoshu priests, fifteen thousand Gakkai members, seven hundred invited guests, and the Japanese and overseas press, including TV, Ikeda touched on issues from the generation gap to the movement's relations with the Japan Communist Party. Much of what he spoke about he'd said in the past, but the free speech issue gave him a platform from which to make shifts in emphasis of such magnitude that some members recall that it took them a year or more to grasp his intent fully.

Ikeda asked the Japanese people to understand that the Gakkai had no dark plans for the nation, even as he offered apologies for its mistakes in the past. He formally committed the organization to the principles of free speech and freedom of religion, and underscored this pledge by calling for the formal separation of the Komeito and the Gakkai. More important, he took members to task for their intolerance and oversensitivity, which had set up barriers between the movement and the rest of Japan. "We must take the lessons of this incident deeply to heart and must absolutely not make the same mistake again," he said.[16] To facilitate this change of heart, he called for moderating shakubuku and for a more thorough democratization of the movement, urging its members to adopt an attitude of openness to others even as they held fast to their religious convictions.

Ikeda's 1970 speech marked a watershed between the shakubuku-driven activism of the early days and the more moderate, secularizing style that would become a hallmark of his presidency. It also marked his coming into his own as a teacher at the age of forty-two—still young by Japanese standards—as he began to articulate clearly the basic principles of his emergent globalizing and universalizing Buddhist Humanism.

Kosen-rufu is a process, not a goal, he told the thousands before him and millions more who would later study his words. It is the mystic law flowing into the future, "the very pulse of living Buddhism within society," a stream that will "broaden and deepen, that will flow steadily and swiftly into the hearts of all people." He saw three principles at the heart of Nichiren's message to the modern world: absolute pacifism, the sanctity of human life, and respect for human dignity. "These principles are universal to humankind, transcending the limits of religion, race, nationality, or ideology. . . . They derive from the essential nature of human existence. Everything starts from this humanism," he explained, in terms he would continue to fine-tune over the next decade. "Our present task is to work to lay a broad foundation encompassing all aspects of society, not simply the realm of politics. And on that foundation, we should construct a vast new society and culture."[17]

• • •

The sea change is reflected in interviews with three pioneer members who recall for me the intense old days in the late '50s in Osaka. I have come to get a firsthand impression of the Osaka incident, during which the Gakkai took the Kansai region by storm, Ikeda was arrested, and the view of the movement as a dangerous organization of the poor and sick became fixed in the public eye. As I hear these senior members talk, I am persuaded that the Soka Gakkai is not only modernist Buddhism but a modernizing movement more generally insofar as it has been a vehicle for people to move from one era of social organization to another, to adjust themselves personally and collectively to the rapidly changing social and political realities of the postwar world.

Japan's second city, Osaka considers itself earthier and more cosmopolitan, certainly more historically important than Tokyo, its density as a city even more astonishing to my eye than the capital. My impressions are, however, limited to downtown as we tour Osaka's Central Public Hall, accompanied by a local Komeito representative, wearing hard hats because the early-twentieth-century Taisho-era landmark is undergoing renovation. It is the auditorium where Ikeda, having been released from prison, stood on a balcony to greet his jubilant supporters.

"It was just about there that they marched Mr. Ikeda in handcuffs through the street," Akiko Kurihara says, a bit perplexed because this part of Osaka has changed tremendously since that time.[18] "But I am sure it was over there," she says, pointing; "that's where we had our demonstrations. Up there, on that balcony, is where Mr. Ikeda greeted us. We all felt so happy that justice prevailed." Kurihara is short, earnest, and high-energy. Dressed in a dark blue dress, looking as if she has had her hair done for our interview, she startles me when we meet by making a deep, almost military bow from the waist. A mother and housewife active for many years in the movement, she admits to me that she is very nervous, which puts us both at ease.

Later, back at the Kansai Culture Center, Kurihara describes in vivid terms her experience of the kosen-rufu movement under Toda, when she and Ikeda were both young, almost fifty years in the past.[19] "Life force was important to me when I started practice. I didn't believe that I had any power. I had a destiny or karma I had to overcome, but no strength to do it," she begins. "The word we used then most often was *conviction*. It was like a password. When we greeted each other, we would say, 'Do you have strong conviction in this practice?'" she recalls, her emphatic tone evoking what the Gakkai would later refer to as the heroic and passionate "Kansai spirit." "We were overflowing with happiness and we wanted to share this with others. 'Did you know you can change yourself? Did you know you can change your destiny?' This is how we talked to other people. We were happy."

She also recalls, however, the naïveté she brought to the movement. She thought that kosen-rufu "would definitely be realized. And when that happened, we'd be disaster-free and nature itself would be happy, would be peaceful, wonderful. And the world would be filled with happy people. That is what I had in mind. A kind of a utopia." Ikeda, however, taught her to moderate her views. "'Life is like pushing a boulder. You can't stop the wind; you cannot shove a huge boulder,'" she recalls him saying. "'But what you can do is put in a wedge. If you use a wedge, you can move the boulder wherever you want it to go,'" she says. "'Faith is akin to that.' At that point, I realized that kosen-rufu was not a final point of destination, but a flow, and that we are already in that flow."

Two men share with me their views about why the Gakkai generated such controversy. The first is Ryozo Nishiguchi, who is quiet and dignified and now a senior leader.[20] "It is true that in the pioneering days in Osaka we were quite aggressive with shakubuku. But I'm still confident that our motivation was purely spiritual, purely religious. We wanted to save people, to introduce Buddhism to them, so the motivation was pure, but maybe the way we did it could have been a little bit less aggressive," he says, positions that called to mind Akiya's reflections on the energy among youthful leaders in the years after the war. "Someone who was shakubukued must have felt a bit intimidated," he adds.

He does not, however, accept as true stories once told in the press about young Gakkai men destroying altars of nonbelievers with axes, describing for me instead how he and other members dealt with *hobobarai,* once a central part of shakubuku. "According to Nichiren, when someone decides to practice, we must ask them to do hobobarai, which means to put away all talismans," he says, a remark that calls to mind Makiguchi's refusal to accept the talisman from the Ise shrine. "This must be done by the person who converted. If someone else does it, it doesn't work because you have to make up your own mind that you are fully committed."

As he talks, I recall that hobobarai has since been deemphasized. Gakkai members now are not pressured to remove symbols or altars of another sect or religion from their homes, a shift that is of a piece with the liberalization of the movement. And it is certainly an intelligent move, given the kind of problems hobobarai created in the past.

"Many people had strong emotional attachments to altars that had been in their families generation after generation," Nishiguchi continues, "and they couldn't do it. In that case, we might help them. In quite a few cases, we did keep at people who could not make up their minds. 'Why don't you come with us?' we might say. 'I'll put your altar on my bike and we'll go to Soka Gakkai and change your temple [affiliation].' Some members were too enthusiastic." When I ask him how Ikeda responded to this problem, he replies, "President Ikeda told us not to lose all common sense. His consistent guidance was to appreciate the feelings and emotions of the person we were trying to shakubuku. But that kind of input often got completely lost in the momentum."

Kazuhito Fukunaka, strikingly handsome, dressed in a green glen plaid suit, concedes that they may have been too zealous when young, but underscores that they saw themselves as standing on important principles.[21] Now a well-respected, retired assemblyman, he tells of his own struggle with neighbors a few years after the Osaka incident, one that he describes as getting a bit out of hand when a small-scale shakubuku campaign gained too much momentum. The situation began after Fukunaka attempted to introduce the Soka Gakkai to the members of his small village, most of whom belonged to the Pure Land sect and ridiculed him for his beliefs. Some months later, he refused to bear his family's portion of the expenses for a memorial service offered to a founder of a rival sect at the village temple. In response, villagers began systematically to ostracize his family, exclude them from village communal rights, and boycott his business.

In Japan back then, he says, "people knew there was a constitution and there were rights protected by it, but their lives had nothing to do with it. So they did not realize they were wrong in drawing up rules to ostracize me," he says, as he begins his story. "It was their ignorance of the law that really angered me." In response, he called in the Young Men's Division to shakubuku the entire village—an act that, he admits, "reflected my own lack of common sense. But as far as my not contributing to the support of the temple—to try to force me was definitely a breach of my freedom of religious expression. I was impassioned. I was angry."

The fracas that ensued, while seriocomic in retrospect, reflects not only how one Gakkai member responded to the new constitution, but how passions could flare in a small controversy of the kind that is easily magnified by the press in the retelling. One cold January morning, young Gakkai men arrived at Fukunaka's house at 7:00 A.M., did gongyo together, and then divided into three groups to shakubuku the village in an orderly fashion. But as Fukunaka tells it, young men eventually began turning up more than once at a house or knocked at both the front and rear doors simultaneously, alarming residents, who locked their doors, chased after them with bamboo sticks and buckets of cold water, or called in the police.

Like the free speech issue, however, the "Fukunaka case" set a precedent, not only in that it encouraged moderation in the Gakkai, but also because it heightened consciousness of rights issues in the village. According to Fukunaka, soon thereafter the villagers "decided to separate or divide the expenses necessary for governing and the religious expenses. It was decided that the religious expenses were to be incurred by the practitioners of that religion, while the expenses necessary to maintain the community would be paid by all."

. . .

I'm having much more fun in Japan this time around, my own sense of ease reflected in a more relaxed attitude toward me on the part of people in the Gakkai. Leaders I interview now seem less determined to set the record straight, less concerned I'll take off on some half-understood tangent—to confuse high energy with fanaticism or group discipline with coercion or some such thing. I'm still unsure about what's going on around me in the streets, but I'm not so charmed by indecipherable neon signs or enthralled by sleek bullet trains. Having done my homework in New York, I don't have a panicky need to figure everything out and am content to just let Japan be itself, while I get down to business.

I have a VCR in my hotel room to screen old movement documentary footage—brief snippets of Toda, and lots of Ikeda, much of it shot in the late '70s when he was silenced by priests but kept in touch by way of videos circulated among members. I see the old familiar sameness and difference all over the place—Kaneko wearing Mary Tyler Moore styles; Ikeda riding around in golf carts and spreading into middle age about the time he quit smoking. And always the bowing and gift-giving and receiving, that formal comportment alien and often off-putting to people in the States.

I'm also collecting videos of culture festivals to take back to Deansboro, a favorite *Osaka in the Rain,* a 1966 marathon with Busby Berkeley extravaganzas and colossal gymnastic displays, members' collective will to discipline untouched by a daylong monsoon, mud everywhere. I've been sent culture festival videos from Singapore, from São Paulo and Bahia in Brazil, and from the United States, all of them displaying the signature high energy of the Gakkai in Japan. I watch and rewatch the São Paulo tape, fascinated by the Japanese-Brazilian folk dances, German-Brazilian marching bands, thousands in a Latin-Afro-Native-Euro-Asian mix performing together to welcome Ikeda to Brazil in 1984, as if it were the most natural thing for Nichiren Buddhists to dance the samba.

But having come to grips with the Gakkai's old critics, I've created a new interpretive problem for myself as fretting over Cold War scholars' dread of Japan's lumpen proletariat gives way to my own, academic disdain for bourgeoisification. "Buddhist Humanism—peace, culture, education—who cares? There's certainly nothing wrong with it, but it's not too compelling either. Who in the middle class, Japanese or American, is not for global peace, culture, and education?" I take to asking Rob, who once again indulges me with his patience.

However, in interviews with leaders in institutions Ikeda established about the time he founded Komeito—the Institute of Oriental Philosophy, the Tokyo Fuji Art Museum, and the Min-On Concert Association—I see dynamic tensions at work in Buddhist Humanism today. Classic and creative tensions between authority and autonomy, conformity and individuality, they reflect the Gakkai's effort to reconcile the collectivism required for a focused and coherent movement with humanistic freedoms.

According to Belgian sociologist Karel Dobbelaere, groups such as these are central to a process he calls "pillarization," the institution-building done by religious organizations to protect their spiritual core in a highly secular world.[22] These and other Gakkai organizations—the Artists' Group; professional associations for physicians, lawyers, and beauticians; the Women's Division Chorus; and many more—are designed to create Buddhist environments in which members can pursue individual interests while remaining within the group. Whether rehearsals for performances or professional get-togethers, meetings begin with chanting and the sharing of members' experiences, and then progress to discussions of how best to live Buddhist values in the modern world. Many of these organizations have their roots in the Toda years but are now less evangelical and more in the spirit of the early Makiguchi, whose humanist pedagogy Ikeda revived as he clarified his own ideas.

These groups strengthen the Gakkai as an institution and also serve as venues in which members learn to hone their spirituality, an often-delicate act of balancing the religious and secular. In his "Faith and Practice: Bringing Religion, Music, and Beethoven to Life in Soka Gakkai," Levi McLaughlin writes about his experience as a non-Japanese participant-observer in the Tokyo Orchestra, one of many Gakkai musical ensembles in Japan. Though much like any other orchestra when in concert, McLaughlin writes, the orchestra is revealed by Gakkai rituals that frame it and Gakkai spirit that pervades it to be "fundamentally religious in character," a quality self-consciously maintained by movement leaders. "The leadership consciously acts," he writes, "to prevent members from drifting into either a realm of individuality and secular pursuit on the one hand or a world of anti-social isolationism on the other."[23]

At the Institute of Oriental Philosophy (IOP), Toru Shiotsu speaks of how the Gakkai interprets the collective symbol of bodhisattvas arising from the earth in terms consonant with a humanistic emphasis on individuality.[24] "Our understanding is unique," he tells me, as we talk in the IOP reception room on the Soka University campus. Under the direction of Yoichi Kawada, a medical doctor with a PhD in immunology, IOP scholars work at the intersection of Buddhism and global issues such as environmentalism and bioethics.

"For us, the phrase 'rising from the earth' is about self-motivation," says Shiotsu, whose recent work is on the Buddhist grounds for human rights. It is not a mystical idea but one about "decisions freely made, about self-motivated individuals who emerge into the world to accomplish something of value. In other Buddhist schools, it is understood more as a mission thrust upon an individual by somebody else," he says, which recalls President Akiya's remark about free choice being at the heart of the Soka Gakkai's understanding of the mentor-disciple relationship. "For us, rising from the earth refers to people who make their own decision to base their life work on compassion. This is a very important distinction for the Soka Gakkai," he notes. "It is an interpretation we're proud of."

At the Tokyo Fuji Art Museum (TFAM), Mitsunari Noguchi, its soft-spoken curator, describes how Buddhism, world peace, and art work together in Makiguchi's ideas about happiness and value creation.[25] As we tour TFAM's collection of Western art from the Renaissance to the twentieth century, I ask about the reviews of an exhibit I'd seen there a year earlier, one of ancient Chinese earthenware whose simple, elegant lines had been enhanced by Harlem Renaissance graphics and Art Deco glassware. "Most reviewers liked it, but some found it not acceptable," Noguchi tells me, saying that TFAM could not have experimented in such a way had it not owned all the pieces. "Mr. Ikeda thought it important to try something new: 'I'm all for it. It's very good for the museum to take a new approach to things,' he told me after viewing it. 'A bold, dynamic presentation.'"

"Please tell me how jades, terra-cotta plates, and jazz posters—or Renaissance masters, for that matter—relate to Nichiren's Buddhism," I inquire, a connection hardly obvious to most outside observers.

"Nichiren's mission during the turbulent Kamakura era was to bring joy and peace into people's lives through the philosophy of the Lotus Sutra," Noguchi explains. For seven centuries his Buddhism was propagated only by priests until Makiguchi recast it in terms of value creation, a development Noguchi calls "very cutting-edge." Now we interpret Buddhism "as a universal principle about how human beings can live their lives in order to enjoy happiness. We believe Nichiren's Buddhism is about cultivating enlightened individuals who can contribute to the betterment of society. Based on this philosophy, TFAM brings different peoples together through art as a contribution to global peace and human happiness."

In downtown Tokyo at the Min-On Concert Association, Hiroyasu Kobayashi, its president, explains the connection between music and Buddhism to me in both social and personal terms.[26] Recalling that many Japanese dismissed Min-On as sectarian in its early days, he notes how they have since come to embrace it warmly, the turning point coming in the '80s after Min-On underwrote a tour by La Scala, among the first Western opera companies to perform in Japan. "I recall President Ikeda saying he wanted average Japanese people to see first-class art, even if we lost a lot of money. It was amazing. La Scala moved to Japan, all but the opera house. Five hundred people. We paid for everything." Min-On has since sponsored exchanges with eighty countries and regions and under written orchestral, dance, vocal, and folk arts performances both in rural prefectures and in major cities. He tells me that it is now Japan's leading promoter of Latin, folk, and indigenous music.

Good-humored and worldly, Kobayashi recalls his discovery of the link between music and Buddhist practice around the time he participated in the 1967 culture festival in Tokyo National Stadium, the one that had so troubled Fujiwara. "I was eighteen. I played drums in a brass band established by President Ikeda, which had about twenty thousand young men in it nationwide. I was very casual about my skill and technique. But as I learned Buddhist philosophy, I saw I had a mission to convey this spirit through the music we performed in the band. Skill and technique became important. I became very serious. I had no choice but to become very serious."

When I ask Kobayashi if Min-On administrators routinely discuss Nichiren's *Gosho* as they pursue day-to-day business, he laughs heartily, then waxes serious. "Well, we probably don't use the word *kosen-rufu* or quote Nichiren, but we do use the phrase *world peace* when we talk among ourselves," he says. "Something I think about . . . it's really a dream I have," he continues, musing aloud. "When world peace becomes a reality fifty years or even a hundred years from now, we hope that people will come to realize the contribution Min-On made through its efforts to promote people-to-people exchange based on music and culture."

More than anything else, the Gakkai's political activism has been a source of controversy, even though it is now widely understood that religion and politics are a natural fit, even where church and state are constitutionally separated. At least since the 1980s, scholars have been commenting on how religion is reasserting itself as a force in local, national, and global politics. José Casanova calls this phenomenon "de-privatization," by which he means that religion is no longer viewed as being limited to personal conviction, but is also to be expressed in social values. Most commentators have focused with alarm on how Islamic and Christian fundamentalists have become active in civil society, but Casanova points out that liberals are also de-privatizing in an effort to strengthen modern rights and freedoms. The overall impact is wholesale shifting of older boundaries between public and private and between secular and religious in societies around the globe, a process that has been ongoing in the Gakkai since the days of Makiguchi.[27]

At the Komeito's unassuming headquarters in Shinanomachi, I meet with Toshiko Hamayotsu, who talks of how the party fits into this picture as a rights-based advocacy organization devoted to political change in Japan.[28] A smart, focused woman, Hamayotsu spent twenty years in law before becoming a Komeito politician and now holds a seat in the Upper House of the Diet. The principle of church-state separation is found in Article Twenty of Japan's peace constitution, she notes, which stipulates that the state must not intervene in the affairs of religions. But to assume the reverse—to say that religious people cannot be active in affairs of the state—would violate Article Fourteen, which stipulates equality of all people, including those with strong religious convictions, under the law.

She then lays out a deeper motive for the Gakkai's long history of political engagement. Hamayotsu shares with other critical observers a concern that Japan lacks a strong tradition of human rights, a reflection of the fact that modern freedoms came to it not by means of struggles at the grass roots, but through two revolutions imposed from above. During the Meiji Restoration, rights were presented as gifts bestowed by the emperor. They were bestowed once again after World War II by MacArthur during the American occupation. Since then, in response to the disastrous role of religion during the war, Japanese people have tended to dismiss religious and philosophical values, a tendency that has stifled the development of principled justifications for freedom of expression, religion, conscience, and the press. In light of this history, Hamayotsu sees Komeito's mission, and to a degree that of the Soka Gakkai, as the clear articulation of Buddhist principles to provide the philosophical ground for human rights and freedoms.

Hamayotsu makes it clear that in Japan, as in the United States, church-state religion-politics issues make for subtle terrain. Categorically denying that Ikeda meddles in the affairs of Komeito—a favorite charge of its enemies—she nevertheless admits to his having proposed its general guidelines, such as that it become a party to protect the rights of ordinary citizens. Thus, on one hand, Komeito does "not exist in order to use its political authority to spread the teachings of the Soka Gakkai, its doctrines," she says. But still, on the other hand, "we do believe that we can express Buddhist values of compassion, humanism, and the dignity of life in making policy."

"I'm a politician," she adds as we part in the lobby. "But I'm very proud to say I'm a disciple of President Ikeda. I see him as a mentor in

life. I believe that to have met my mentor has contributed to the rich-
ness of my experience as a politician."

. . .

By the mid-1970s, Ikeda had clearly articulated peace, culture, and education as the pillars of Buddhist Humanism, but even today the Gakkai's
understanding of them remains unsystematic and fluid. There is no cat-
echism pinning the three principles down, no hard-and-fast definitions.
Instead a wide variety of activities is tucked under the umbrella of each,
all three understood as together expressing the substance of Nichiren's
understanding of the dharma in a voice tuned to modern democracy
and a globalizing world.

One can, however, discern a tendency to associate a principle with
each of the presidents. The Gakkai links its commitment to peace to
Toda's 1957 call for the abolition of nuclear weapons. Its chief organization devoted to peace is the Toda Institute for Global Peace and
Policy Research, founded by Ikeda in 1996, which has offices in
Honolulu, Okinawa, and Shinanomachi. But Gakkai peace work is a
multifaceted educational effort to foster awareness that peace is not an
absence of war but a value to be created, whether through Gakkai
exhibits and publications, by expressing support for the United Nations
or working in local non-Gakkai initiatives, or by cultivating harmonious
relations among peers, neighbors, and family.

Culture most immediately reflects Ikeda's interest in art, music, literature, and philosophy, which he has displayed since he was a young
man. This principle is expressed in formal organizations such as Min-
On and TFAM, whose missions encompass both intercultural dialogue
and popular education. It is expressed in the Gakkai tradition of the culture festival, which empowers members by encouraging them both to
discover their own talent and to discipline it. It is apparent in Ikeda's
exuberant appreciation of novelists and artists, whom he delights in
citing in his many inspirational tracts, numerous essays, and countless
speeches. It is surely the ideal of culture that accounts for the presence
of Raphael, Tolstoy, Whitman, and Leonardo on the campus of Soka
University.

Education, of course, goes back to Makiguchi and his thwarted
efforts to reform Japan's prewar educational system, but Ikeda has, in
recent decades, made education his own first priority. As a value, education infuses all aspects of Gakkai spirituality but is most concretely

expressed in its schools—kindergartens in Singapore, Hong Kong, Malaysia, Brazil, and Hokkaido; high schools in Tokyo and Kansai; universities in Hachioji and Southern California.

The spirit of the Gakkai is so tied to its schools that I make a special trip to the Kansai Soka schools, the long drive through the hills and farms outside Osaka a welcome relief from my busy schedule. The middle and high school buildings, modern and clean and tucked up under a range of deeply wooded hills, provide a respite from the pressured density of the city. "Uphold the dignity of life," I read in a glossy brochure, one of the five principles for the Kansai school system formulated by Ikeda. "(2) Respect individuality; (3) Build bonds of lasting friendship; (4) Oppose violence; (5) Lead a life based on both knowledge and wisdom."[29]

Rob and I are welcomed by Shigeyuki Matsuda, president of the Kansai schools, and representatives of the faculty, who share an hour of their time briefing us on the Soka spirit.[30] Much of our discussion is about how teachers balance efforts to give a spiritual foundation to an essentially secular education for a student body that includes children from non-Gakkai families. Unlike Soka University, all faculty here are practicing members, a policy designed to ensure that Buddhist values infuse the educational environment. Gohonzons are displayed in the school and dorms, and students chant daimoku on important occasions, such as before athletic events. Non-Gakkai students may participate voluntarily, and efforts are made so that they feel neither coerced nor excluded.

Buddhist elements in Soka education are also evident in small ways— in the emphasis placed on opposing militarism and creating peace; in a schoolwide campaign against bullying; in the way harmony and helpfulness pervade the ideals of the school. More striking is the effort by students to reestablish the firefly population in the region, which had been devastated by agribusiness and industrial pollution. "They go into fields to collect fireflies, care for them in our culture house, then hatch eggs and feed the babies," Matsuda says, clearly pleased by the success of this program. "They hatch one hundred thousand each year because the survival rate is only two percent." Such activities reflect both the Buddhist value of interdependence and the hands-on pedagogy of Makiguchi, he tells me. "Students learn how precious life is, see how much effort it takes to have even a single firefly in the beautiful, natural environment. They understand how a single life depends on the ecosystem." He laughs warmly as he recalls broaching the subject with Ikeda.

"He thought I should do it and appointed me chair of the Fireflies Committee!"

The idealistic streak in Soka education catches me off guard when, over a lunch of noodles, fresh vegetables, and miso soup, a boy of about ten asks me, in a piping voice and amazingly good English, "Professor Seager, what is your dream?" The look on his face is so earnest that I know I must try to tell him the truth—the first of many occasions during the day when I will be forced to be both more sincere and more idealistic than I usually care to be.

"My dream . . . hmm . . . my real dream just now is to live in a trailer in the desert, where I can sit in the sun and reflect on life untroubled by the controversies of the world," I say, but add, "You see, I'm beginning to think about retirement."

From the blank look on his face, I can see that the concept of retirement does not compute, so I give it another try. "When I was your age," I say, getting into the spirit, "I dreamed about going to Asia, like my grandfather did many decades ago. For a while, I dreamed about Iran. Then India. But that dream never came true until I was an old man and came to Japan."

The boy gazes at me thoughtfully, clearly wanting more information. "So, you see, I am fulfilling my dream by sitting here eating lunch and talking with you. Never did I think my dream would come true this way!" His eyes widen and a look of astonishment spreads across his face, as he takes in the idea that he is the fulfillment of the dream of a gaijin professor from America.

After lunch, I am conducted to the spacious library where I am to speak with older students about my work. I'm one in a long line of intellectuals, social activists, athletes, and philosophers from the corners of the world who, having been drawn into Ikeda's orbit, are asked to contribute to the education of Soka students. I feel strangely ennobled as I step up to speak, a clutch of Japanese students looking intently at me, both putting me at ease and seeming to demand the best I have to offer.

Taking a cue from lunch, I talk to them of my dream as a way to encourage them in their own, beginning with my youthful fascination with Alexander the Great, who while still a young man led his troops to India. That was the start of my journey, which eventually led me to Harvard, where I studied Buddhism and Hinduism. Mari translates, but I can see that some students follow my English.

"All of that led me here to Japan, where I have had wonderful opportunities—to speak with President Ikeda, to visit Shinanomachi, to meet pioneers who knew Presidents Makiguchi and Toda well," I say, laying out for them, like a good Buddhist, the chain of causes and effects that brought me to them. "I've learned how your parents and grandparents struggled through the war and postwar years and in the past decades, when your country grew powerful and rich, to attempt to make the world a better place. Please take seriously that I am very honored to be here," I say, oddly moved to hear myself say aloud what I've come to think about the Soka Gakkai. "But I want to hear what's on your minds. I intend to relax a bit. Please tell me about your own dreams and how you hope to achieve them."

One young girl, prim in a tartan plaid uniform skirt and white blouse, a bit shy and blushing, begins in English, but soon shifts to Japanese. "My dream is to be a teacher. I want to know all that my teacher knows and, when I become a teacher, I want to embrace all students with the sense that 'I like you.'"

"That's a fine dream," I say, into the swing of things but thinking it also my role to offer realistic bits of guidance. "Sometimes that's not so easy. Students can be difficult," I say, meaning to tease her. "But my classes go best when I enjoy my students and they enjoy me."

A young woman, a bit older than the first, raises her hand, then stands up very straight. "Firstly, since I've never lived in any English-speaking countries, please forgive my poor English," she says, formally and near flawlessly. "My dream is changeable, but I want to be a strong woman. Now I feel I want to be a politician in Japan. To go to school at the new Soka University in America. After I graduate, I will have strong power and will come back and change corrupt Japan."

"That is a noble calling," I say, "one that President Ikeda would very much appreciate. Just a few days ago I spoke with Toshiko Hamayotsu, a Komeito politician and a strong woman. I am sure she would appreciate it too. But let me add this—if you do go to the United States to study, you might stay for a few years after graduation. There are many strong women in the U.S. of different races and cultures. And there are different ways to be strong. Learn a lot in another country, then you will be ready to come back to take on the Diet."

One young man tells of how he traveled to Taiwan for a Gakkai youth meeting, where he learned about child abuse in violent homes. "I want to work in the United Nations or an NGO [nongovernmental organization] for children. Now I study English very much because English is my method for my dream. I am very happy, but what can I do to end the suffering of those children?" he asks, clearly distressed by the pain he had witnessed. "I want . . . I think I should . . . I really can't find out what can I do to alleviate all these sufferings."

"The things you are doing, learning languages and thinking about NGOs, are important," I begin, hoping to address his distress. "Begin networking with people who do work that inspires you. There are many in Gakkai networks to help you. But you must accept that you cannot save all the children of the world. You may do small things. Or very large things. But you cannot end all suffering. If you try to, you will only hurt yourself."

The afternoon wheels by quickly as, one after another, the students share with me their dreams, while I enjoy my role as wizened gaijin, mixing gentle cautions about the real world with the kind of hopeful outlook that does not come to me easily or instinctually. *Ann*—a hard-working idealist if ever there was one—*would be so proud of me,* I think, in an off moment while Mari is busy translating.

Another young man stands up to speak, a senior who wears the old military-style Soka uniform, high-necked with brass buttons, dashingly romantic in a nineteenth-century way, which is being phased out in favor of blue blazers. He is tall and thin but strongly built, with a swarthy complexion, not ethnically Japanese like most of the other students. He talks softly but directly, his English very good and with an accent that sounds British.

"I was born in Malaysia and raised there for about fifteen years," he begins. "My teachers there taught us about history, in 1945 or 1942, I don't know, when the Japanese came to Malaya and committed many atrocities. I was abused by my classmates because my father was Malaysian but my mother was Japanese. That's all I want to say."

The room is silent, but I can't tell whether everyone is ill at ease or I've been startled into alertness. The young man speaks with no rancor and asks nothing of me, but seems to have pushed us all into deep water. I flounder, looking for a few words.

"All of us, as we strive to build a better world, must deal honestly with tragic events that have happened and will continue to happen in history," I begin, trying to find a path through the situation. "I've not had the kind of experience you've had. But there are places, like Vietnam, where people might abuse me because I'm from the United States, because of horrors we inflicted on them in one of our wars."

Struggling to get my bearings, I decide to talk to them about something I do know about—race relations and American slavery. "Slavery in the United States is as bad as any history gets," I say to all in the class, keenly aware that World War II and its legacy must still shape the Japanese character in intimate ways I cannot fathom. "Sometimes I have been in situations when people have been angry at me because of that history. At times like those it's important to keep a good heart and to try to understand. I find having good African American friends is a key," I say, wondering if he has close friends at school, surprised to hear how very much I sound like Ikeda when I conclude by telling everyone that they "can build bridges together across history with friends."

"Should I teach them about this history in Japan?" he asks.

"Teach whom?"

"Other students."

"Certainly. I hope that in Soka school there is room for frank discussions about this terrible history. Can you talk about that history here?" I ask.

"Yes," he replies, which relieves me because I'm not sure what I would do had he answered no. "So then, dialogue really is important, as President Ikeda always tells us," he adds, returning to his seat, seemingly satisfied.

A few minutes later, when we all emerge together into a sunny courtyard in front of the school, a festival is in full swing—the girls' fife-and-drum corps plays, young men of the cheerleading squad run through drills, parents and teachers mill about chatting.

As our car drives up, President Matsuda asks us to pause for a moment because a choral group wants to sing the Kansai Soka school song, which they have prepared in English to honor my visit. A small group of young men and women scamper into formation around a flagpole, the Soka school "banner of glory" flying at the top.

Oh, the hopeful sky spreads endlessly.
The scent of beautiful flowers floats on the hillside.
All of you, learn true justice.
And your wisdom will be brighter.
Look up at, look up to the banner of glory.

Mari gently edges us toward the car because we are running very late. But as we start to move, I'm struck again by how in Japan a small tableau that I want to dismiss as corny or just too much can take on the power of an archetype, defying all sense of irony. My habitual cynicism seems a world away as I behold the clutch of students, primly uniformed, alert and upright, broadly waving good-bye to me, as they sing.

Oh, the *man'yo* flowers are all at their best,
Pretty fireflies dance everywhere.
Our school can be praised as a symbol of peace.
With shining eyes, hearts of you and me
Are filled, filled with the banner of glory.

Can I—can the world—ever live up to them? I wonder, aware that wishing does not in itself create a world of hope, aware that youthful idealism dashed can itself breed cynicism, as our car pulls slowly through the gate and heads out to the highway.

Oh, in Kansai, the mentor and disciples
Are a poem sounding like a glorious melody.
Together you and me
Will fulfill our promise to achieve world peace
With joy and glee,
We are sure to be champions with the banner of glory.
We are sure to be victors with the banner of glory.

CHAPTER 6

Countervailing Trends

Two countervailing trends marked the Soka Gakkai in the decades after the watershed free speech issue in 1970: the first was an ongoing process of liberalization; the second, mounting tensions between progressive laity and traditionalist priests. Both helped to give Ikeda's long presidency its own distinct character and reflect how he, like Toda before him, virtually re-created the Gakkai by recasting the original hybrid philosophy bequeathed to it by Makiguchi.

In many respects, liberalization advanced naturally as members explored ways to express Buddhism in contemporary terms—a process led by Ikeda, who modeled for them hearty and good-humored ways of engaging with the world. His Buddhist Humanism evolved into a worldly, idealistic faith infused with reverence and piety grounded in the gohonzon and daimoku. But Ikeda also fleshed out this humanism through his travels and writings and, above all, through his networking with intellectuals, artists, and activists and his citizen diplomacy with political leaders in countries around the globe.

Perennial conflicts between Gakkai laity and priests, which date at least from Makiguchi's refusal to accept amulets from the Ise shrine, flared periodically but resulted in an irreparable breach only under High Priest Nikken Abe in 1991. The Gakkai now refers to a "first priesthood issue" around 1979 and a "second priesthood issue" around the time of the excommunication. Although details differ in each, both incidents were rooted in struggles between traditionalists and champions of innovation, a familiar feature in modern religions that invariably results in pain and recrimination on all sides. The climax to this struggle—at once dramatic, tragic, and ironic—came in 1998 with the demolition of the Sho-Hondo, the grand temple conceived by Toda to fulfill Nichiren's prophesied kaidan, which Ikeda and High Priest Nittatsu had built together and dedicated to world peace.

•   •   •

Ikeda's network-building and his dialogues played a key role in developing the liberal spirit of Buddhist Humanism as it evolved from the '70s into the '90s. It is easy to dismiss the dialogues and Ikeda's many honorary professorships and degrees as evidence of his tireless self-promotion. This view has had a particular appeal to his enemies, who view his cutting a high global profile as part of a scheme to raise the office of Gakkai president over that of the high priest. Since the 1991 excommunication, they have delighted in charging Ikeda with consorting with drug traffickers and dictators. On Web sites styled as cult alerts with obscure, presumably unofficial, links to Nichiren Shoshu, they cite, for instance, his acquaintance with Manuel Noriega, whom he met in 1974 during a stopover in Panama, and with Fidel Castro, his partner in a 1996 dialogue that was the climax of a Min-On–sponsored cultural exchange.[1]

Such spurious charges distort the meaning of Ikeda's networking and the resulting dialogues with Oxford sociologist Bryan Wilson, Indian scholar-statesman Karan Singh, Norwegian peace activist Johan Galtung, Nobel laureate Linus Pauling, and many others. These meetings serve a number of constructive ends, most basically that of satisfying Ikeda's passion for self-education. They have played a crucial role in his personal journey into cosmopolitan complexity, becoming both pilgrimage and mission—much like his first trips abroad, when he and his colleagues first began to peer beyond the horizons of Japan. In this capacity, they have helped him to shape his emergent humanism, even as they enable him to carry Nichiren's Buddhism around the world.

These activities are also an important part of Ikeda's work for Gakkai members as their mentor and president. At home in Japan, where *Seikyo Shimbun* covers his many meetings, Ikeda's travels become causes leading to positive effects that yield the benefit of linking rank-and-file believers to the larger world. Japanese members not only take pleasure and pride in his accomplishments, but also grow in their knowledge of issues in the Americas, Africa, Europe, and the Asian mainland. Conversely, for members in other national movements, Ikeda's visits and his networking with local figures help to keep them linked, in a particularly immediate way, to Japan and the rest of the global movement.

Ikeda's networking became so central to the new spirit of the Gakkai that his inaugural dialogue overseas, with British historian Arnold Toynbee in 1972 and 1973, has taken on legendary proportions. Fortunately, reflection on the encounter between the two is available in a more insightful form than Polly Toynbee's report of her trip to Japan in 1984, briefly discussed in chapter 2. Noted historian William H. McNeill, in his biography *Arnold Toynbee: A Life,* writes about the circumstances that gave rise to the dialogue and suggests what each man seems to have seen in the other, just a few years before Toynbee's death and when Ikeda was only beginning to grow into his role as a mature leader and teacher.[2]

A prodigious scholar best known for his ten-volume magnum opus, *A Study of History,* Toynbee created a sensation in Britain with the publication of his first three volumes in 1934, as Europe struggled with the legacy of the First World War and drifted toward the Second. With the publication of another three in 1939, Toynbee gained a following in the United States, where after World War II he was toasted as sage for the American century, a reputation secured by a 1947 cover on *Time* magazine.

Much of Toynbee's popularity rested with his claim to discern patterns or laws in the rise and decline of the twenty-one civilizations he placed at the center of history, an argument that gave his sweeping narrative an appealing, explanatory power in an age of global crisis. Much also rested on his spiritual orientation, which—though Catholic, conventionally Protestant, and decidedly post-Christian at times—suggested a transcendent force in the making of civilization. This perspective surely appealed to Ikeda. But by the time Toynbee published his final volumes in 1954, he had come under attack by scholars who viewed his method as flawed in many ways, most significantly his use of the decline of Rome and rise of Christianity as a template into which he forced the history of other civilizations. Toynbee's status as sage continued to dim over the course of the '60s, in part thanks to his too-avid pursuit of lucrative publishing and speaking contracts, particularly in the United States. But even as his scholarship passed out of fashion, he remained a kind of cultural monument in the West, though his magisterial image was tied to a rapidly passing era and his books were rarely read.

But according to McNeill, enthusiasm for Toynbee soared in Japan after he made his third trip there in 1967, where he was hailed as a gaijin sage, a wise man from the West. His reputation in Japan rested on his being both a historian and a religious thinker. As early as 1954, a Tokyo businessman sponsored a translation of *A Study of History,* but an abridged version appeared in Japanese in 1966 about the same time as did Karl Marx's *Das Kapital,* while demonstrations were raging over the Japan-U.S. security treaty. As a result, these two very different interpretations of history vied with each other for the public's attention at a time of acute crisis. While visiting Japan, Toynbee gave lectures titled "The Coming World City" and "Mankind's Future" at Kyoto Sangyo University, his principal host, and at the Imperial Palace before an array of dignitaries including the emperor, prime minister, and minister of education.

It appears that Ikeda's initial interest in Toynbee was piqued by this 1967 visit. After his departure, Toynbee the historian was picked up by Japanese intellectuals who viewed his work as an antidote to Marxism. They founded the Toynbee Society, which flourished even after the historian's death in 1975. The more explicitly religious aspects of his thinking gained a much wider reading after he signed a contract for 3,500 pounds with the *Mainichi Shimbun,* one of Japan's major dailies, to publish his views on life in a ninety-part series. This took the form of a dialogue with Kei Wakaizumi, a professor of international relations at Kyoto Sangyo University who, like Toynbee, was disillusioned by America's role in the Vietnam War and disturbed by the alienation of the new generation.

According to McNeill, it was Wakaizumi who introduced Ikeda and Toynbee, the two men soon corresponding about time, place, and the consideration of fees, with the result that the historian invited Ikeda to come to London in 1970 for a dialogue. "When I was last in Japan in 1967, people talked to me about the Sokagakkai [*sic*] and about you yourself. I have heard a great deal about you. . . . I am going to read some of your books and speeches translated into English," Toynbee wrote to Ikeda. "It is my pleasure, therefore, to extend to you my personal invitation to visit me in Britain in order to have with you a fruitful exchange of views on a number of fundamental problems of our times which deeply concern us all. . . . I might suggest some time next May . . . as we usually have a lovely spring in my country."[3]

Ikeda found it difficult to make time for the trip, but the two men corresponded before their formal meetings, which eventually were to extend over five days, first in May 1972 and again in 1973. "Our discussions swept through a vast panorama of subjects," Ikeda wrote in *Chuo Koron,* a Japanese monthly, about his and Kaneko's first visit, "from the meaning of life to science and religion, history and civilization, learning and education, war and international affairs, social problems, literature and art and women's issues."[4] Ikeda oversaw the translation of his side of the dialogue into English and the arranging of a text suitable for publication under the title *Choose Life,* which was soon translated into half a dozen languages. Toynbee handled the preface, which he wrote in the third person. "In spite of the difference between the authors' religious and cultural backgrounds," he wrote, a "remarkable degree of agreement in their outlooks and aims has been brought to light. . . . Their agreement is far-reaching; their points of disagreement are relatively slight."[5] McNeill observed that "convergence between East and West was . . . what Toynbee and Ikeda sought and thought they had found in their dialogue," noting that the historian viewed the broad areas of agreement between the two as "reflecting the birth of a common worldwide civilization."[6]

But it is easy to discern more specific intellectual connections between the two, one man forty-four years old, the other in his eighties. One was a shared conviction that the great sweep of history had a structural unity and was infused throughout by a spiritual dynamic, an idea that Toynbee himself, at that stage in his life, readily likened, in very general terms, to the Buddhist notion of karma. Toynbee also argued that the growth of civilization was stimulated by what he called Challenge and Response, the dedication of a creative minority to the overcoming of obstacles, a view that thoroughly resonated with Ikeda's experience and his activistic Buddhist spirituality and philosophy. Toynbee's view that Western society, while threatening to absorb other civilizations, was itself in a state of decline fitted well with Nichiren Shoshu doctrine of the age of mappo. Both men also shared a conviction that the next chapter in history was to be the emergence of global civilization, although Ikeda expressed more optimism than Toynbee about it being achieved through peaceful means. Toynbee attributed this divergence to a temperamental difference traceable to the contrast between Ikeda's Mahayana Buddhist background and his own, more tragic views grounded in Christianity.

McNeill also suggests that Toynbee's interest in Ikeda was rooted in the Gakkai's rapid rise in postwar Japan in the face of vehement opposition, a phenomenon that recalled the decline of Rome–rise of Christianity template that structured his history. "Soka Gakkai was exactly what his [Toynbee's] vision of the historical moment expected," McNeill writes, "for it was a new church, arising on the fringes of the post-Christian world, appealing principally to an internal proletariat, and deriving part of its legitimacy from an ancient and persecuted faith." McNeill notes how Toynbee defended the Gakkai against charges made by individuals familiar with its controversial history in Japan. "I agree with Soka Gakkai on religion as the most important thing in human life, and on opposition to militarism and war," Toynbee remarked on one occasion. On another, he defended Ikeda: "Mr. Ikeda's personality is strong and dynamic and such characters are often controversial. My own feeling for Mr. Ikeda is one of great respect and sympathy."[7]

It is not difficult to imagine an aged Western historian with a long-standing interest in globalization and Ikeda, a young man, still very much the junior by Japanese standards, being taken with each other, and the happy success of the Toynbee-Ikeda dialogue accounts for much of its legendary status. But it is equally, if not more, important for the subsequent history of the Gakkai that Toynbee urged Ikeda to expand his networks and gave him his first set of contacts. "As we were about to part upon completing our discussion," Ikeda wrote, "Dr. Toynbee handed one of the interpreters a list of the world's leading intellectuals that he recommended I seek out," among them Aurelio Peccei, founder of the influential think tank the Club of Rome, and René Huyghe, an eminent French art historian.[8] Ikeda pursued these leads, which eventually resulted in new dialogues and new publications, marking further steps both in his personal education and in the Gakkai's maturation.

Ikeda later transformed his networking into a kind of citizen diplomacy, the record of which is found in *Peace Builder: Daisaku Ikeda* and *Memorable Encounters, Daisaku Ikeda: Dialogues for Peace*. These are collections of photographs of Ikeda meeting François Mitterand and Corazon Aquino; Margaret Thatcher and John Major; Turgut Özal and Hassan Gouled Aptidon, former presidents of Turkey and Djibouti; and many others. With no explanation of why these meetings happened or what they represent, one is inclined to dismiss them as routine photo ops, but there are stories, rationales, and outcomes behind each.

For instance, Ikeda first met Nelson Mandela in 1990 just after the South African leader's release from prison, in the course of his world tour to marshal support to end apartheid. One might assume that Ikeda courted Mandela, but the situation was the reverse; the story was recounted to me by the head of the Gakkai's African Affairs Division, Kazuichi Namura.[9]

In the mid-1980s, Oswald Mtshali, a South African writer whose poetry was influential in the anti-apartheid movement, read Ikeda's *Glass Children* and was inspired by his remarks about empowering youth. He later praised Ikeda as a profound Eastern philosopher in a series of articles that Mandela read while imprisoned. Some years later, Mandela requested a meeting with that philosopher during his visit to Japan, with the result that he and Ikeda met for a first dialogue in Tokyo at the offices of *Seikyo Shimbun,* with a second held later, in 1995, in the government's state guesthouse near the grounds of the emperor's palace. The favorable publicity Ikeda gained from these meetings rankled his political rivals, but more important are the concrete results. The meetings strengthened existing links between the Gakkai and the African National Congress, resulting in Gakkai-sponsored anti-apartheid lectures, a traveling exhibit, and student exchanges between Japan and South Africa through Soka University.

Ikeda's meeting with Zhou Enlai was also equal parts politics and serendipity.[10] In 1968, Ikeda called for the opening of relations between China and Japan in an address to twenty thousand Gakkai students, an idea that caught the attention of a nonmember politician influential in Japanese diplomatic circles. He soon arranged dialogues between Zhou Enlai and Komeito party representatives, who as members of the opposition party could operate informally and outside established channels to help pave the way for formal recognition. These encounters also led to the meeting between Ikeda and Zhou in 1974, which led in turn to youth exchanges between the two countries, exhibitions of Chinese art, visits between China and Japan of dance companies and music ensembles, and the establishment of permanent links between Chinese educational institutions and Soka University.

Like his dialogues with intellectuals, Ikeda's diplomacy fulfilled important functions in the movement by enriching Buddhist Humanism and placing Nichiren and his Buddhism before the world. More concretely, Ikeda's diplomacy forged living links between nations and peoples by laying the groundwork for student and faculty exchanges at Soka University, public cultural events by Min-On and TFAM, and scholarly conferences sponsored by the IOP. It was, moreover, the kind of public relations that could ease the way for national Gakkai movements considered suspect by their governments, such as those in Cuba and Korea.

As important, Ikeda's diplomacy expressed his Buddhist Humanism and had a spiritual meaning. Ikeda's ease in moving among dissidents and prime ministers encouraged members to become citizen-diplomats each in their own way, to become global citizens in the contemporary world. Speaking at Columbia University in 1996, Ikeda likened the humanistic ideals of Makiguchi to those of John Dewey, noting the importance of both to his vision of globalization.[11] Evoking the Mahayana view of the universe as a web of relations, he argued that cosmopolitanism is not determined by the number of languages one speaks or by how many countries one has visited. True cosmopolitanism is the possession of the wisdom to perceive the interconnectedness of all forms of life, the courage to respect differences among peoples and cultures, and the imaginative empathy to extend genuine compassion to all who suffer in the world.

Ikeda's networking and diplomacy find a natural extension in the Gakkai's commitment to multilateralism and the United Nations. "I grew up in the shadow of fascist militarism," Ikeda wrote recently. "The members of my generation, on whose psyche war left its indelible mark, were greatly inspired and excited to learn of the founding of the United Nations. . . . Under Mr. Toda's tutelage, we were regularly exposed to the ideal of global citizenship."[12] As early as 1973, to honor Toda's call for the abolition of nuclear weapons, the Youth Division collected ten million signatures in support of both disarmament and the United Nations.

The Gakkai's institutional presence there, however, dates from 1981, when Soka Gakkai became a registered nongovernmental organization (NGO) in the Department of Public Information. In 1983, SGI (Soka Gakkai International) received consultative status with the Economic and Social Council of the United Nations, and in 1997 it opened offices in both New York and Geneva. "Opinions are of course divided about the U.N.," Ikeda observed, "and there are those who deny that it has any meaningful potential. But it remains that the U.N. is the only existing forum where all nations can gather to discuss and seek solutions to the pressing problems facing our world. As a citizen of our world, I consider it only natural that we should support the U.N., so that it can fulfill its potential for peace."[13]

.   .   .

Short, a little round, very robust, Ikeda greets me on the top floor of the *Seikyo Shimbun* building with an embrace so unexpectedly warm that I flush. "We are taking good care of your wife's cherry tree," he says, shaking one hand, his other grasping my shoulder.[14] "Your wife is always by your side, Dr. Seager. Buddhism teaches that we can meet again and be reunited—as siblings, as parent and child, as relatives, or as lovers. We can move freely throughout the cosmos and be born again on a star of our choosing. Yes, Professor Seager, life does possess this unfathomable capacity and potential."

Ikeda speaks in a tone both intimate and bracing, his convictions about the order of things so natural and persuasive that I feel as though I've been chasing Ann through many lifetimes. "But for you to persevere now is an expression of the highest possible love for her," he continues, bringing me down to earth. "That will be your greatest victory. In the deepest realms of our lives is a wellspring of sublime joy. I believe your role from now on, Dr. Seager, is to demonstrate and share this truth with others."

Disarmed, I offer words of thanks even as I collect data in one corner of my mind, knowing that I'm getting a one-two punch that is classic Ikeda. First comes lofty spiritual guidance, then what Gakkai members call an "encouragement"—the exhortation to become all that you can possibly be. I'm flattered, even moved, that he sees in me the kind of person who might tap into cosmic joy, even though I'm dubious. But I find myself wondering, for the first time since I've become involved with Ikeda and the Gakkai, whether my critical disdain is related to my intelligence and academic education, as I like to think it is. It may well be that I'm just spiritually indolent and existentially lazy.

Ikeda then reads to me in Japanese two brief poems that Nichiren wrote for a disciple, Myoshin, a lay nun who had lost her life partner, the solemn cadence of his voice moving me although I do not comprehend a word. Oblivious to Rie's running translation, I savor the moment, then tuck a printed English translation of them into my inner coat pocket.

"Well, let's get on with the interview," Ikeda continues, once again hale and nimble, with a small shrug and a grin, walking alongside me, hand still on my shoulder as if we were buddies, Rie a few steps behind. "Let's have an enjoyable dialogue. Our discussion is for humanity, it's for the future."

We spend the next two hours sitting at a low, Japanese-style table chatting informally as we dine, a sense of intimacy between us even though Rob and a small entourage of reporters and aides share the meal, take notes, laugh at our jokes, and watch us intently. I find being in the spotlight with Ikeda more ennobling than discomforting. Conversing through interpreters, I can enjoy our lively, wide-ranging conversation but can also withdraw periodically into thoughts of my own, gauging my responses to him and honing a next question.

"I have never had an interviewer ask me about being 'Edokko'! You are the first!" he says with a laugh. "I've met with hundreds of people and none of them have asked this." Having read much of his writing, I'm more interested in Ikeda the person than in his ideas. So I've asked him to comment on his being raised in the urbane merchant culture of Tokyo, using a term that refers to old Edo and carries a special meaning. It is comparable to asking someone how being a Manhattanite or a Knickerbocker rather than a New Yorker may have shaped their personality.

"It is said that Edokko are known for their optimism and generosity, but that they spend each night what they earn each day," he begins, working off notes prepared in response to a few broad questions I submitted to his office several days earlier. "It is said they are honest to the point that they give too little thought to the consequence of what they say. They tend to be good-natured and as a result are easily deceived. They are feisty, contentious, impatient, and tend to make decisions quickly. They like to stick up for the underdog and have a strong sense of justice," he continues. His eyes almost merry, he adds, "With this kind of character, Edokko have rarely been people of great note," sort of winking as he speaks, his expression signaling that now he is teasing.

Whether it's the prepared notes, the Japanese language, the interpreter, or Ikeda himself, the casting of his remarks in the third person is distancing. I want him to reveal more of himself, so I press him. "But does that really describe you, President Ikeda, or not?"

Laughing at my bluntness, he goes off notes and answers with a recollection. "My mentor, Mr. Toda, used to tell me: 'You are an Edokko— good-natured and generous. You want to help others and don't think of the sacrifice. But remember, others may not be like you. No matter what you do for them, the fact is that they may forget everything,'" he says. "Sometimes it turned out exactly as Mr. Toda predicted. I've been betrayed by people I did everything I could to help."

Not knowing how much self-revelation I can expect from a prominent, public Japanese man, I stay with this line of questioning, telling him of my visit to his old Ota haunts, asking him to talk about the old days. I may get some of what I'm after when I think I see him flush, maybe even beat back a tear—a casting back into memories of laver harvesting? Of his mother, perhaps? Or of the hard war years? Or maybe such an emotional display, however modest, is wishful thinking on my part? I try to drive the question home by talking about his disciples in the United States and their great affection for him, asking, "In your youth, did you ever imagine that people on the other side of the world would love you?"

Ikeda pauses, thinking, and then talks about Ota, slowly at first but then animated. He recalls the death of his brother in Burma; a fragment of an old family mirror that he has kept for many years; his long, pensive walks on Morigasaki beach. He tells me that his young friend who became a Christian, who played a prominent role in his own spiritual quest, disappeared one day, and was never seen or heard from again. His point seems to be a Buddhist lesson in impermanence, the tone of his voice suggesting melancholy, which recalled to me the poems he had read as we greeted.

"Being Edokko, I did have grand hopes and dreams, even if these had no basis in reality," he says, chuckling to himself. "I remember the day my second brother's wife introduced herself to me in our garden in Morigasaki. I offered to help her in any way I could and suggested that she not work too hard at being a good wife, as it could be hard on her health. That is a typical thing for an Edokko to say, by the way," he adds. "She gave me a very serious look and asked, 'Daisaku, what do you want to become when you are older?' I replied, 'I will do something that will astonish the entire Japanese nation.'" He smiles again. "That, too, is the kind of thing Edokko are prone to say. My sister-in-law remembered that and later said, 'You really did what you said you would.'" He raises his eyebrows as if he too is astonished that he grew up to be a religious leader with disciples around the globe.

While Ikeda is talking and Rie preparing to interpret his remarks, I realize I feel completely at ease, my legs tucked under the table, shoeless, eating crabs, mushrooms, and various pickled things, adequately if not elegantly managing chopsticks. Stories about Ikeda come back to me—how he corresponds with members who write to him, keeps a watchful eye on people with special problems, delights in presenting small gifts out of the blue to encourage people. As a new round of dishes is served, I recall Minoru Harada, his former secretary, telling me how Ikeda lives in accord with Nichiren's injunction to spend each day as if it were one's last, so he puts his full effort into each person he meets lest they never meet again. I find myself wondering if I will ever see Ikeda or any of these marvelous people again, once this project is finished.

I then tell Ikeda of my interest in the remarkable life of his mentor, which turns our conversation to Toda, a man to whom Ikeda attributes all that he is today. This ascribing of a disciple's accomplishments to the mentor is common in Gakkai circles. A young woman may work long hours to master gymnastic techniques, a man may devote a decade to developing a program at Soka University, but in their telling, they ascribe their success to Ikeda. Many outsiders find this practice off-putting, but I now see it as a key to the mentor-disciple relationship. Individuals become disciples because they find Ikeda's Buddhist Humanism an inspiring vehicle for self-actualization and a way to make the world a better place. They look to him for guidance and encouragement as they seek to realize that vision in a personally meaningful way. The spiritual bond that exists between mentor and disciple is so intimate that to make a fast distinction between his inspiration and one's own accomplishment is not viewed as particularly relevant.

"If there were more books about President Toda in English, the Soka Gakkai would be more widely and more deeply understood," he notes. "He was a man of intense, passionate conviction. To be perfectly honest, he surpassed President Makiguchi." This statement shocks me, because Ikeda has gone to great lengths to foster a Makiguchi revival. "The dynamism of his action, flashes of genius, well-balanced judgment of social conditions . . . I have yet to meet anyone who can match Mr. Toda in any of these regards." As Rie speaks, I recall watching old footage of Ikeda and Toda walking together under the ancient trees of Taisekiji, a look of loving admiration passing between them. "You must have been afraid of not being able to fulfill Mr. Toda's expectations," I say, trying to keep our conversation running in a personal vein.

"I was filled with a sense of pride and determination that no matter what it took, I would respond to his expectations," he replies, his voice pitched with intensity. "I had a profound sense that betraying my mentor's expectations was absolutely unthinkable; to do so would be the Buddhist equivalent of falling into hell." As he describes himself as a young man, I recall his writing in his diary that to bring someone into the faith was a far better gesture of friendship than to treat him to a movie. "I was weighted by a heavy spiritual ballast, leadlike in its weight, so it was impossible for me to find joy in the shallow pleasures of life. Deep down in my heart, I burned with resolve, my soul ignited by flames," he says, his idealism today no less emphatic than half a century ago. "But President Toda always treated me as if I were a golden egg," he says, musing again, his tones fond and warm. "He cared for me more intensely than he would have his own child. With his very life. It was truly extraordinary."

We then talk of the abuses and good uses of religion and the challenges young people face today, the ease of our conversation making time slip quickly away. His handlers grow restless, concerned that he get sufficient rest, so we exchange gifts, he giving me a collection of his nature photographs, I giving him a book about San Xavier del Bac, a mission church outside Tucson, Arizona, where I observed the first anniversary of Ann's death. I take a moment to point out to him the Cristos, santos, virgins, and old altars, wanting to convey something to him about my own spirituality, such as it is.

"I feel as if the two of us went back to Morigasaki beach after all these years," he says, picking up on my Christianity and that of his lost friend, as we step into our shoes assisted by an elderly kimono-clad woman, preparing to part company. He looks older to me now, tired and maybe even a bit frail. "I hope you will enjoy new sights and vistas. I hope we will meet again as good friends. I also hope you have a chance to see the cherry tree which we planted in honor of your wife," he says, then adds, almost as an aside. "I would like to plant a cherry tree for you also, so the two of you can be together. You can be assured that we will take good care of you both."

. . .

A week or so later, Rob, Rie, and I return to Makiguchi Memorial Garden to see Ann's tree and to plant one of my own. The ceremony this time around is abbreviated and much more relaxed, only the three of us this time, and one young woman and man to bear the shovel and watering can. Ann and I seem to be in a Filipino neighborhood: a tree on one side of us is dedicated to a married couple and, on the other, one to a lawyer apparently alone who belonged to the Knights of Rizal, a charitable organization in the Philippines.

Afterward, I wander off by myself for a time, enjoying leafing trees and budding blossoms, glimpsing once again the bridge where I'd stood with Shibata a year before feeding koi, the whole glen now bathed in warm, quiet sunlight. I unfold and read Nichiren's poems that Ikeda had read to me for Ann, the two of them marvelously appropriate. "Last year's sadness / The pain of this year's months and days," the first began, seeming to ask me to recall all that I've been through since I was last in Japan. "Sad thoughts never dispelled / never made clear and bright."

The second spoke more of futurity, but with that bittersweet ache one often associates with Buddhism, cherry trees, and Japan.

With time,
the petals that scatter the fruit that fall from trees
will bloom, bear fruit, and ripen once more.
How could it be
that those who have passed away
will not return to us?

A bit later, Rob, Rie, and I sit for a time in the sun near my two trees talking about relationships—Rob about being a husband and father, Rie about her marriage to Shibata, me about Ann.

. . .

Ikeda's original call for liberalization was an appeal for a change in tone in the Gakkai, not for a wholesale recasting of doctrine. But even so, Nichiren Shoshu traditionalists periodically charged him with dangerous innovations, straining his relationship with Nittatsu, the high priest from 1959 until his death in 1979.

"I have innumerable fond memories of our encounters and interactions," Ikeda wrote to me in 2001, more than two decades after Nittatsu's death. "High Priest Nittatsu and I worked in complete harmony and unity of purpose toward the construction of the Sho-Hondo." He was "a forward-looking, open-minded individual, who deeply appreciated the importance of the Soka Gakkai's mission and activities." But Ikeda also recalled the "constant and indeed strenuous effort to build and maintain good, cooperative relations with the priesthood." As he sees it, the central issue was a difference between a group that spread "Buddhism as a living faith in society, promoting peace, culture, and education for the sake of humankind" and one "inclined toward a rigid adherence to tradition and to clerical authority."[15]

In retrospect, the alliance between liberalizing Gakkai and conserving priesthood was a classic case of a center that could not indefinitely hold, and the image of Nichiren Shoshu stoutly anchored to Japanese traditions and the Gakkai eager to set sail for parts unknown has a good deal of merit. But this dichotomy should not suggest that priests resisted, while the Gakkai embraced, the prospect of globalization. On the contrary, for many years the two worked hand in hand to develop a global reach. It is more a case of tensions between laity and priests taking on different guises over the course of forty years, many of them issues of equity versus hierarchy grounded in a traditional religious culture that is distinctly Japanese. These tensions were exacerbated by

Ikeda's increasing cosmopolitanism and his openness to the aspirations and values of people in the growing organizations overseas. As his globalizing Buddhist Humanism moved into the foreground, it was perhaps inevitable that traditionalism must recede—a process that would be abruptly halted by Nikken, who saw himself as having to reassert the authority of priests.

Japaneseness runs deep in issues between the laity and the priesthood—disputes over incomes derived from rituals, charges of improper disposition of ashes of the dead, factional struggles among priestly families, and more. Running through it all was a priestly preoccupation with an etiquette that reflected class, status, and the expectation of lay deference toward priests, the breach of which led clerics to confuse criticism with blasphemy. In his recounting of events, for instance, Nichijun Fujimoto, a priest and general administrator of Nichiren Shoshu, thought Ikeda's having remarked that "someone who's a high priest ought to think of the happiness of believers . . . not about power" both "denigrated and scorned" Nikken.[16] The finer points of this etiquette were obscure for many Japanese and usually wholly opaque to members overseas. Thus issues of great import within Nichiren Shoshu were often far removed from members' concerns, which meant that struggles Ikeda found constant and strenuous often went unobserved, only to surface dramatically in major blowups.

The upshot of the first priesthood issue, which came to a head in 1979, is described easily. Ikeda resigned his position as the third president of Soka Gakkai–Japan and became its honorary president. He then turned his attention to his role as the first president of Soka Gakkai International, an umbrella organization founded in 1975 to nurture national movements around the globe. Thus Ikeda relinquished the administrative responsibilities of the presidency, while remaining spiritual teacher with a free rein to develop his Buddhist Humanism in the context of a global community.

Events that precipitated the crisis are more difficult to recount—lawyers' intrigues, threats of extortion, and libelous articles—in a tangled plot that is, perhaps, now impossible to puzzle out completely.

In his article "Why Did Ikeda Quit?" Daniel Metraux discusses three key issues, the first about a difficult Nichiren Shoshu doctrine. In the Nichiren Shoshu tradition, Nichiren is understood to be the original, primordial Buddha. His teachings supplant those of Shakyamuni, who is considered a later Buddha, for the entire duration of the current age of mappo. When some Gakkai members praised Ikeda as a Buddha and

The Human Revolution as a kind of new *Gosho*, priests saw it as an attack on this doctrine, tantamount to heresy. A second issue was tied up with Nichiren's third secret law. The Myoshinko, a small group of lay conservatives, denied that the Sho-Hondo could in any way be the prophesied kaidan because its construction had *not* been sanctioned by the state. An antimodernist camp in Nichiren Shoshu, the Myoshinko was disbanded by Nittatsu in 1974 and its leaders expelled. A third issue was the Gakkai's building of *kaikans* or community centers to be used for both cultural and religious activities. In the view of traditionalists, these kaikans directly competed with Nichiren Shoshu temples and undermined the authority of priests.[17]

The second priesthood issue, which culminated in 1991, also had a tangled plot, one involving lawsuits and allegations about fraudulent audiotapes, inaccurate transcriptions, and forged documents, a story that became more complex as charges were made, retracted, and later restated. It also has its own cast of characters, such as the Shoshinkai, a group of about two hundred disaffected priests who banded together to press issues voiced by earlier clerical critics. They blamed their inability to secure permanent positions in temples—without which they had no income from performing rituals for laity—on the Gakkai's building of kaikans.

Standing at the center of these controversies was High Priest Nikken, whose obscure motives, widely discussed and said to be common knowledge by the Gakkai, give this priesthood issue an element of Japanese gothic. After he took office in 1979, Nikken first suppressed the Shoshinkai but within a decade implemented what is called Operation C, a plan allegedly to discredit Ikeda and to either ruin or take over the Gakkai. Some suggest his goal was to destroy the accomplishments of his predecessor, Nittatsu. In this scenario, the Gakkai is seen as a pawn in a power struggle among a few priestly families. Others see Nikken as seeking to control Taisekiji's considerable wealth. Having enriched the temple for decades, the Gakkai no longer had a use and had become nothing but trouble. Another line of interpretation focuses on Nikken's personal psychology and his mother, who is alleged to have been a nun and concubine of the sixtieth high priest. In this telling, Nikken's behavior reflects the influence of a mother who inculcated priestly ambitions in her son from infancy.

Whatever Nikken's motives, one cannot miss the shift in the Gakkai's mood from respectful disbelief to anger and counterattack in five volumes of documents published as the crisis unfolded.[18] Gakkai leaders took up damage control as members in a hundred countries suddenly

discovered they'd been excommunicated and quickly became privy to
rafts of information, much of it very obscure. The entire debate over
the doctrinal significance of the Sho-Hondo was rehashed, for instance,
with the Gakkai critiquing Nikken's interpretation of Nittatsu's modern
understanding of the kaidan, all parties citing *Gosho* chapter and verse.
Some of it seems patently ridiculous, such as Nikken's charge that
singing Beethoven's "Ode to Joy" at Gakkai meetings was blasphemy
because Friedrich Schiller's lyrics contained references to Christianity.

To appreciate the complexity of this incident, picture it as a cross-
cultural and multicultural globalization crisis operating on a plane of
nuanced Buddhist philosophy and Japanese ecclesiastical politics.
Important and subtle debates took place in Japanese in Shinanomachi
and Taisekiji, but their outcome had to be translated into Spanish,
English, Chinese, and other languages and broadcast to members by
e-mail or fax. Over the course of several years, an astonishing amount of
sectarian vitriol also appeared on the Web as rank and file in both camps
joined the fray and reports, spurious and otherwise, about Ikeda's
forays into the cocaine trade with Manuel Noriega and Nikken's wom-
anizing in Seattle proliferated in a half-dozen languages.

The similarity of this schism to the break between Protestants and
Catholics led Jane Hurst to call it a "Buddhist Reformation." She sees
the issue at stake as comparable to the challenge laid down by Martin
Luther and his idea of a "priesthood of all believers," a radical concept
in that it attacked the power of the church by locating religious authority in the people. Hurst also limns the conflict in terms of the Triple
Gem, a traditional formula used to express the essence of Buddhism in
terms of the Buddha, his teachings, and the community. According to
some Nichiren Shoshu authorities, the Buddha is Nichiren; his teachings are condensed in the dai-gohonzon in the possession of Taisekiji;
and the priesthood is the community.[19] In this reading, laypeople, such
as members of the Gakkai, can be *followers* of the bodhisattvas of earth
but cannot be among the bodhisattvas themselves, because that status
is reserved for priests.

As the dust from the struggle settled, both parties, and certainly the
Soka Gakkai, seemed to be happier going it alone. Members who
believed priests to be essential to their spirituality stayed with Nichiren
Shoshu, but most remained within the Gakkai, their loyalties tied to
Ikeda and his modernist Buddhism. Some 560 temples, more than 350
of them said to be constructed with Gakkai donations, were settled on
Nichiren Shoshu in what amounted to a costly divorce.

Nikken barred Gakkai members from Taisekiji, so tozan ceased, which meant that a symbol and experience no longer bound the global Gakkai community together; but this function was soon taken up by leader and youth meetings among members from different countries. In limited respects, Shinanomachi and Makiguchi Hall also began to serve as religious centers, although the discussion meetings held in homes and community centers remain at the heart of Gakkai spirituality. Kaidan is now understood to be any place where the faithful practice Buddhism, an interpretation of the third secret law that the Gakkai claims reflects Nichiren's original intention.

In a last-ditch effort to make the Gakkai toe the line, Nikken refused to issue gohonzons to new members—in effect, cutting them off from the energy source of Nichiren's spiritual charisma. In response, Tokyo headquarters began to issue its own gohonzons inscribed by Nichikan, the twenty-sixth high priest and an important eighteenth-century scholar and teacher. Nichiren Shoshu stalwarts ridiculed the Gakkai for its "fraudulent" gohonzons, suggesting that they lacked the potency of the dai-gohonzon. But this kind of charge seems to have had no real impact on Gakkai members' thinking—an indication of the depth to which Ikeda's modernist Buddhism had permeated the movement both in Japan and overseas.

Events climaxed in 1998 when Nikken ordered the Sho-Hondo demolished, which brought to an end, in a remarkably concrete way, Toda's aspiration to fulfill Nichiren's prophecy. At that time, Shoshin Kawabe, a priest at the Washington, D.C., temple, argued one final position bluntly but clearly. Reflection on doctrine revealed that the Sho-Hondo had the "potential" to be the kaidan, but it was not. It existed only for the convenience of Gakkai pilgrims, who no longer came to Taisekiji. Thus it "has completely lost the significance of its existence. . . . it is no longer good for anything."[20]

. . .

These tangled issues begin to become concrete to me during a visit to Taisekiji, an impressive temple complex near Mount Fuji, the legendary sign of all things Japanese, which I glimpse fitfully between the fast-food restaurants and strip malls that line the highway in Fujinomiya city. The cabdriver who shuttles us out to the temple makes clear that spiritual conflicts have concrete consequences when he complains about business having fallen off by more than a third after Gakkai members stopped making pilgrimages. Shops and restaurants in a small commercial enclave on the temple grounds are either closed and apparently abandoned or open but empty. The husband-and-wife owners of the restaurant where we eat an indifferent meal are more interested in watching soaps on TV than in cooking.

Taisekiji sits on a broad plain at the base of the tapered slopes that climb toward Fuji's peak, a magnificent setting chosen for its *shishin-sou-o*—its auspicious geocosmological properties—by Nikko, Nichiren's successor in the Nichiren Shoshu lineage. Given all my research, I can't help but see Taisekiji in terms of Gakkai history. I picture Toda in his palanquin passing the torch to youth in 1958. I see Nittatsu in priestly robes and Ikeda in formal wear officiating together in October 1972 at a cycle of rites to mark the Sho-Hondo's opening—a completion ceremony on the first, the solemn transfer of the dai-gohonzon to the mystic sanctuary on the seventh, a dedication ceremony on the twelfth, to name only three among many. This ceremonial cycle was followed by the World Peace Culture Festival: hundreds of Japanese women playing the koto, morris dancers from the United Kingdom, flamenco dancers, French folksingers, and African pop musicians, all performing in the crisp, clear air of autumn, on an immense plaza in front of the Sho-Hondo called The Garden of the Law, Mount Fuji serene in the distance.

I visit Taisekiji with Rob and two other members, Joan and Mariko, so I hear little good about Nikken but many wonderful recollections of tozans taken fifteen or even twenty years in the past, as we walk the temple grounds.[21] The quiet I consider pleasant they find ominous, the head temple in their experience a solemn yet joyous place thronged with millions of pilgrims every year. Ancient landmarks remain, such as the elaborate Mieido, built in the seventeenth century, and the five-story pagoda that dates to the eighteenth, but much has changed under Nikken, who demolished pilgrims' lodgings and the Grand Reception Hall built in 1964 and cut down hundreds of mature cherry trees donated by Soka Gakkai and planted by Nittatsu.

Even so, happy memories come easily. Joan, who is from the United Kingdom and works in Shinanomachi, recalls sleeping on tatami mats in big rooms crowded with pilgrims on overnight stays, waking to picnic-style breakfasts that were not very good but certainly adequate. Each dormitory had a gohonzon for practice, but the goal of each pilgrim was to chant before the dai-gohonzon in the mystic sanctuary in the Sho-Hondo. Everyone got a ticket that was considered "very precious" and cued up in long lines, four abreast around here, Joan says, gesturing to take in the long, narrow tree-lined stone avenue that is the central axis of Taisekiji.

Mariko, who is along as translator, says that she never stayed the night but came on day trips with her mother, who went on tozan over eighty times. I ask how her mother, given such piety, views the excommunication. "She's happy," Mariko says. "Members were expected to go to the local temple on the thirteenth of every month, give donations, and listen to a boring lecture from a priest for about an hour. My mother never did. She didn't like it. She wasn't afraid to speak out. So she wasn't particularly affected by the priesthood."

The affection Gakkai members hold for elements of the old regime, even as they dismiss them as irrelevant to their spirituality, becomes clear as random memories emerge while we stroll up a gradual incline under arching trees, alongside a gentle stream, past small temples and ancient stone embankments. "Toda used that temple for his lodging in the old days." "I spent a night in that one once." "Do you remember traditional ceremonies like the Airing of the Scrolls?"

"We used to do *ushitora* gongyo at two in the morning," Joan recalls fondly, "between the hour of the dog and the fox or something, which dates back to Nichiren. That time is thought to be very significant, so every night they did this and it was meant to be really good stuff if you went."

"It was the hour of the tiger and ox, not fox," Mariko corrects her, "and it was done for the attainment of kosen-rufu."

Joan recalls lectures at two in the morning in classical Japanese, which she never comprehended but loved because of the cadence of the archaic language. "I doubt Japanese members understood much either," Mariko adds. "Priests would be there," Rob throws in. "The high priest would be there sometimes. Sometimes he wouldn't. I never understood why he was or wasn't. And then you would see laity falling asleep, priests falling asleep. You know, I mean, it's two in morning."

The pathway ends in the Mieido, which contains a likeness of Nichiren carved in the fourteenth century. It is situated at the crest of the slope, and beyond it lies an immense open field in which the Sho-Hondo is conspicuous by its absence. We all stand together for a few minutes, saying nothing. The nonexistence of the vast convex roof designed to recall a crane in flight and the huge pillars that managed to evoke both the pharaonic and the high modern takes our breath away.

"It was like a dream," Joan eventually says softly. "It was like world peace, happiness, international unity, people here from all different countries. So you did have this feeling—this is the dream of how people can be together."

"You wore your best clothes," Robs recalls. "People from all cultures. We were so diverse. Members from all the SGI countries. There would be this mixing going on with members from all over the world, not just from here in Japan. That was the reality of kosen-rufu. The merging of cultures and people in such an auspicious time."

"I remember seeing members from overseas, sometimes in their native costumes. Very impressive," Mariko sighs. "My mother was furious when Nikken destroyed the Sho-Hondo," she recalls. "She is still furious."

. . .

Back in Tokyo, I probe priesthood-laity, Nichiren Shoshu–Gakkai issues more deeply in three interviews: one with the architect of the Sho-Hondo, two with former Nichiren Shoshu priests who have no relationship with either the temple or the Gakkai today.

Educated in the Roman church, I'm comfortable with clergy, enjoy deferring to nuns and priests, and know a bit about ecclesiastical culture. For all my secularity, I have affection for orthodoxy in these times when tradition is so easily discarded in favor of the new. As a result, I find the break between priesthood and Gakkai unfortunate. But these priesthood issues remind me that the idealism of Gakkai members, which part of me wants to dismiss as being . . . what?—too sentimental? too bourgeois? just much too much?—has been tested and found to endure through more than one great struggle. Their idealism has, moreover, been strengthened by their emancipation from an institutionalized tradition within which they had worked for years before it showed itself to be both burdensome and irrelevant.

Kimio Yokoyama, the architect of the Sho-Hondo, was a young man when he began to do work at Taisekiji but is now in his seventies.[22] He has taken time to come to Shinanomachi to talk to me, although the tenor of his remarks as we begin suggests that he and the Gakkai have long been out of touch. Yokoyama designed banks and schools, but his professional life was closely tied to Nichiren Shoshu, and he worked on a number of large temple projects underwritten by the Gakkai. I requested this interview to learn what laity-priesthood tensions looked like to a secular, creative artist. So I am astonished to learn how large was Yokoyama's own personal stake in the issues, his family being Nichiren Shoshu parishioners and his wife, High Priest Nittatsu's daughter.

Yokoyama's recollections of working on the Sho-Hondo are both revealing and heartbreaking. He lovingly recalls discovering the temple's "inner necessity," striving to unite its function as a mass pilgrimage site with the need for formal solemnity in what he calls "the joy of use." Ikeda inspired him with his view that the Sho-Hondo must embody Buddhist nondualism by uniting the physical and spiritual, Nittatsu with his desire that it be both sacred and humane. The idea of a symbolic crane in flight came to him only gradually as he wrestled with the Nichiren Shoshu tradition, which rejects the use of the human image as an object of worship, favoring instead the abstraction of Nichiren's gohonzons. This aniconic sensibility resulted in Yokoyama's creation of a modernist temple both opulent and austere. He talks of how he was well aware of doctrinal controversies surrounding the building of the kaidan, but describes his relationship with both Nittatsu and Ikeda as supportive and open, neither inclined to stifle his creative freedom.

As Yokoyama talks of reconciling traffic flow and access for the disabled with high design, I recall a video shot during the heyday of global tozan—long lines of devotees mounting a processional staircase that rose majestically on the side of the immense, high platform that formed the Sho-Hondo's base, their obvious happiness exalted, not crushed, by the temple's monumentality.

"Personally, when I look back on it, the fact that I was able to complete this project is nothing less than a miracle," he says, speaking seriously but with the hint of a grin that suggests warm memories. "When I look back at what enabled me to do it, I think it was my interactions with President Ikeda, to see how utterly committed he was, literally betting his life on everything," he explains. "And at the same time, there would be pilgrimages and I would see believers coming to the temple, people who had strong faith in Mr. Ikeda and his vision. To encounter that and to feel their expectations, their tremendous hopes—without that I couldn't have survived the pressures and the tensions of that project for eight full years." Musing for a few moments, Yokoyama recalls that when "President Ikeda thanked me, the words that he used literally meant 'You shortened or shaved off days of your life; you expended your life to fulfill this project.' And I could feel that President Ikeda knew exactly what I had gone through, that he fully understood everything that I had been through."

As I listen to his words, I recall another video, one shot in 1998 from the roof of the Gakkai's art museum near the temple grounds. Heavy equipment yanks at one of five Luxorian columns that formed a portico along the Sho-Hondo's facade, eventually bringing it down. The wing-spread roof evoking a crane in flight shudders for long moments before folding in upon itself in a huge cloud of dust.

"I need to ask," I say, "what do you make of Nikken's charge that sea salt had corroded the concrete, that steel supports had rusted, and that the Sho-Hondo would have collapsed if an earthquake had hit the Fuji region?"

"These were excuses for destroying the building that had no basis in fact," he says, clearly agitated, noting that third parties verified the soundness of the construction on a number of occasions.

I tread lightly but must also ask what he thinks moved Nikken to order the demolition. "My honest reaction," he begins falteringly, tears threatening, his face twisting with a grief that conveys more powerfully than words the loss of his masterpiece, a loss so deep that I can see in it my own loss of Ann: "I can't understand. I've thought about it a lot, but I cannot find any valid rationale."

. . .

After being associated with the temple for years, Takudo Hosoi and Hosho Shiina severed their relations with Nichiren Shoshu after Nikken took office. Both men have insiders' views of the pressure and politics within the institution, although those of the first are more intimate, the second more sociohistorical. Both help me to see past the vitriol, rumor, and rhetoric of struggle to some of the basic issues that led to the excommunication or schism. Both also surprise me with the pointed and quite similar opinions they express about the singular personality of Nikken.

Hosoi is head priest at Tokyo's Jisshuji, a temple once affiliated with Nichiren Shoshu but now independent, after Hosoi and the temple's board voted to part ways with Nikken.[23] A man around sixty, dressed informally but in robes, Hosoi, like Yokoyama, had a deep personal stake in the issues, being one of three sons of Nittatsu to become a Nichiren Shoshu priest. The other two brothers remain within the organization for reasons he prefers not to discuss but suggests are financial.

Having grown up in Nichiren Shoshu, Hosoi speaks authoritatively about nuances in the relations between laity and priests, such as how Toda pointedly used the word *gosoryo,* meaning "respected priest," to refer to clergy who worked hard for kosen-rufu, but *bozu,* a derogatory colloquial term for a monk, for those who did not. He recalls Ikeda as being more generous and indirect than Toda, but Ikeda too expected respect from priests and Nittatsu was, in turn, very candid with him. "They didn't fight, but had such an open relationship that they could be really frank," he says. "It might seem like they were throwing criticisms at each other, but they were not."

Hosoi also gives satisfying concreteness to struggles too often painted as having been waged between cosmic forces of darkness and light. He says he was a Shoshinkai sympathizer but appreciated the Gakkai because the two groups balanced each other out, one traditionalist, the other modernist, while most priests stood somewhere in between. He also describes politics as circling around distinct issues— one being that older parishioners understood Buddhism exclusively in terms of funerary rites, so they did not like the rise of the Gakkai. For their part, Gakkai members sometimes went overboard in their affection for Ikeda and zeal for kosen-rufu. Many priests appreciated that the Gakkai carried a modern message based on Nichiren's teaching to people around the world, but they tended to be unrealistic about their role in the kosen-rufu movement. "Some young priests did not understand the raison d'être of Soka Gakkai," he says. "They felt, 'We want to be the ones to lead them. We want to be their teachers.' So they were very frustrated."

In Hosoi's view, Nikken is a man who seems to be driven by arrogance, anger, and jealousy. When he first became high priest, he praised Ikeda, referring to him as "sensei." But within a few years, he began to dismiss the Gakkai president as merely a lay leader, eventually seeing his presence as unwelcome. "Nikken wanted to be revered as the ultimate leader by lay believers," he says. "But world figures did not come to Nikken, but to Daisaku Ikeda. Daisaku Ikeda is the one who's invited to countries worldwide. He's the one who meets with heads of state. I really think that the essence of the issue is a kind of envy."

When I ask him about the demolition of the Sho Hondo and other projects at Taisekiji that his father had worked on for years, Hosoi tears up and shakes his head in disbelief—"The insanity of Nikken's impulses! For me not to be too affected I have to come up with some kind of rationale, you know, and my rationale is insanity."

I get a more dispassionate reading from Hosho Shiina, a fit, compact man dressed in a dark suit and T-shirt who looks forty but must be older given his years in Nichiren Shoshu.[4] Shiina took his priestly vows in the sixth grade, the third generation of Nichiren Shoshu priests in his family. He served in New York in the '80s, during the heyday of the collaboration between the temple and the Gakkai in the United States.

During that time he and Rob occasionally worked together on projects on the East Coast. He left the Nichiren Shoshu priesthood in 1993 in the wake of the excommunication.

Shiina sketches the schism between Gakkai and priests on a broad canvas, which sets the entire priesthood/tradition versus Gakkai/modernism tension in a satisfying social and historical perspective. You must understand Nichiren Shoshu's parochialism, he explains, referring to the geographical isolation of Taisekiji and its long tradition of control by a few wealthy, rural families. Prior to its incorporation in 1912, by order of the government, it was only an informal association that had recruited its high priests from other sects for nine generations. Its Buddhism was lax yet conservative, backward-looking, oriented to life in the countryside, and protective of established interests.

When the Soka Gakkai entered the picture, he says, "Nichiren suddenly became a living presence in the religious life of laity and believers." Its impact on the established community was "an unprecedented event. There were many within the priesthood who had never heard the word *shakubuku*." Toda's demand that laypeople have an informed commitment was shocking and anxiety-provoking. "It was literally the heavens were astonished and the earth moved!" he says.

United by the crises of war, defeat, and occupation, Toda, Ikeda, and a succession of high priests worked together in a relationship Shiina likens to a good marriage, one in which a couple do not stare at each other looking for faults, but stand back-to-back to look out on the world together. High Priests Nichijun and Nittatsu understood what the postwar era required, but priests from the old families did not. Both of them "endured a lot of resistance, harassment; their efforts were undermined. Both had very weak support bases. They had not been part of the traditional establishment but appeared on the scene in a cometlike fashion, and there was a lot of intrigue and resistance directed against them."

In contrast, Nikken came from a traditional, priestly bloodline despite what Shiina refers to as his mother's "unfortunate background." "You have to look at the personal, and in that sense I think Nikken is very talented politically," he says. "His ability to manipulate things, to move things, you could even say his genius, you have to take very seriously. But it all comes from a very mean-hearted spirit that I think is a fundamental characteristic of his basic life condition."

Despite all the rhetoric to the contrary, Shiina sees doctrinal issues as having played little part in the struggle. "The majority of the priests, to be very honest, didn't make any effort to understand what was going on. For the majority, it was a question of economic stability—'The Gakkai has brought us prosperity we've never known before; let's go along for the ride.'" At the same time, he thinks Nichiren's intent and legacy have been misconstrued by priests. Priests' claims to be the sole agents of kosen-rufu are "very clumsy, very unnatural, because Nichiren didn't specify anything of that kind. He laid out the principle and core idea—kosen-rufu is the propagation of Nam-myoho-renge-kyo—and that's very simple. He didn't specify who was to propagate it or how it was to be propagated. . . . If we go back to Nichiren, the question of who's a priest, who's laity is just not even on the map."

. . .

On the evening before we depart from Japan, Rob and I sit at a Starbucks gazing across a trough of tracks and speeding trains at the huge Takashimaya department store complex. On overhead walkways and promenades, thousands of people are engaged in intensely private cell phone conversations under a warm sky blushed with a setting sun. *This is the modern Tokyo of legend,* I'm thinking to myself, *teeming, massive, vibrant.* The Tokyo that inspired the cityscapes in *Blade Runner.* Microwave towers spike off the roof of Shinjuku Station, its walls pulsing with immense digital displays—head shots of celebrities, advertising animes, hieroglyphics shimmering in a darkening sky in which a pale moon has begun to rise.

We've been playing pachinko—blinking lights, plinking sounds, steel balls flying through comic-book graphics—men in cramped parlors sitting on small stools feeding machines, looking simultaneously bored and enthralled. "One old Gakkai commentator called Japan in the '50s a vast pachinko parlor," I tell Rob, "the idea being that Japanese are so robotic they'll grasp at mindless games and mindless religions like the Soka Gakkai as a source for numbing solace. A missionary, I think, who saw godless heathen and Communists around every corner." I try not to be too dismissive, recalling my own flip-flopping over Ikeda, the Gakkai, and Japaneseness, which seems now a very long time in the past.

As we sit sipping our lattes, I'm mulling over what to make of all I've learned, torn just now between orthodoxy versus innovation issues that are gripping, but not my own. In the midst of all the activity of the past few weeks, I've noticed that I'm becoming accustomed to my inability to make the leap of faith to embrace the Gakkai's optimism; I doubt I ever will. Maybe I'm simply in possession of a cranky life condition.

Whatever else I may think about Ikeda, Nikken, and all the rest, I know that I deeply value the Gakkai's understanding of its epic history for the many modern parables it contains about genuine happiness and the obstacles to it that seem always to be in the road—militaristic elites, conquering gaijins, and atomic weapons; scheming priests and overly rambunctious zealots; market booms and busts; sickness, old age, death. That I become a genuinely happy person remains an aspiration, one both dauntingly cosmic and very intimate. That life is always about dukkha, however, seems a simple fact to me, one that I can embrace because the appalling realism of the dharma makes tragedy the starting point for hope.

CHAPTER 7

Zuiho-bini

Rank-and-file Japanese members, not Tokyo leaders, spearheaded the globalization of the Gakkai, a process shaped by circumstances in each country. The Brazilian movement grew out of a large Japanese immigrant community, the U.S. from the efforts of war brides, the British from those of businessmen's Japanese wives, all three developments taking place as Japan rose to postwar prominence. In contrast, the Singapore Soka Association was founded by two Japanese men in the 1960s, but is now largely ethnic Chinese. The origin of the South Korean group can be traced to Koreans living in Japan who maintained close contact with their homeland. Singaporeans, Koreans, Malaysians, and others in East and Southeast Asia had to wrestle with the legacy of World War II, in the form of distrust of a religion associated with the conquering Japanese. SGI–South Africa took shape only in the '80s, by contrast, and its members recall various factors in its formation—local Japanese families, South African sailors returning from Japan, the influence of the movement in the United Kingdom—all of which came together as the nation took on the dismantling of apartheid.

In the course of these different histories, each national movement began to take on its own characteristics as members adapted their faith to local needs, languages, and cultural styles. The principle behind this process is referred to as zuiho-bini, which means adapting Buddhist precepts to different cultures. This principle is said to have its source in Shakyamuni's original teachings and to have guided the transmission of the dharma across Asia. Nichiren reflected on this principle in a brief tract in which he urged his disciples to be sensitive to the time, place, and culture in which they were propagating, and to develop a knack for what to teach and to whom, so the mystic law could thrive in new settings.

At the same time, however, Soka Gakkai practice and philosophy have stayed remarkably consistent around the world. Members everywhere chant daimoku in Japanese phonemes before the gohonzon and evoke the concept of kaidan. Nichiren's *Gosho* and the ten worlds are central to Gakkai philosophy, which is still taught in graded classes first developed in Japan in the '50s under Toda. In Gakkai movements around the world—some seventy-six officially constituted national organizations, with practitioners in another 110 countries—members see themselves as bodhisattvas arising from the earth to teach and preach, as assembling on Eagle Peak, now as in the past and in the future.

Ikeda's Buddhist Humanism mediates the process of adaptation, on one hand, and the maintenance of consistency on the other. Functioning much like a shorthand or a conceptual lingua franca, its pillars of peace, culture, and education enable movements in different countries to take their own directions even as they all share a common agenda. Practice and doctrine are shaped by Ikeda, by study departments in Tokyo and in national movements, and by a growing cadre of Soka Gakkai intellectuals, all of them working within a broad tradition that encompasses Nichiren and his many interpreters, whether ancient sectarian scholars or Toda and Makiguchi. Less a systematic philosophy and more a spirit in the modernist vein, Buddhist Humanism seeks to inspire, empower, and unite people around the globe by basing its appeal on the universal human experience.

.   .   .

Adapting the Gakkai to new settings, however, has forced an examination of what is essential and what is specifically Japanese, a question Catherine Cornille studied in "New Japanese Religions in the West."[1] Sometimes conflicts emerge with what she calls "nationalistic undertones," as in the case of Tenrikyo or Mahikari.[2] Tenrikyo teaches that the Jiba, a place near the ancient imperial city of Nara, is where the world was created, while Mahikari continues to regard the emperor as divine—both religious myths with ancient Japanese roots that are not easily transplanted into different cultures. Sometimes tensions are more ethnocentric in kind, as in movements like the Gakkai, which have deliberately abandoned nationalistic myths associated with the war.

With its modernist approach to Buddhism, the Gakkai retains few archaic Japan-centered myths to hamper the process of zuiho-bini, although Japaneseness has played a number of important roles in its transmission overseas. At times, it has been constructive in creating the Gakkai's international religious identity. Ideas central to its vision of global kosen-rufu often reflect Japanese origins, such as the convictions that Nichiren is a new Buddha for the mappo age and that propagation is a kind of Japanese mission to Asia and the rest of the world. This missionary impulse is also reflected in the Gakkai's commitment to world peace, which is its response to Japan's militarism and to the destruction of Hiroshima and Nagasaki.

At other times, Japaneseness has been a source of tension to be worked out in face-to-face relations among members, an intimate process at the heart of the unique ethos of each movement overseas. Oftentimes tensions arise over minor matters of cultural style, as when early Japanese leaders taught U.S. members that it was important to chant daimoku sitting on their knees. This is known as *seiza*, a posture common in Japan where sitting on tatami-mat–covered floors, rather than in chairs, was the norm for many centuries. Most non-Japanese found seiza painful, and leaders eventually came to see it as nonessential to practice. Such changes have been made in other Buddhist movements coming to the West, such as in Zen, where it is no longer considered essential to meditate sitting in the lotus position.

More substantive conflicts arise when received Japanese traditions touch on more prickly issues such as gender roles. Separation of the sexes remains a common practice in Japan, which is reflected in the Gakkai's tradition of having men's and women's divisions. This separation is further reflected in a division of labor in which women exercise a great deal of influence within the Women's Division and in the broader institution, but men tend to take on most public leadership roles and often lead the chant. The Japanese also honor distinctions based on age, with a long tradition of juniors who are thirty or forty years old being expected to defer to elder leaders. Such values often came into conflict with those of non-Japanese members, especially in the West during the '60s and '70s, when becoming a Buddhist was often tied to a search for an alternative lifestyle, at a time when radical egalitarianism and revolutionary feminism were both very much in vogue.

The adaptation of Nichiren's Buddhism to new settings has been greatly facilitated by Ikeda, whose championing of the principle of zuiho-bini is of a piece with his liberalization of the Gakkai. Buddhism "does not exist apart from society, apart from reality," he wrote in 1994, a position that echoes those he powerfully argued in his 1970 address in the wake of the free speech issue. "We must respect society's ways and try to harmonize with them."[3] At the same time, while his Buddhist Humanism owes much to Toda and Makiguchi, it is less overtly political overseas, which has eased the Gakkai's acceptance in societies where church-state separation has long been the norm, as in the United States, or where political activism is suspect or discouraged, as in Singapore or South Korea.

As I look at the Gakkai now, after several years of study and reflection, I take my cues from Robert Epp, one of the few academics to interpret Ikeda's religious ideas. He sees Ikeda as a leader who has not forgotten his modest origins but draws on them to communicate with ordinary people, whose instincts he trusts and whose spiritual needs he seeks to address. Epp calls Ikeda a modern exorcist who teaches "an inner revolution of viewpoint," thus freeing people from the demon of alienation by proposing "a meaningful picture of the world and a relevant plan of action to deal with it." He praises Ikeda's philosophy for its universality and exportability, calling Buddhist Humanism a "redemptive therapy" applicable to everyone because it enables people to affirm their lives and those of others in the midst of the chaos and artificiality of mass society.[4]

Epp traces much of Ikeda's success to what may seem a paradox to Westerners: his teaching that self-esteem is discovered only within groups, a communitarian element Epp suggests is related to Ikeda's own Japaneseness. For Ikeda, conscience and culture need not be in conflict but can work together in harmony—a proposition often seen as antithetical by those who champion the free individual. Epp sees this Japanese social ideal epitomized by the Gakkai's culture festival in which amateurs voluntarily strive to be professionals, to submerge themselves in a group, only to discover themselves as individuals with particular talents and interests. "They become freed of their passive, onlooker roles and become actors," Epp writes, and "when that happens they stop being 'nobodies.'" To become somebody is to discover a role in the world, as Ikeda urges his disciples to do in one of his Whitmanesque odes, expressing aspirations whose essential sanity and healthfulness, however sentimental and romantic, are hard to deny:

> People, now is the time to stand
> In the footlights and take the lead

Now is the time to dance, to leap
With heads held high—to launch
A new pageant of history.[5]

• • •

A sprawling grid city in the American Southwest, Tucson is not the first place one expects to find evidence of the principle of zuiho-bini. My trip here was not for research, however, but to say good-bye to Ann with a visit to Mission San Xavier del Bac, the old church outside the city where I observed the first anniversary of her death. With a second year now past, I hope to put grief and confusion behind me.

I begin each day with mass among Indian kids from the Tohono O'Odham reservation and a handful of Anglos, communing with the Cristos and santos I'd shared with Ikeda, imagining Ann, like one of the saints who populate niches on the altars, secure and at peace in a mansion in Christian heaven. But every afternoon I go out into the desert at Ez-Kim-In-Zin among tall, thick-limbed saguaro cacti, yellow poppies, and purple lupine, where I read Ikeda—*The Wisdom of the Lotus Sutra: Learning from the Gosho* and *Unlocking the Mysteries of Birth and Death*, a work thick with philosophy that I find I can't relate to my thoughts and feelings about Ann.

From time to time, I break into a few rounds of Nam-myoho-renge-kyo just to hear it roll across the desert. The sensate pleasure I take in enunciating each syllable and projecting myself into the still, dry air puts a point on the power of chanting as practice. Jacqueline Stone, the noted Princeton scholar, writes that when Nichiren identified daimoku as the first of the three secret laws, he drew on a philosophical distinction between "principle" and "actuality." Principle was associated with silent meditation in which one contemplates Buddha as principle within one's mind. Nichiren drew on a different tradition, however, which teaches one to actualize the Buddha within oneself through chanting.[6]

Each time I let a Nam-myoho-renge-kyo fly, I picture it actualizing an awakened essence of the Sonoran Desert and its expressive energy enlivening me. I imagine myself one with scorpions, rattlers, and cacti and wonder at the fact that this little phrase captured the spirits of Ikeda, Toda, and Makiguchi. Nam-myoho-renge-kyo is the engine behind all of the shakubuku activities—the resistance to State Shinto, the postwar political campaigns, even the Buddhist baton-twirling in the Gakkai's patriotic American parades.

For my book *American Buddhism,* I did lots of SGI-USA research—interviews, informal conversations, visits to home meetings, mostly in Chicago and Los Angeles. Wanting a fresh take, I hunt up the Tucson center; there I meet Dan Summers, an engaging thirty-something African American, a military man who is raising a Gakkai family along with his opera-singer wife, Renee.[7] As we chat, I watch a Women's Division meeting across the hall where some twenty Latina, Asian, African American, and Caucasian women practice under a banner that reads "Chant to bring President Ikeda to Tucson on his next American visit," their drone a soothing accompaniment to my conversation with Dan.

"Do they expect Ikeda to come?" I ask skeptically, gesturing toward the women. "People chant for many reasons, seeking benefits," he replies. "A visit from President Ikeda would be a great benefit, but we can't make it happen. It's not magic. Often the benefits we get are not ones we seek but help us nevertheless to change our karma in unexpected ways." After hours of reading about Lotus Buddhism and Kamakura Japan at Ez-Kim-In-Zin, I need a local reality check. "Should I see in those women a rainbow coalition of bodhisattvas arising from the earth?" I ask, charmed by imagining what Nichiren might make of the assembly on Eagle Peak touching down in a New World desert. Incredulous at my question but amused, Summers replies, "Well, of course. Most certainly."

Of Buddhist organizations in America, SGI-USA claims to be the most diverse; meditation groups are predominantly white, and most traditional temples are tied to a particular ethnic community. David Chappell, a scholar of Asian Buddhism, gave substance to this claim in 1997, when he compiled information on SGI leaders in nine American cities. Of 2,449 district leaders, he found some 39 percent to be European American, 27 percent black, 19 percent Japanese, and 6 percent Hispanic. "At the local level," he writes, "SGI-USA cannot be called a Japanese Buddhist group without serious qualification."[8]

That an organization with roots in Japan came to embody the diversity ideal of mainstream America testifies to the successful implementation of the principle of zuiho-bini. How it did so is tied up with the movement's rich history, which Chappell divides into two phases, the first a "period of evangelism" that began in the '60s, the second a "period of dialogue" set in motion by Ikeda during his 1990 American visit, on the eve of the break with Nichiren Shoshu.[9]

The roots of SGI-USA's diversity are in the first, formative period—three decades during which the movement was called Nichiren Shoshu of America or NSA. James Dator's 1969 sociological study, *Soka Gakkai, Builders of the Third Civilization,* provides an early glimpse into NSA but only hints at the Gakkai's later demographic complexity. "The 'typical' American member is a white male in his twenties or thirties, in the military but of less than officer rank," Dator writes, "married to a Japanese who was a member of the Soka Gakkai before they met, converted by his wife."[10] Most came from Catholic or working-class Protestant backgrounds, converted between 1961 and 1964, encountered the Gakkai while stationed in Japan, and on returning to the States settled in California, Hawaii, or Chicago. One crucial fact that Dator notes only in passing helps to account for the current diversity in SGI-USA. "While two thirds of the members were white, it is significant to note that Nisei [second-generation Japanese Americans] and Negroes account for about one sixth each of the membership. Most group photographs of Soka Gakkai meetings show at least one male Negro."[11]

Dator also provides a glimpse into early shakubuku activities. The wives of GIs looked up Japanese-sounding names in telephone directories and bused out to neighborhoods to make visits, their aim to propagate the practice and to increase the well-being of other women who had moved to the United States. For several years, little effort was made to convert the general public; but this changed in 1960, when Ikeda appointed George Williams, a Japanese born in Korea as Masayasu Sadanaga, to lead the organization. Shortly thereafter, NSA began to grow and diversify rapidly and to take on its distinct character. In response to Williams's call for propagation suited to a time of radical social change, women stepped up their door-to-door solicitation and their native-born husbands, among them African Americans, became increasingly active in shakubuku activities.

Black men and their Japanese wives must be credited with an important role in creating the diversity that is now an SGI-USA hallmark, although little research has been done on their shakubukuing the inner city. Dator hints at the energy invested in propagation when he quotes one African American calling for "wall-to-wall shakubuku" to spread "True Buddhism to the Negroes for a better life filled with *kudoku,* divine benefits."[12] James Gardner, a black leader in Chicago, only suggests to me the history of this little-known phase when he reminisces about Gakkai pioneers on Chicago's South Side in the '70s, when he first began to practice.[13] "There was Mr. Chapman, Charles Chapman; and Almeda Bailey's father, Lee Roy, he was African American too. And Mrs. Kazuko Simms and Mrs. Kuniko Chapman—they spoke little English.

And then Malvin Wright came along—we trusted him. Before I joined it was real small, like over a storefront, at Pulaski and Lawrence, I think. You might be talking forty people."

Inspired by the civil rights and black power movements, African Americans began to join the Gakkai in increasing numbers around 1971, as they sought spiritual alternatives to Christianity, with its long history of racism, and took to the Gakkai's message of positive outlook, benefits, and inner transformation. Soon large groups of black practitioners began to emerge in Los Angeles, Chicago, and New York, who then spread the movement to Boston, Cleveland, San Francisco, Philadelphia, and Detroit.

The Gakkai's rapid diversification made for textured race relations among blacks, whites, and Japanese, their face-to-face relationships important to the creation of the movement's unique character in America. Gardner recalls, for instance, that the "seed" of his practice was planted by Japanese who lived in his South Side apartment complex, but he was then too preoccupied with street life to do more than to learn to chant. A few years later and on parole he was reintroduced to Nam-myoho-renge-kyo, this time by a black woman living in the projects. "I needed a job, a place to stay, some wheels, needed to get my whole life back together. Strangely enough, those things happened."

Gardner was soon deeply involved in the movement, recalling that it was "not a perfect organization" when it came to race. He had no particular problem with Japanese, although he found them to be a "strange breed" whose trust was difficult to earn and whose Japaneseness came through in their emphasis on "discipline, discipline, really being disciplined with yourself. American leaders are not disciplined at all, like a real motley crew." He recalls Japanese pioneers as compassionate but strict. One leader, Mrs. Kiyoko Cheng, "could look at you and tell you what was happening. She knew when to pat you on the back." But despite many white SGI friends, he recalls a big race issue as being a "North Side, South Side sort of thing," with white North Side members displaying a sense of ownership at headquarters, which at that time was located on the North Side, and dominating the leadership. "We've made tremendous headway in the last ten years or so, as far as African Americans having top positions," he notes, a shift he attributes to Ikeda, whom he describes as "my modern-day mentor."

Patricia Walker, a Chicago black woman, recalls how race issues unfolded differently for her, but to much the same effect.[14] At fourteen, she was shakubukued by an African American teacher who taught her to chant. Ten years later, never really having practiced but with a new interest in Buddhist philosophy, she tracked the teacher down and asked to be taught to chant once again. "She said just jump back on and I did and I never stopped chanting."

Walker never felt that she was in a Japanese movement because she practiced on the South Side: "Everybody on the South Side was African American, so I was with my people, so to speak." She recalls black friends asking how she could trust the Japanese or questioning her racial identity because she'd taken up Buddhism. But race became significant only when Walker moved to Boston, where she became chief of an all-white district and the only African American at leaders' meetings. Together with the few local blacks, she soon began to address the issue. "I remember joking—if I hear one more folk song . . . it doesn't have to be rap, but just something different. As an African American, one wants cultural expressions familiar to the heart." Boston was "never cross-cultural," she recalls. "In the early '80s, we were all this one shakubuku steamroller, but you looked up front and noticed black hair or long hair, but you did not see anyone with a 'fro."

Like Gardner, Walker sees things as having improved dramatically in the past decade and also attributes this to Ikeda, who lifts up Martin Luther King Jr., Rosa Parks, George Washington Carver, and Sojourner Truth as exemplifying the principles of kosen-rufu. "When President Ikeda started to use individuals from African American history as examples, then I say okay, we're on the road."

Asian and Hispanic Americans have had comparable, positive experiences in SGI-USA, which routinely holds monthly meetings in Chinese, Korean, Spanish, and Japanese in most major cities. These assist immigrants to negotiate Americanization by enabling them to maintain their first language and cultural identity even as they acclimate to the English-speaking mainstream.

In the case of Hispanics, SGI sponsored a national Spanish-language meeting in 1998 and regularly supports Latino festivals in major cities. It publishes a Spanish-language newsletter, *Arco Iris de Miami,* and encourages networking among Spanish-speaking members from the United States, Puerto Rico, Mexico, and other Latin countries. The *World Tribune* includes a four-page biweekly Spanish-language insert for more than four thousand subscribers.

All these efforts reflect SGI's interest in addressing the needs of its minority members. But they also reflect the strategic intelligence, the knack

for zuiho-bini on the part of Gakkai leaders—a quality that owes a great
deal to Toda's political acumen, which he passed on to his disciple, Ikeda,
who in turn entrusted George Williams with developing the United
States movement. The upshot—the effect of these causes—is that "it is
safe to predict that SGI-USA will continue to expand its Hispanic membership in the future," Chappell writes. It "is the only Buddhist group in
America prepared for the emergence of Hispanic culture as a dominant
feature of the United States in the twenty-first century."[15]

. . .

The demographics of the SGI-USA also shifted dramatically in a somewhat different direction starting about 1965, when Williams encouraged
members to shakubuku hippies and other young people in search of
spiritual alternatives on the streets of America's cities. It is easy to imagine the pioneering Japanese women—enthusiastic, still quite young,
speaking in charmingly broken English—as they first ventured onto the
streets to pass out business cards printed with Nam-myoho-renge-kyo,
inviting young seekers to gatherings devoted to Asian philosophy where
they could learn to be happy. Like Zen and various Hindu movements,
SGI-USA grew rapidly as the counterculture burgeoned in the midst of
riots, war, and experimentation with drugs and radical lifestyles. In a
manner reminiscent of the high-energy campaigns in Japan under Toda
and during Ikeda's early presidency, the Gakkai took to the streets and
quickly boosted its membership by thousands. Some of the newcomers
passed through the organization quickly, while others stayed for life.

The earliest of the new recruits soon profoundly affected the movement, as youth-culture types began to shakubuku their peers by making
pitches suited to their needs and capacities, whether for sanity, liberation, ending the war, saving the world, or immediate gratification. "I
have heard longtime members from the East Coast to the West Coast,"
Chappell writes, "recall their amazement in the 1960s when, as young
hippies, they asked NSA leaders if they could chant Nam-myoho-renge-
kyo to get girls or drugs, and were told that was okay." This uncondi-
tional openness, however, "did not result in a loose organization
featuring drugs and sex, but in a remarkably tight and caring group,
which nurtured supportive friendship." According to Chappell, the
"real benefit" for new recruits was the chance to break through old
social barriers to join people from other backgrounds in cultivating a
more positive attitude toward life.[16]

When seen in the larger context of Buddhist history generally and that of the Gakkai in particular, it is clear that what came to be known as "street shakubuku," however spontaneous its origins, was also zuiho-bini in action. Members offered Americans the opportunity to become Buddhist in the midst of social extremes that, however outrageous in retrospect, constituted a norm for many during the '60s. Their intent was to persuade people that daimoku, even when chanted with no understanding and for dubious benefits, possessed a real power as spiritual practice, a strategy not unlike Toda's in the years immediately after the war. Nam-myoho-renge-kyo was presented as a kind of doorway through which people could step in pursuit of whatever they construed as happiness while, almost unbeknownst to them, they began to walk the Buddhist path. In the process, street shakubuku also became the Gakkai's contribution to what sociologist Steven Tipton called "getting saved from the Sixties," the efforts by alternative spiritual movements to rescue people from the self-destructiveness pandemic during that period.[17]

The getting-saved message is crystal clear in *Hippy* [sic] *to Happy*, a half-hour video made by members in 1969, which is both a wonderful period piece and a rich source for Gakkai history.[18] Its protagonist is a young white male who, when the story opens, sits serenely on a misty Pacific beach, casually dressed in sport coat and tie, reading *The Complete Works of Daisaku Ikeda*, one of Ikeda's early English-language publications, and *Politics in the Metropolis*, then a standard political science reader. As narrator, the man recounts his being "lost in the ranks of the revolution" and finding Nichiren's Buddhism, a journey seen in flashbacks of his life as an aimless surfer, a stoned hippie, and an avid seeker buying contemporary classics such as Alan Watts's *Psychotherapy East and West* and Hermann Hesse's *Siddhartha*.

"One day in the bookstore, I saw people with shining eyes and faces and I wondered what their secret was. I resented the warm, happy vibrations they sent out," the narrator recalls, describing his experience of being shakubukued in a way that happened in real life to thousands of Americans. "Suddenly they approached me and spoke of a philosophy. Their faces and voices . . . spoke for them, of a hope, maybe regeneration. Would I go to a meeting and hear more?" He is soon seen at a gathering of some thirty people, mostly whites but blacks too, all of them clean-cut, where he hears about the human revolution, life-force philosophy, and value creation, curious but wary and cool, protected by dark sunglasses, until his cynicism begins to give way and he decides to give Buddhism a try.

Hippy to Happy makes the case for the Gakkai in its '60s-era shakubuku heyday in terms of a contrast between order, purpose, and meaning on one hand, and chaos and despair on the other. Vignettes of earnest Buddhists are juxtaposed with contemporary footage of street people, zonked-out dancers at be-ins, and angry demonstrators. The Gakkai spirit is conveyed by mystic vocalization, easy-listening jazz, or upbeat tunes recalling *Godspell* or the early years of the British invasion, in contrast to dissonant cacophonies that accompany the narrator's flashbacks to his life in the "unhappy crowd."

The central message of *Hippy to Happy* is far from being reactionary, however. On the contrary, it powerfully asserts that the revolutionary aspirations and visionary hopes of a generation can be fulfilled only by the kind of human revolution taught by Ikeda, while keeping its overt Buddhist proselytizing light. With a message of individual transformation and progressive social change, the Gakkai comes off as a Buddhist phalanx in the "Clean for Gene" wing of the hip generation, those young people who only a year before the video's release had cut their hair and straightened themselves up to campaign for Eugene McCarthy.

"We weren't really thinking in terms of zuiho-bini," Larry Shaw tells me.[19] "It was a spontaneous, synergistic thing worked up by friends who knew one another from Beverly High," he says, referring to a distinctive and quite spectacular Los Angeles style of street shakubuku that emerged in the '60s. Now fifty-something and a psychotherapist, Shaw played the seeker in *Hippy to Happy*. Once a surfer himself, in and around the Southern California counterculture for years but never really a hippie, Shaw recalls "being adrift, and we just drifted into this formalized, rigid really, movement. Cleaning up was part of the philosophy of its leaders—smart, very high energy, with an incredible work ethic, 99.9 percent of them Japanese." Shaw recalls George Williams and others as "really knowing how to encourage and inspire young people. And, of course, at that time we had no leaders—the Kennedy and King assassinations, the war, the whole thing. Some people went to India, some to the Maharishi. We went a different way."

Shaw, who was a West L.A. *chiku bucho* (district leader) around 1963, recalls how the power he and his friends discovered in practicing led them to recast shakubuku to get it into step with the times. The generally staid, hour-long introductory meeting held at seven o'clock each evening, which at the time was still conducted mostly in Japanese, gave way to freewheeling get-togethers as young English-speaking kids proselytized in restaurants and on streets, inviting "guests"—college students, longhairs, Romanian sailors, tourists from Tennessee, just about anyone—to check out a cool Buddhist scene with chanting, beads, some people maybe a little stoned, in meetings in Hollywood, the San Fernando Valley, Santa Monica, or downtown L.A. "We'd have five, six meetings a night, six nights a week, at all hours. They were maybe twenty minutes long—get 'em in; move 'em through; get 'em chanting for whatever they want; send 'em home with a gohonzon in their purse or backpack or luggage," he says with a laugh, recalling times that were both very good and over the top, as we converse in a West L.A. restaurant. "We might get ten, twelve people a night to accept a gohonzon," he said, while the Japanese got one or two. "One month February 1969, I think—we had 969 shakubukus, something like that."

Shaw recalls that many Japanese leaders disapproved of this style of shakubuku at first, fearing a lack of respect for practice, and threatened to bring Americans into line by disbanding their group and integrating them all into Japanese-led districts. Innovation won out, however, as they came to see the Americans' success as indicative of a new strategy for a new place and time—which is to say they recognized that street shakubuku L.A. style was an expression of zuiho-bini. "Around that time they more or less unleashed us," Shaw recalls. "We were flying by the seat of our pants—out every night, sometimes in Westwood near UCLA, sometimes on motorcycles on the [Sunset] Strip. But each night we'd go back to report to those Japanese guys, to tell them what we'd been doing, looking for their encouragement. They'd always hammer home that our success was not our accomplishment, but the power of the gohonzon at work. This was them teaching us humility, well, ego-breaking."

The high energy '60s-era campaigns gave way about 1976 to what was called "phase two"; this was a cooling-down period, quieter in tone, during which many members turned their attention to study, personal development, and starting Buddhist families. The '80s, however, saw renewed propagation but in a style more suited to the Reagan era. In *Soka Gakkai in America*, Phillip Hammond and David Machacek write that strategic shifts made over three or four decades resulted from "conscious policy-making" by Gakkai leaders. "Rather than reject sacred American values such as individualism, capitalism, and the family, Soka Gakkai embraced them."[20] This was especially so in the '80s, when new expressions of shakubuku emerged that mixed Japanese precedents with progressive political values and American patriotism.

During this decade-long phase, the culture festival, established in Japan in the '50s, came into its own in the United States, most dramatically in mass celebrations like the Aloha—We Love America rally in 1982 or the New Freedom Bell tour in 1987, for which a two-ton replica of the Liberty Bell was forged to mark the bicentennial of the signing of the U.S. Constitution. These festivals showcased a style of evangelism that was a fusion of Buddhism and Americanism and that appears to have been the brainchild of Williams, its ideological content laid out in his *Freedom and Influence: The Role of Religion in American Society,* published in 1985.[21]

Most of the book is a standard academic interpretation of American religious history from the Puritans to the present, but it is set within a Gakkai frame of reference that emphasizes why Nichiren's Buddhism can best fulfill John Winthrop's vision of the City on a Hill. Individually and collectively, the argument runs, Americans can overcome the nation's negative karma—evidenced in slavery, racism, assassinations, the Vietnam War, and the like—to realize their true greatness. American society, however, has a long tradition of seeking answers in outside powers: in an almighty God or, in his absence, the psychiatrist, physician, or lawyer. What the nation needs is the empowering inner orientation of Buddhist Humanism, which has a capacity to wed individual uniqueness and public good in a way suited to a pluralistic society.

Daniel Golden, a reporter for the *Boston Globe,* sounded an alarm at what he feared was the Gakkai's cultlike hyperpatriotism, a replay of old criticisms in Japan.[22] He saw the New Freedom Bell—which toured dozens of cities and hundreds of schools, its meaning explained in a pamphlet, "The New Common Sense," written by Williams—as a sobering lesson in how to "co-opt" America's sacred symbols. Hammond and Machacek are correct when they write that the Gakkai's amiability allowed it to be "barely noticed" during the cult scares of the '70s and '80s.[23] But Golden's lengthy piece reflects widespread suspicion of the Gakkai's unapologetic mix of Buddhist conviction and patriotism, their flag-waving, Reagan-era spectacles ominous to many who had come of age during the cynically hip '60s.

What Golden completely missed, and what becomes clear only when seeing SGI-USA in a comparative perspective, is that Williams was retooling both the Japanese culture festival and the Gakkai's long-standing commitment to the public good and personal happiness. In other words, what Golden missed is that Williams, whose leadership style Chappell describes as "brilliant and charismatic," was evoking the venerable principle of zuiho-bini to restate a basically progressive agenda in terms suited to a new decade.[24]

The patriotism and bell tours read differently today—more traditionally corny than ominous—as seen in the 1987 video *The Sun Rises: The
Bell of Peace and Happiness.*[25] The tour begins on the bridge in Concord,
Massachusetts, local minutemen at hand, in a heavy April snowstorm,
but by July 3 the bell has made a twelve-thousand-mile circuit of the
country to arrive in Philadelphia, where it is presented to the city.

A high point of the tour is at City Hall in Los Angeles, where Gakkai
celebrities jazzman Herbie Hancock, Ron Glass of the *Barney Miller*
show, and Patrick Duffy of *Dallas* (all looking a bit chagrined) toll the
bell along with Mayor Tom Bradley, who gets a big hand from African
American members. That afternoon, the NSA brass band plays fanfares
in a pregame extravaganza at Dodger Stadium—men's gymnastics teams
form human pyramids topped by Asian boys waving American flags,
wearing tricornered hats, 350 Gakkai girls perform a cape dance to Neil
Diamond's song "America." Their exuberance compensates for the lack
of the spit and-polish of the Japanese originals, as does getting Dodgers
manager Tommy Lasorda and Astros coach Yogi Berra into the act,
escorted by Williams to the platform to toll the bell along with local
little leaguers. Actor John Astin (Gomez in the old *Addams Family* TV
series) gives an address crafted to speak to Pacific Rim Los Angeles—"It
is our cry that there be no more Alamos, no more Pearl Harbors, no
more Hiroshimas, and no more wars"—as ten thousand red, white, and
blue helium-filled balloons rise into the sky over Chavez Ravine.

• • •

Those old, superintense days seem a world away as I talk with Matilda
Buck, the first non-Japanese woman to head the U.S. Women's
Division, and Danny Nagashima, who is likely to be the last Japanese
male general director of the American movement.[26] We chat in a sunny
room in SGI-USA headquarters on Wilshire Boulevard in Santa
Monica, California. With the Third Street Promenade and the palisades
overlooking the Pacific Ocean only a few blocks away, I can't help wondering if it's Japaneseness or Gakkainess that accounts for the movement's knack for choosing really good real estate.

The two American leaders make an interesting pair. Buck is a tall,
lean, casually chic white woman in her fifties, who describes herself as a
"suburban Brentwood housewife," a status about which she displays
much ambivalent good humor. She has had one failed marriage with a
surfer, which was a part of her rebellious early years. She admits to

almost losing a second with a conservative Republican WASP, which she saved by chanting. He now chants too. Nagashima, who is in his first year as head of the movement, is fifty-two, short and roundish rather than wiry and lean. In conversation, he is all smiles and lively eye movements, and he bristles with energy. When walking, he is prone to quick movements and little bows that must reflect the twenty-four years he spent living in his native Japan.

Both Buck and Nagashima talk easily about the frustrations and rewards of working cross-culturally. "If I am going to preach world peace and global citizenship, I must live it in the day-to-day," Buck explains; she talks of how pioneer Japanese women, who could be "very direct" and "tough," forced her to look into the depth of Buddhist teachings. Her hope is not for a thoroughly American-style movement in the future but for a "fusion" of the United States and Japan. "A big, big piece of this is President Ikeda," she says. "We are founded on the master-disciple relationship, and he is—well, he is Japanese. Nichiren is Japanese."

Nagashima is familiar with many of the cross-cultural issues that surface in SGI-USA from his work in a Japanese trading company in New York. The challenge here is to keep the spiritual teachings authentic while planting the dharma in "different soil, different cultures, different nations. That's zuiho-bini," he says, "and it's a process that is not easy. For example, myself—however much I try to be American . . ." he begins, but then trails off with an embarrassed grin and what sounds like a weary sigh. "Unfortunately, I am not able to see clearly, so I am making so many mistakes." He understands that his role is to realize Ikeda's vision for America, not his own. "Personally, I want to accord with his [Ikeda's] heart. What he wants to accomplish, I want to pursue. I really want to learn what he is expecting in America, and go exactly with that."

The Victory over Violence (VOV) campaign epitomizes both Ikeda's humanistic emphasis on peace, culture, and education and the mood of SGI-USA around the year 2000. Reflecting the Gakkai's perennial concern to develop young citizen activists and leaders, VOV is entirely the work of the Youth Division and is their response to the 1999 Columbine High School shootings. Conceived as an expression of Gandhian nonviolence and the spirit of Martin Luther King Jr., the VOV campaign has grown to include a traveling exhibit, some five thousand student-led discussion groups, a nonviolence curriculum, and culture festivals built around themes such as Makiguchi's resistance, Gandhi's work in

India, and the heroism of Rosa Parks. "Victory over Violence is trying to create a new wave of respect for life," Darin Nellis, a VOV cochair, tells me.[27] Columbine "epitomized the downplaying of the sanctity of life that pervades my generation. Our objective is to get to the heart of that lack of respect for life to try to regenerate or re-stoke excitement for it. . . . In a sense, we see Victory over Violence as the nonviolence movement of the twenty-first century."

The current character of SGI-USA began to take shape during Ikeda's February 1990 visit to Los Angeles, which opened the new phase that Chappell called a period of dialogue. Of nearly thirty trips he has made to the United States, this one was of particular importance for two reasons. First, Ikeda called for a change in the tone of the movement by steering members away from the kind of frantic propagation that had become an NSA hallmark. He also emphasized his egalitarian readings of the Lotus Sutra in an effort to undercut a hierarchical mindset that persisted among both members and leaders. That Ikeda's visit occurred on the eve of the break with Nichiren Shoshu may have been serendipity, karma, or strategic thinking, but it hardly seems purely accidental. Precisely what role this visit played in the unfolding of events is unclear, but members now look back on it as a watershed, one that marked their abandonment of an older sectarian mentality and the embracing of a new openness to the world.

In retrospect, there appears to have been little new in Ikeda's teachings during the tour, which suggests that the U.S. movement may have been a Gakkai hinterland, its members out of touch with ongoing changes taking place in Japan. In gauging their effect, one must factor in events behind the scenes, which no one has recorded yet. More easily imagined is the sheer delight members took in being in Ikeda's presence, his teasing humor, easy ways, and personalized touches needing no translators.

Ikeda's teachings reflect what has always been his strength—the unpacking of the Lotus Sutra and *Gosho* in ways that make them applicable to people in a particular time and place, while maintaining the transcendent universality of the Buddhist worldview. Thus to the Youth Division, he teaches that chanting is like driving a car in the direction of truth and happiness. Without regular maintenance in the form of daily practice, Buddhism cannot get you where you want to go, which is to be united with the mystic law–life force of the universe. At a conference of adult leaders, he evokes Franklin Roosevelt's New Deal and John Kennedy's New Frontier as he argues that equal rights is an essential teaching of Buddhism and precisely the value he hopes to see manifest in the American movement.

One is justified, I think, in hearing in his remarks not only a criticism of authoritarian tendencies in the American movement but also echoes of the growing crisis in the Gakkai's relations with Nichiren Shoshu. "All people are equal. There are absolutely no distinctions of superior and inferior among human beings. Differences of position in an organization are temporary and provisional." Members must "feel free to speak their minds to leaders and say what they feel has to be said—for we are all equally good friends who are dedicated to the same cause."[28]

Ikeda's guidance to the Women's Division, delivered in "Buddhism Is the Mirror That Perfectly Reflects Our Lives," is considered a particularly memorable teaching, and many members, both women and men, recall it as the central message of his visit.[29] This "mirror guidance" is also classic Ikeda insofar as he weaves proverbial wisdom, *Gosho,* the history of mirrors, and the negative example of Oscar Wilde's *Picture of Dorian Gray* into an exposition of how to realize the absolute happiness of Buddhahood within daily life, with all its suffering and frustration.

Just as a mirror is indispensable for putting oneself in order physically, so too people need mirrors to order themselves spiritually. For the Gakkai, the purest mirror is the gohonzon because it represents the true nature of the universe infused with the awakening of the Buddha. When used in practice, it functions as a template that enables people to assess the quality of their life conditions. It also provides an image of perfection to aspire to as each polishes his or her own inner mirror by chanting Nam-myoho-renge-kyo. Ikeda stresses, however, that human relations are also mirrors because each person possesses an inner Buddha nature that deserves utmost respect and reverence, a fundamental truth that he hopes will infuse the entire organization and inform all future efforts at propagation.

During the ten years that followed that visit, after coming through the excommunication to arrive on a new plateau, SGI-USA achieved a stable state, with a committed membership Chappell estimates at approximately fifty thousand.[30] The ethos of the movement today has been described by Hammond and Machacek in terms of a sociology of demand and supply, which is in essence a sociologist's way to describe zuiho-bini.

In their analysis, the emergence of spiritual alternatives in the 1960s amounted to the deregulation of the religious market. Successful religions met market demand with an existential supply that spiritual consumers found worth purchasing —that is, meaningful enough to commit to. In this frame of reference, adjusting the movement as it came out of Japan to America's racial, ethnic, and linguistic diversity, emphasizing community, and accommodating patriotism and middle-class lifestyles are all adjustments made by Japanese leaders on the supply side. On the demand side—what American consumers went shopping for and found—are values such as self-expression, personal autonomy, a libertarian spirit in matters of sexual practice and orientation, and a lifestyle grounded in a sense of social responsibility. Hammond and Machacek hit the right tone when they describe SGI-USA today as a kind of soft-sell Buddhism that has adopted "a low tension position close enough to the American mainstream religious culture to be a realistic alternative," but "unique enough to maintain its distinctive appeal."[31]

. . .

A flight to Singapore takes me into new terrain, into the regional weather system I'd found so intriguing on Japanese TV in the Hotel New Otani, back on that first trip to Japan. My cherry-tree romance and paranoia about cultic Japanese seems a world away, but I'm still hung up on bourgeoisification and a bit in the dark on peace work, a commitment that seems too obvious for me to grasp, a posture vis-à-vis the world like being pro-oxygen or pro-music. But even as I'm thinking this, the electronic flight map in the cabin marks our position as due south of Ho Chi Minh City, which reminds me of events during my tumultuous coming-of-age—napalmed villages and nightly body counts, countercultural rebellion and antiwar riots, the self-immolation of Buddhist monks in Saigon streets.

How did that fevered chain of causes and effects cascade into the age of globalization as described by Thomas Friedman in *The Lexus and the Olive Tree,* that paean to the '90s boom with its cool dot-coms, sleek financial markets, and benign American dominance? And now the world Friedman celebrated has also been swept away, the market still in a tailspin. Rob tells me to take it as a Buddhist lesson in impermanence, but I am not sure whether I find this new wrinkle in globalization exhausting or exhilarating. Rob tells me it "just is."

I prefer Benjamin Barber's fretting in his 1995 book *Jihad vs. McWorld,* which I read fitfully as the plane soars over the South China Sea. Barber's stark picture of a world torn between fervid consumers and Muslims who resist the commercialization of their culture is persuasive and satisfying. It also suggests to me how Ikeda's values define a contemporary middle way in classic Buddhist fashion. Ikeda is no anticonsumerist ascetic, but he is nevertheless the antithesis of Barber's "complacent denizen of McWorld." No "angry brother of Jihad," he nonetheless champions the triumph of spirit over the calculations of the market. The fact is that when Barber calls for the creation of "communities of cooperation" of citizen-activists self-consciously dedicated to the global public, he could just as well have called for "global kosen-rufu."[32]

As Rob naps in the seat next to me, I recall impressions gleaned from a battery of briefings we received in Tokyo on Asian national movements—the Gakkai's appeal to the English-speaking middle class in India; its ability to bind different income groups together in Hong Kong; its attractiveness to Catholics in the Philippines because of its emphasis on personal initiative. With some eight hundred thousand to nine hundred thousand members across Asia, the Gakkai has overcome the stigma of its Japanese origins, thanks to Makiguchi and Toda's reputations as war resisters and to Ikeda's cultivation of networks in nations once invaded by Japan. Everything we heard confirms Daniel Metraux's observation that the Gakkai's success in Asia stems from "its appeal to individuals living in rapidly urbanizing and industrializing societies." To East Asian countries with ancient Buddhist traditions of their own, it brings a modernist message of personal empowerment and social responsibility, providing upwardly mobile, career-oriented individuals with "a strong sense of optimism, happiness, and a meaningful 'extended family.'"[33]

As we make a final approach to Changi airport, I see a hundred ships waiting to enter Singapore's massive container facility, one legacy of the city's status as an Asian entrepôt in the British imperial age and still a lifeline of the multiethnic state. Any romance I harbor about Thomas Raffles, however, soon gives way as I zip down a crowded, rush-hour expressway, unable to imagine Singaporeans reading by kerosene lamps, radioless, often living with no plumbing as recently as the '50s.

Today Singapore's heft as a city recalls the compact density of Boston, but its heat, light, and color seem to synthesize Miami and L.A. This sense of familiarity is heightened by the casual style of leaders of Singapore Soka Association, the SSA—Ong Bon Chai, Michael Yap Gim Chuan, Sandra Sin, and Weng Fong, all of them Singaporean Chinese speakers of Mandarin and English. Their friendly ease immediately puts us all on a first-name basis as we chat over drinks at the

Laguna Club on a patio overlooking fairways and greens, a scene that evokes not so much the Raj as a warm evening in some pastoral corner of Orange County, California.

A man in his mid-fifties, Ong Bon Chai, who likes to be called B. C., is general director of SSA. Over dinner, we explore local issues, about which I know little aside from a few ideas gleaned during the outcry against Singapore during the "caning incident" in the '90s. "The Michael Fay case, of course. Americans assumed caning is Asian," B. C. says, referring to charges of Oriental barbarism made in the U.S. press. "But it is actually a legacy of the Indian Penal Code introduced by the British during colonial times." To understand the debate about Singapore—about repression, conformity, Asian values, and the like—you must understand its geopolitical position, a tiny nation posed between two giants, Malaysia and Indonesia, either of which could end its existence with ease. At independence in 1965, Lee Kuan Yew, the city-state's architect, called for a society unified by a new Singaporean identity with an emphasis on Confucian values, political uniformity, and a strong bureaucracy. Singapore's success demands the constant creation of educated, disciplined, and productive citizens, who are its chief resource. This has led, B. C. says, with a wry smile, to a way of life that is "competitive and at times stressful," and a political landscape that is "considered by many uneventful."

After dinner we attend an SSA meeting and B. C. asks me to say a few words about my impressions of Ikeda, so I find myself seated before some four hundred Gakkai members, mostly Chinese, all of them eager to hear my thoughts about their teacher. Recalling my Kansai school experience, I decide to use this opportunity to engage members and to clarify what I actually think about Ikeda, pleased that I will be speaking through translators, which will buy me time to think on my feet.

"President Ikeda is twenty years older than I am, one full generation. But when I read his history of the Gakkai in the early days, with his references to many world events, I cannot but recall developments that shaped my own youth—Sputnik and Yuri Gagarin, the Cuban Missile Crisis, the American military presence in Japan. This hits home to me that however different his life in Japan, yours in Singapore, and mine in the United States, we have all been parts of a single, global society for some time now, even if we have only begun to talk about globalization very recently. I have studied the history of the encounter between East and West for years, but only now am I seeing it firsthand, from the side of Asia. The life and work of Daisaku Ikeda are for me a touchstone for understanding one outcome—a good outcome, I think—in that long, often tragic history."

As the translator speaks, I wonder where to go next—my work on the World's Parliament of Religions? Buddhism in the U.S.? Here in booming Singapore as back in Japan, the old East-West dichotomies I learned in the academy seem irrelevant and, worst, uninteresting. So I decide to go with something more intimate that I know they will enjoy.

"My first visit with President Ikeda was very rushed, and it took place in the reception hall in Makiguchi Hall, which is very formal. At first, I found him a bit scary," I say, which immediately elicits laughter, my first tip-off that many in the audience speak English. "But later, when I saw photos of the two of us together, I was struck by how happy I looked. Despite my discomfort, I guess he put me at ease.

"The second meeting was far longer. We spoke for several hours over a Japanese-style dinner and, I am happy to report, neither of us was in a hurry to have it come to an end. We drew our conversation to a close only when President Ikeda's aides signaled it was time for him to retire." This remark draws sighs from many in the audience, which suggests just how lucky they consider me to have had so much time with their mentor.

"Let me share with you my main impression of Ikeda as a person and thinker, keeping in mind that I know about many of the controversies that have surrounded him during the past forty years. Above all, I see him as a person deeply shaped by the Cold War who has developed a keen sense of how relations between peoples—nations, cultures, civilizations—cannot help but be political and spiritual in the grandest sense of both terms.

"I see him as a man, a Japanese man, whose vision is deeply informed by the experience of his country—its rapid modernization, wars, devastating defeat, and successes in the postwar years. When I first heard Ikeda speak last year, I was surprised by his outspoken criticism of Japan. Even though we spoke together through translators at our meetings, I watched his face and listened very carefully to the tone of his voice. I saw how passionately he believes in genuine internationalism as both a political and a religious value."

I see many heads nod as I speak, then watch others as they listen to the translator. During the pause, I check my inner compass, wanting to say nothing motivated by a wish to charm them with a disingenuous portrait of their leader.

"I also detected a note of dismay, maybe even confusion, when Ikeda and I talked about what young people experience today. We agree that the current obsession with financial markets and consumer goods provides little sustenance for a generation. Occasionally it felt as if he and I were commiserating—two old men reflecting back, each in our own way, on our good old days and the passion we experienced in the struggles that marked our youth." I note with some relief that a wave of chuckles spreads across the assembly.

"I'm not Buddhist, but a Roman Catholic," I say, beginning to wind down, "who is well aware of grave mistakes made in the name of religion. I am also a historian and think it very important for you to understand how for several centuries, when scholars spoke of global religion, of humanistic religion, they spoke exclusively in Christian terms. For many years, globalization meant westernization and Christianization.

"Scholars now think in terms of something new—the globalization of the religions of Asia, chief among them Buddhism in its many forms. That the Soka Gakkai plays an important role in this owes a lot to Nichiren, Makiguchi, and Toda. But it owes much more to your mentor, Daisaku Ikeda, who has worked hard, often behind the scenes, to give your religion its global reach. I want to be clear here," I add. "I am not attempting to flatter you or your teacher but to give you what I think is an honest assessment, having wrestled deeply with the history of the Gakkai.

"But there is one last thing I must add," I say, thinking about a point I've been mulling over for some time, seeing this as an opportunity to let it fly in public. "The working title of my book is *Nichiren's Lions,* an image in the plural, because I want to draw attention to you, members and disciples, as the builders of the Soka Gakkai. I want neither to startle nor to offend," I continue, wondering if I need to tread lightly, "but Makiguchi, Toda, and Ikeda would be nothing without you and the millions of others who answered their call."

The idea floats in the auditorium for a moment as I wait for the translator to catch up with me. Faces seem to be approving. "If I judge President Ikeda correctly—and I think I do," I continue, sensing that I have the room with me, "I am sure he would applaud me for saying that it is you who are Nichiren's real lions in the modern world, not he."

In the next few days, I learn how SSA moved from the margins of Singapore into its mainstream in three phases—a founding era between 1967 and 1980; then an expansion phase; and finally its maturation into a stable, distinctly Singaporean, institution over the course of the '90s.[34]

Concern about the Gakkai's Japaneseness was softened by its first general director having been a Japanese man who settled in Singapore when young and married a Singaporean Chinese woman. The early organization had strong ties with Malaysia and was administered through Hong Kong, so Tokyo was kept at a distance, even though ties to Japan remained important. It was a donation from Ikeda, for instance, that enabled SSA to purchase a center in the early '70s, a modest two-story bungalow in Geylang, which B.C. describes as "a red-light district." Elderly people, many of them illiterate Chinese women with old-fashioned ideas about Buddhism, concerned more about benefits than social transformation, defined the ethos of the group well into the '70s. But as the children of older members and younger new recruits took up Ikeda's Buddhist Humanism, the SSA entered its second phase, growing rapidly during the '80s by appealing to young, well-educated, professional Chinese, a group also targeted by evangelical and charismatic Protestants.

The activities of the SSA today must fit within legal perimeters designed to maintain unity among Singapore's diverse population—primarily Chinese Buddhists, Taoists, and Christians; Malay Muslims; and Indian Hindus and Sikhs. The Constitution guarantees religious freedom, but this freedom is circumscribed by the Maintenance of Religious Harmony Act, which enables the government to restrict proselytizing deemed insensitive or too aggressive and the mixing of politics and religion.

As a consequence, Gakkai traditions forged in Japan have adapted and taken on new meaning in accord with the principle of zuiho-bini. The politicized citizen-activist of the Toda era, who shakubukued Japan in the name of participatory democracy, has become the citizen-patriot working to contribute to the collective identity of Singaporean society. The culture festival has been transformed into an SSA tradition of participating in biennial events for Singapore youth, the Chingay Procession on Chinese New Year, and the National Day parade: large-scale, state-sponsored ceremonies designed to unite the island nation. But the SSA fife-and-drum corps, gymnastic groups, and the like still fulfill the same religious goals as the Japanese originals—rehearsals and performances are framed by chanting daimoku; participants learn self-expression, to overcome obstacles, and to work well in groups. Members also understand their voluntary service, whether raising funds for the disabled, supporting public health education, or providing outreach to the elderly, to be work for global kosen-rufu.[35]

The SSA keeps me on a tight schedule, much like the Gakkai in Japan, with a similar energetic intensity that may owe something to Japaneseness but may be a by-product of the city. A day may begin with a tour of the city; a visit to Sri Mariammam Temple, Singapore's oldest Hindu shrine; or a drive past large public-housing blocks with spacious, modern mosques that replaced ones destroyed by redevelopment in the '70s and '80s. Malay Muslims, who comprise about 16 percent of the population, hold a uniquely sensitive place in Singapore's multicultural landscape because the identification of race and religion is strong in the community, which has many ties to Malaysia, where Islam is the dominant religion. As a result, proselytizing Muslims is discouraged because of its potential to be a source of communal conflict, a situation taken for granted by most Singaporeans and respected by the SSA. A few Christian groups have been censured under the guidelines of the Maintenance of Religious Harmony Act, however—a move that some Western rights advocates decry as evidence of Singapore's repressive society.

By ten I am usually immersed in stories from Chinese, Indian, Japanese, and Eurasian members, today with teachers, businessmen, businesswomen, and a physicist turned construction engineer, all of whom tell me what Buddhism means in a rapidly changing society.[36] They talk of their varied routes to the Gakkai—through a personal tragedy, a search for inner peace, an effort to escape a family's superstitious beliefs, a need for something more than the Christianity encountered in the Boy Scouts. Some entered the Gakkai despite their families' alarm at their taking up a Japanese religion, others specifically because they were impressed by Makiguchi and Toda's resistance. None regrets the break with Nichiren Shoshu, because it was Ikeda, not priests, who showed them how to overcome obstacles in their daily lives through chanting and faith in the gohonzon. "When I first started practicing," one tells me, "I took as my guide President Ikeda saying how every day is a series of struggles. Success yesterday does not guarantee success today. Defeat today does not mean defeat tomorrow. That's from his *Youthful Diaries*. In the early days, we xeroxed parts of it to read together. Now it is my bedtime reading."

The engineer, a man raised in a Hindu family, recalls the Gakkai giving him new resources that helped him to negotiate Singapore's high-stress society and economy. The move from Hinduism to Buddhism was not difficult, he explains, because both teach tolerance and karma; but Hindus talk about God, while Buddhists do not. "That struck me as something apart," he recalls. He started chanting because of the

Gakkai's message that individuals can make a difference, which he considered "a very profound concept." It took time for him to accept Ikeda
as personal mentor because he did not want to emulate a human being,
to have a "master," but decided he could learn from him as a person
who had overcome his own problems to become a great man.

Chanting now plays a crucial role in maintaining his sense of self.
"The construction industry—it's basically uncivilized, like a war zone
in peacetime. Everybody fighting to complete projects. How do you
avoid losing control over yourself? My greatest benefit from practice is
to see beyond the construction industry." Soka Gakkai gives people
"the opportunity to excel, to bring out greatness from within, to
develop that potential." He shares that experience with others through
shakubuku—not like in the old days in Japan, in a mass movement, but
through conversations with acquaintances and friends. "The spirit of
Buddhism today goes beyond overcoming sickness and poverty," he
insists. "Now we talk about value creation, what you can do to make a
difference in another's life and in society. This has a very profound
impact on you. You want to be a dynamic player, rather than passively
observing the environment. It's tremendous!"

One early afternoon, I visit Soka Kindergarten, whose principal talks
at length about how Makiguchi's theories encourage creativity in more
than 250 students from both Gakkai and non-Gakkai families, while
preparing them to perform competitively in Singapore's public
schools.[37]

On another afternoon, at Soka AnLe Temple, Yuhan Watanabe, a
priest who was raised in a Gakkai family, recounts his own harrowing
experiences in the Nichiren Shoshu priesthood.[38] "Nikken only trusts
priests who have parents who are priests. He directly told people like us,
like me—my parents are Gakkai members so I'm not a child of the
priests—he told us that we are half corrupted. We are not clean. That
kind of discrimination was very strong. It was all over the head temple."
After the excommunication, Watanabe worked with other reform
priests to re-educate Gakkai members before being recruited to come
to Singapore by B. C., who thought it important for members to practice alongside a good priest. Now Watanabe works with laity, helping
them to instruct new members and, when requested, performing ceremonies. "I cover about 50 percent of the religious ceremonies and am a
member of the Ceremonial Department, which is comprised of senior
members and leaders . . . but I do not make decisions." He now sees his
seminary education as having been very superficial. "I gained my

knowledge of Nichiren's Buddhism more from the Soka Gakkai before I was ordained as a priest."

Things quiet down during a leisurely visit with Gwee Yee Hean, a friend of SSA and a sometimes collaborator with Ikeda, at his home in the Bukit Timah district, near the old site of Singapore University.[39] Because he is an English speaking academic, I anticipate an informative conversation, but still I'm surprised at the ease of our talking together. The tone is set when Gwee gestures to sweep in a view of his street, which is lined by houses, some large, some small, but all having a patina of wealth and prestige. "It's fortunate we bought years ago," he says offhandedly. "I couldn't touch it today, although Singapore real estate is down just now"—a comment like a thousand others I've heard in Boston, L.A., and New York City.

A slight man, calm but with a great deal of intellectual energy, Gwee has had a long and varied career as an academic. He was in charge of teacher training at the Ministry of Education in Malaya in the '50s, a lecturer at the Singapore Institute of Education, and a professor in the Faculty of History at Nanyang University in the '60s and '70s. He then served as chief executive of the Industrial & Commercial Bank until his retirement, when he became principal of the Nanyang Academy of Fine Arts, an institution whose educational endeavors run from painting and sculpture to fashion design. A self-described trader in ideas who now works as a consultant, Gwee converses widely with me on topics ranging from the troubling aspects of genetic engineering to the growing instability in financial markets, all over cool drinks in the spacious living room of his home. We talk of how our work depends on grants and grant makers—governments, businessmen, well-heeled nonprofits—that underwrite academic books, research, and conferences, both of us fully aware that our chat is funded by a Gakkai organization, though we let that fact go unstated.

Gwee first came into contact with the Gakkai in 1987 when a faculty member at Soka University asked him to consult on a symposium on the Pacific basin, a project that eventually lasted four years. During this time, he met Ikeda on a number of occasions and became a supporter of SSA. Like many academics, Gwee admits to having no strong religious convictions of his own. But he is impressed by the contemporary quality of Gakkai values at a time when secular-humanist and Confucian-style ethics have become out of date. "My initial exposure to Ikeda was through reading his university lectures and a number of his dialogues," he recalls. "I did not see him as a religious leader until I later met him and came to know the SSA. I was initially impressed that he promoted a progressive humanism in terms of peace, culture, and education, which struck me as to the point, very relevant."

For thirty years president of the South Seas Society, an old-line institution devoted to Southeast Asian history, and recently honored with a Festschrift published by Beijing University, Gwee is a scholar to be reckoned with. So I ask him for his frank opinion of Ikeda as we move to the terrace for durian and mangosteen, local delicacies considered the king and queen of fruit, and compare notes on recent events in the Gakkai.

Gwee followed the priesthood issue from a distance but was unaware of the Sho-Hondo's demolition, which he calls "appalling." He has heard the rumors that Hiromasa Ikeda may succeed his father, despite the fact that it will look very Japanese if there is a hereditary succession. I'm impressed by his down-to-earth assessment of Ikeda, whom he describes as a networker and bridge builder, a mover and shaker who likes to see things get done that are important to him. With the Gakkai's resources at his disposal, he is "an academic's Santa Claus"—someone who funds research without compromising a scholar's integrity. Between bites of the male durian, which tastes uncannily like sweat, and the sweet, female mangosteen, which goes down very easily, I ask Gwee why he thinks Ikeda seems always to be surrounded by controversy. "When you become a great man," he replies, speaking as if Ikeda's greatness is simply a matter of fact, "there will always be people who do not like you."

• • •

On the following day, my last in Singapore, I awaken to a view of brilliant sun on the harbor and its vast container facility, which I can see clearly from my room high up in the Copthorne Hotel. Over morning coffee and juice, I get dizzy thinking about all the DVD players, designer dresses, Nikes, salvage tires, and invasive species in transit via the cranes, rails, and ships in the industrial landscape before me.

Every American should see Asia firsthand, I think, *where people experience modernity as exciting, as liberating.* After a century and a half of overdevelopment, Americans seem stodgy, maybe just war-weary, by comparison. The BBC financial report, however, reviews new and dire downturns in the global economy. I try to remain aloof from the contagion spreading among panicked market spin-doctors and political economists, but feel lucky to have my hideaway in Deansboro.

The day brings new rounds of interviews, punctuated by a quick shopping trip in the old downtown, where we eat in a Victorian-era market square. I am reminded again of the food court mentality of Boston's Quincy Market, where leisure-oriented merchandising thrives amid the charm of the good old days, which softens the bustle of newness.

By evening I'm wired, so I put tape recorder and notebook aside to relax with a few Gakkai young people over a late dinner at the Singa Inn Seafood Restaurant. Salty smells from the ocean and the hot, humid air are calming and envelop our table under the trees like a soothing balm. I nestle into a comfortable chair to enjoy a few drinks while four young men and women, all of them ethnic Chinese, describe their work in the SSA with an enthusiasm that crackles like lightning. *Valedictorian material*, I think, noting how one speaks impeccable English and lays out her arguments with awe-inspiring clarity and crispness.

I have been goading them on a bit, calling them Generation M, the millennial generation, a phrase I borrow from a speech of Singapore's prime minister printed that morning in *The Straits Times*.[40] "He says you were born with silver spoons in your mouths and have the world at your feet. But you just wait—he thinks you'll be buffeted by global forces beyond your control and by regional economic uncertainty," I say, in a tone not quite ominous. I am curious if young people of faith will be able to keep that faith when the going gets rough, so I want to provoke them. "Please, tell me, how do you factor bad economic news into your vision of global kosen-rufu?"

As good students do, they bite down hard on the question and launch into a lively discussion of Buddhism in the contemporary world, their words striking me as more than the Gakkai drill even though they are pure Ikeda. Their affluent lives, so unlike their grandparents' or even their parents', mean responsibility, not privilege, they say. Education, leadership, and service can meet the challenge of the twenty-first century. They speak with intense certainty that owes something to their youthfulness, to their religious conviction, and also to a diligence inherited from the Gakkai in Japan. But I recall B. C.'s remark about the stressfulness of living in a society that considers smart, productive people its greatest resource, so I wonder if I'm merely hearing the high pressure of the Singaporean lifestyle.

But their enthusiasm is infectious, and I am soon drawn into a debate over *shoju* and shakubuku, two terms with a long history in Japanese Buddhism. They use *shoju* to refer to dialogue or conversation designed to persuade people rather than convert them, a style of propagation now preferred to old-style shakubuku in SGI movements around the world. But they also use the phrase *shakubuku spirit* in a way that suggests the original meaning of *evangelical,* which is something like "spreading the good news." When they lapse into Mandarin to debate among themselves I lose the thread of the conversation, but the overall impression is clear. Propagation for this generation means persuading people to empower themselves and others in order to contribute to the public good, which is the essence of Ikeda's Buddhist Humanism. From time to time I glance over to watch Tay Eng Kiat, an affable man and a senior leader, who says very little but justifiably glows with pride.

Eventually, wearied by too much talk about social responsibility, my attention drifts to thatched huts far across the patio, at the side of an oval pool where a band plays and performers execute what the menu describes as "cultural dances," which must evoke the Malay peninsula of yesteryear. Waiters arrive with half a dozen seafood dishes—lobster salad, steamed fish, butter prawns, various preparations of crab—which I am told are Thai and classic Cantonese cuisine. Food turns the discussion away from the Gakkai, about which I have learned quite enough for one day, to pleasantries: what they study in school; what they will do after college; where I live in New York, about which they know nothing other than the city—as a yellow-blue moon rises through the trees along the shore of the Strait of Singapore.

CHAPTER 8

World House

On the drive from Los Angeles International Airport to Aliso Viejo, a newly incorporated city in Orange County, California, it's hard not to recall my train ride to and from Hachioji less than two years earlier. Then I was on my way to Soka University–Japan and my first Ikeda sighting; now I'm off to the dedication of SUA, Soka University of America. Then I was still raw from Ann's death and wet behind the ears about all things Japanese, as cynical about the Gakkai's idealism as I was intrigued by its controversies. Now, having come to an understanding of both the Gakkai and Japan, it's as if I've already begun to contemplate a new life.

Indistinguishable from much of Orange County, Aliso Viejo is lushly landscaped and tastefully overdeveloped, a new, largely residential community that, after a few qualms about SG being an Asian cult, embraced SUA as a cultural and economic asset. It also adds a stunning visual element to the new city, its summit perch, dun-colored stucco walls, strong vertical lines, and low-pitched, California-Mediterranean roofs calling to mind a Dalai Lama–Tibet–Potala Palace–style Buddhist city on a hill.

The mood of the crowds that cluster under the tall, recently planted palms is festive, the opening a fulfillment of Ikeda's long-cherished dream of a school to educate Pacific Rim leaders. With its contemporary lotus ponds, rooftop colonnades, and dramatic views of pristine chaparral canyons, SUA was, quite obviously, very expensive. According to some, Gakkai trustees were cautious about making the financial commitment required to create a university, but Ikeda's enthusiasm con-

171

vinced them. More astonishing, reliable sources report that the Gakkai not only created a $200 million endowment for SUA but paid cash for its eighteen buildings and 103-acre campus. This approach to institution building, I am quite certain, has a lot to do with how the Gakkai does things in Japan.

I'm amused by the notice of SUA's opening, "Zen and the Liberal Arts," that Rob clipped for me from the *New York Times* educational supplement.[1] Apparently, Nichiren draws a blank with reporters at America's newspaper of record, who, like most people in the United States, assume that Buddhism plus Japan can equal only Zen. I'm particularly intrigued by its report that twelve of the twenty-one faculty members, most of whom are neither Buddhist nor Gakkai, gave up tenure elsewhere to become part of this Buddhist educational experiment. Tickled by what I imagine to be their fuzzy fantasies about Japanese Buddhism—mossy temples, starkly abstract rock gardens, monks in quiet contemplation—I know from chats with some on the faculty that utopian expectations have begun to give way to testy academic politics and threats of litigation.

I explore these developments with SUA's president, Daniel Habuki, who holds a PhD in agricultural economics from Washington State University and has had years of experience with Soka education, first as a student, then as a teacher and administrator.[2] One of only a few native-born Japanese working at SUA, Habuki is tall and lean, an affable man who seems harried and distracted today, preoccupied with details of the dedication and by the fact that faculty-administration difficulties need to be resolved before the arrival of students on campus, now only a few months away.

Only marginally interested in academic politics, I am nevertheless fascinated to hear Habuki talk of his frustrations in getting SUA up and running. With a laugh and a shrug, he admits to his complete failure at implementing a consensus-driven management style that, theoretically, ought to work well in a small educational institution with a noble global mission. Bred to the Japanese manner that expects to give and receive deference, Habuki sounds war-weary as he recounts how often he has been charged with naïveté. With his hands-on, student-friendly, non-hierarchical approach to leadership, he seems to be bending over backward to avoid any hint of the autocratic style that many Americans associate with Japan. But a new dean of the faculty, a get-tough American, has just come on board, and rumor has it he has been charged with whipping things into shape.

I'm more curious about how Nichiren Buddhism fits into an American liberal-arts education, a question Habuki sees as both an important and a difficult one. As he speaks, I find myself reflecting on the fact that Jews and Catholics have had well over a century to figure out ways to express their distinctive and ancient values in secular institutions of higher education. Both groups have also learned to navigate the shoals in transatlantic internationalism, while the Gakkai is just embarking on a transpacific experiment in undergraduate education.

As Habuki sets Soka education in historical perspective, I begin to see how his job building SUA entails cross-cultural daring because for the first time I grasp how experimental the university really is. In many respects just another small liberal-arts college, it is also the latest, most self-consciously internationalist step in a larger Japanese Buddhist educational enterprise. Makiguchi's westernizing reformism, Toda's occupation-era strategies for democratic empowerment, Ikeda's liberalization and globalization all come out here in the wash. Knowing what I do about members' faith and their diligent energy, I can imagine the pressure Habuki must apply to himself each day as he works to realize his mentor's vision for SUA.

Habuki's English-speaking skills mean we need no translators, so I must watch that I do not periodically drift into reverie. But as he talks of his own education in Soka schools, I see SUA as embodying the centuries-long process of encounter between West and East in all its complexity—Japan's defense against the West by re-creating itself in a Euro-American image; its marvelous hybridization of the art, culture, technology, and ideals of two civilizations; its sending back into the world many achievements as it rose from its crushing defeat in World War II, among them Soka Gakkai International and SUA.

Habuki describes the Makiguchi-Toda-Ikeda teaching lineage of Nichiren Buddhism as centered on the concept of "self-awakening education." Before Ikeda founded Soka schools, the Japanese movement was essentially a mass educational endeavor, one in which ordinary people awakened themselves by practicing Buddhism and strove to realize Buddhist values in their daily lives. For some thirty years, there have been Soka schools, Habuki explains, but only now are people prepared to reflect systematically on the role of Nichiren Buddhist Humanism in the liberal arts. "It's my hope and dream that some SUA graduates will go into academic fields to develop Soka education in terms of methodology. We are Ikeda's disciples, his followers," Habuki says, referring to himself less as an academic than as the son of parents who joined the

Gakkai in the early days. "As disciples we tend to agree with everything," he explains, noting that he has learned much from working with faculty who do not share his experience. "What we need now are people who can discuss and debate Ikeda's intention and the import of Soka education in academic terms."

The pride of donors both large and small, Japanese and multicultural American, who have made the university happen infuses the weekend with the joyful sense of purpose I've come to associate with the Gakkai. Immersed in the crowd, I feel once again, as I did at that first leaders' meeting at Makiguchi Hall, that SGI is an intense and immense international family. As I chat with members, I find some have a particular enthusiasm for SUA's emphasis on Pacific Rim cultures and languages—Chinese, Japanese, English, and Spanish. Others are invested in it educating students to environmentalism, internationalism, or nonviolence. Whatever their vision, members' sense of ownership of SUA is strong and, as we talk, I recall Hiromasa Ikeda describing exhibits in Makiguchi Hall as testimonies to the faith of ordinary members, concrete proofs of the benefits of their faith, study, and practice. That just a half-century ago Toda struggled to build a political-spiritual movement in the ruins of Japan among the despised, poor, and sick seems incredible.

My efforts to interpret the SUA landscape also remind me of Raphael, Whitman, Socrates, Curie, and the other luminaries who grace the Hachioji campus, and I recall with fondness how intrigued I was by their familiarity and out-of-placeness. Here their status as Soka paragons seems taken for granted, but SUA's design highlights peace more than culture or education, as evidenced by Mohandas and Kasturba Gandhi and Linus and Ava Helen Pauling halls, which along with the Daisaku and Kaneko Ikeda Library create the symbolic—and conspicuously gender-sensitive—heart of the campus.

As warm sunshine envelops the clusters of guests who mill, chat, and snack on the promenade around Peace Lake and Fountain, Rob and I enjoy an unexpected meeting with Rie. Our work together—research trips, numerous interviews, informal conversations, our two afternoons in Makiguchi gardens remembering Ann—have created personal bonds. We also find we have a new bond in our shared awareness that the world has seismically shifted since our first meeting in Tokyo. That was during the wild-eyed market boom of the high '90s, which continues to give way to deepening angst over faltering global markets. For Rie and other Japanese, the demise of the dot-coms has not been the occasion for panic, Japan's bubble economy having burst in 1990–91. For me, these new, rougher, if more reality-oriented times put an appealing, almost in-your-face edge on the lofty didacticism of Ikeda's mottoes for SUA— "Be philosophers of a renaissance of life; be world citizens in solidarity for peace; be the pioneers of a global civilization"— sentiments I'd once have dismissed as charmingly irrelevant.[3]

·   ·   ·

From the start, figuring out what to make of Ikeda was a cornerstone of my project—tyrant? beloved mentor? politico?—a puzzle I began to resolve only once I'd understood him as a Japanese man and a Cold War–era leader, an internationalist and idealist, a romantic who was also sufficiently hardheaded and pragmatic to build and lead a highly dynamic movement. As I grew to admire his disciples' consistency in expressing empowerment for self and others in ways both healthy and sane, I also came to trust Ikeda according to the principle—which I think is both Buddhist and Christian—that by the fruit you shall know the tree. Whatever else I might make of Ikeda, Toda, shakubuku, Buddhist evangelism, high-energy religion, and Japan, I willingly admit that Nichiren's lions impress me.

Still new angles on Ikeda's idealistic-pragmatic internationalism are revealed in interviews over the next few days, two of which are with men who both are about my age and have worked closely with the Gakkai in recent years. Both are American religious leaders, both astute players in a globalizing world. Both have also become what appear to be Ikeda's international spiritual-political allies, although the nature of their alliances differs significantly. The first is Dr. Lawrence Carter, chaplain at the Martin Luther King Jr. International Chapel at Morehouse College in Atlanta; the second is Los Angeles–based Rabbi Abraham Cooper, an associate dean at the Simon Wiesenthal Center.

I meet with Carter at SUA, where he is scheduled to deliver the keynote address at the formal dedication.[4] Just a month earlier, Carter inaugurated what he calls the Gandhi-King-Ikeda Community Builders Prize at the King chapel at Morehouse, the first award going to Prince El-Hassan bin Talal of Jordan, the president of the Club of Rome and a man widely praised for peace work in the Middle East. I am most curious to hear Carter's thoughts about why he has linked Gandhi and King to Ikeda, who is not only living but seems, I think, to be in a different league from the two immortals. An enthusiastic talker, Carter lets the story out easily, but to understand his rationale, he says, we must begin at the beginning. So I first get a crash course on the historical-spiritual connections among Henry David Thoreau, Gandhi, and civil rights leader Howard Thurman, a legacy of nonviolent protest that found its ultimate American expression in King.

The presenting problem for Carter is that this vital legacy has been steadily losing steam over the past several decades, and he talks frankly of his years of frustration in attempting to promote King as a global thinker. At the suggestion of Walter Massey, president of Morehouse, and other colleagues, Carter began to change tactics by emphasizing King's Gandhi connections in his networking, teaching, and preaching. He also established a Gandhi Institute for Reconciliation, a kind of global spiritual-political clearinghouse, at Morehouse. "The big shock was that we had been programming around the name of Martin Luther King Jr. for twenty years, but no one paid attention to that in relation to international peace. It wasn't until I identified him with Gandhi and linked Gandhi to Martin King that it sent a signal to the government of India and beyond Christendom. No one paid me any attention until I hooked Gandhi to King."

For Carter, Ikeda and the Gakkai represent a second and important opening to nonviolent rights advocates beyond Christendom, a relationship established in a rapid sequence of events in the year 2000. It began in January when Ann Ford, an SGI member and professor at Clark Atlanta University, paid him a visit. Impressed by his vision, she asked Carter if he'd like to meet with SGI representatives. A few weeks later, a contingent of Japanese, Caucasian, and African American members arrived at Morehouse.

According to Carter, they hit it off immediately, all of them sharing their passion for and spiritual perspectives on global rights issues. In April of the same year, when Carter launched the Gandhi institute during Spiritual Awareness Week at Morehouse, Gakkai people were there, among them SGI-USA's director Danny Nagashima, along with Coretta King and other rights leaders. Carter soon found a platform for his campaign to revitalize King's legacy by speaking at Gakkai events such as Victory over Violence campaigns at the University of Michigan and in the Caribbean. "They began to see I wasn't saying anything different from what Dr. Ikeda was saying, so they thought that I should meet him." Shortly thereafter, Carter made his first trip to Japan.

I enjoy hearing Carter talk about his experience of what I've come to think of as the Japan-Gakkai treatment. "They took such wonderful care of me. I mean, it was unbelievable," he says. "I'd never had an experience like that in my life. There was not a place I went that I was not welcomed by a throng, with gifts and flowers and fruit. And applause. They treated me like I was the head of state." Carter also brought gifts of his own to Ikeda. One was a reproduction of an oil painting of Ikeda and Kaneko that Carter commissioned for the Hall of Honor, a gallery of heroes of nonviolent civil rights protest in the King chapel. A second was Ikeda's induction into the Martin Luther King Collegium of Scholars, another of Carter's operations at Morehouse.

Carter makes clear that India-Gandhi and Japan-Ikeda connections have greatly enhanced his work at Morehouse, strengthened his ability to revive the King legacy, and added a whole new dimension to his networking. As he talks, I begin to see the overtures made between him and Ikeda as a kind of courtship. Both bring themselves, their issues, and a few gifts to the ceremonial table as a way to feel each other out, to explore whether there is substance and spirit enough for the forging of an alliance. A key criterion is mutual benefit, a motive I used to see as self-serving but now understand to be a sane way to proceed in a world of competing interests, most of them profit-driven and having little to do with spirituality and peace. In Carter and Ikeda there is, moreover, a nice cross-cultural fit —to gain benefit is a Gakkai-Japanese religious value, and enlightened self-interest is classically Puritan-Protestant American. As Carter talks about internationalizing his student ministry, I marvel at both the beauty and the practical advantage in a Buddhist teacher and a Christian preacher striking a deal to get King into Japan and Ikeda into Morehouse and the broader African American rights community.

But as Carter begins to theologize, it also becomes clear that there's more than pragmatism at work in his building a bridge between the United States and Japan, between Christianity and Buddhism, between King and Ikeda. "There is room for plenty of traffic between these traditions and a subterranean truth that runs underneath them," he tells me, as he segues into a discussion that is half teaching, half preaching. He talks of one aspect of this truth in terms of the ancient mystical tradition that sees ultimate reality as transcending all concepts and names. "People want to know how I can feel comfortable in Christianity, a religion that is theistic, but relate it to a nontheistic religion," he says, referring to a potentially explosive issue for a public preacher in a region in which many influential people are Protestant conservatives. "It's very simple. There are many names for that power, that force, that principle, that law which governs the universe," he says, taking delight in the rhythm and resonance of words. "In Buddhism they talk about divine law, sacred law, divine principle, sacred principle, mystic law. To me, all of those are names for what Christians call God."

Carter finds a second common thread in his humanistic reading of Jesus. He tells us that Clayborne Carson, editor of the King papers, writes that King never, in any of his sermons, invited anybody to be Christian. "His message was to follow Jesus," Carter notes, "and that's where I'm at. Some Christians fixate on Jesus as God but there are plenty of scriptures that suggest Jesus did not want to be worshiped, that Jesus was like Buddha, like Muhammad, like Gandhi, like King, like Ikeda—a very enlightened person."

He develops a third commonality around the concept of "world house," a metaphor central to King's later Vietnam War–era teachings, when he began to link rights issues at home to materialism, militarism, racism, and poverty around the globe. Carter explains how Christianity teaches that all people live, move, and have their being in God and that there is no separation between one person and another. It is in this context that "Martin King talked about a world house, the beloved community," he says, in which "injustice anywhere is a threat to justice everywhere." Carter understands King's views as parallel to Ikeda's on global justice, which are "built on the interconnectedness of all things, a powerful part of Buddhist teaching."

I get another view of how Ikeda engages with justice issues in King's world house in conversation with Rabbi Abraham Cooper in West Los Angeles at the Simon Wiesenthal Center, an international Jewish human rights organization, where he has worked since 1977.[5] A longtime activist and recognized expert on hate literature on the Web, Cooper also spearheaded the center's work in Asian Pacific Rim nations, working with scholars in China and taking on popular anti-Semitism in Japan.

"The whole idea that anti-Semitic stereotypes would take hold in a continent where there were virtually no Jews, in an influential nation like Japan, was, to say the least, unacceptable to us," he tells Rob and me, recalling his shock at finding Japanese editions of *The Protocols of the Elders of Zion,* an anti-Semitic forgery, in the shop in the Shinjuku Hilton. For years, he pressed his case with Japanese publishers, advertising executives, and other media representatives but was always frustrated by their expressions of polite concern that never resulted in serious engagement with the issue. He describes his struggle to build effective relationships in Japan: "We took on all the big boys in the Japanese media world. We had seminars. We've had all sorts of discussions.

But the truth is, the only partners we found to help us bring our concerns to the Japanese public are the people from Soka University, under the leadership of Daisaku Ikeda."

Cooper admits to an initial reluctance to cultivate a relationship with a Japanese Buddhist group that has a significant presence in the United States because, like many Jewish leaders, he is troubled by the high number of Jews who've embraced Buddhism. He was encouraged, however, by friends who knew the Gakkai's work in Japan and by their telling him they were Buddhists who'd "gotten rid of their idols," a reference to the Nichiren Shoshu–Gakkai tradition of venerating the gohonzon instead of images of the Buddha.

Eventually, he met with Gakkai representatives over dinner in a Tokyo restaurant. "I grilled some of their top people. It was more or less a friendly interrogation, me trying to find out if these guys had some hidden agenda." He recalls being particularly impressed by Rie, who worked as his translator. "No matter what I threw at her—it was just unbelievable. I was talking about Jewish stuff, so I know now how many hundreds of hours of research must have gone on in advance. It was incredible. I have to tell you, the meeting turned out to be a pleasant shock. I'll use that term. It was a real pleasant shock, and it set the stage for my first visit to their headquarters."

An Orthodox rabbi with degrees from Yeshiva University and Jewish University of America, Cooper speaks eloquently but often colloquially, which makes it easy for me to see in him my own initial reactions to Japan and the Gakkai. I know exactly what he means when he talks of his first impression of Makiguchi Hall: "It makes the Lycée look like a dump. Holy mackerel, what's going on here?" I relive my own impressions of Gakkai youth leaders in his astonishment: "I mean, anyone who goes there for the first time . . . you see five thousand freshly scrubbed students. And they're all waving at you!"

Cooper recalls seeing a tabloid ad on the train in which a photo of Ikeda was juxtaposed with that of the leader of Aum Shinrikyo, the radical group that released sarin gas in the Tokyo subway in 1995. Such image manipulation is common in the Japanese media, but it did not resonate at all with his impressions of Ikeda, whom he met for the first time around Hanukkah. "That first meeting was very interesting," he recalls. "It dawned on me after about three minutes that Ikeda knew all about Hanukkah. I was explaining it but, yeah, he knew all about it. He seemed like a nice guy, very approachable. A really sharp guy, very open."

Unlike Carter, Cooper does not theologize as he talks of why he has found Ikeda to be an important ally, shedding a different light on the character of the networking so central to Ikeda's presidency. He describes a connection that is warm, sympathetic, and spiritual in the sense that both parties bring to the table a shared concern for human dignity, honor, and rights but make no attempt to forge a common spiritual perspective. This pragmatic approach to alliance is underscored by a shared interest in concrete outcomes. On one hand, Ikeda gets from Cooper tangible input into the Gakkai's ongoing effort to cultivate a cosmopolitan spirituality among its members and to strengthen the human rights tradition in Japan—a goal in keeping with the thrust of the movement under Makiguchi and Toda and with the mission of Komeito. On the other, Cooper gets substantial, very concrete support for his work against global anti-Semitism.

The first collaborative effort between the Wiesenthal center and the Soka Gakkai was in 1994 when they created together a Japanese version of the center's traveling Holocaust exhibit, The Courage to Remember. To tailor the exhibit to Japanese sensibilities, the Gakkai sent a team of graphic artists from Tokyo to Los Angeles. Using Anne Frank material in the center's archives, they reshaped the exhibit to highlight Frank and her diary, a work that is much beloved in Japan as the intimate reflections of a young girl, but is only dimly understood to be Holocaust literature. Another addition to the standard exhibit was devoted to Chiune Sugihara, a wartime Japanese diplomat posted in Lithuania who wrote visas for Jews in defiance of his government, thus saving thousands from almost certain extermination in Nazi camps.

Through the influence of Ikeda and Soka University, the revised exhibit opened at Tokyo's city hall, where it was viewed by seventy-three thousand people in eleven days. After that, it toured sixty cities in thirty-nine of the forty-seven prefectures of Japan, including a stop at Peace Park in Hiroshima, eventually being seen by almost two million people. "I have to say—I mean, it's almost embarrassing—but the quality of the exhibit in Japan is fifty times more powerful than any other place we brought it, and it's still in rotation," Cooper says. This collaboration also led to the kind of engagement at the heart of a Soka education: eighty-one Soka University students came from Hachioji to Los Angeles to present one thousand origami cranes to the Museum of Tolerance, a public education arm of the Simon Wiesenthal Center.

Cooper talks of a second collaboration slated for 2002 when the center and the Tokyo Fuji Art Museum plan to mount a joint project in

Japan called Friedl and the Children of Terezin. This will be an exhibit
of the artwork of Friedl Dicker-Brandeis—Bauhaus paintings, theater
sets, costume design, and book bindings— and that of children she
instructed while they were all imprisoned in the ghetto of Terezin, a
Czech town near Prague. It would eventually be seen by 350,000 people
in Japan.[6]

Cooper says that since he began to work with the Gakkai, he has
found additional partners in Japan, some of whom he greatly admires;
"but if you ask me who is our best friend in Japan, who 'gets it,' it's
Ikeda." As we part, he shares with me two impressions of Ikeda. The
first is that he seems to miss the good old days, when the Gakkai was the
underdog and they all had to have great courage, before there were
beautiful buildings, schools, and art museums. "I got the feeling that
he would like to see more initiative from the younger generation and
maybe even from people around him."

The second was a brief episode that took place in Los Angeles in an
almost impromptu meeting with Ikeda, just two days before the opening of the Museum of Tolerance. "We still had dust up to our knees,
and Ikeda shows up with his wife and entourage. I think we had a day
or two notice. He was actually our first visitor to our museum. He
comes, of course, with medals, which he presents to the head of the
museum and says, 'Bless this place.' He loved the museum but just blew
in and kind of blew out. It was a wonderful gesture of solidarity."

． ． ．

As May gives way to June and the start of a hot summer, I'm back at
work on the book in Deansboro, pleased to have established a beat and
tone that do justice to the Gakkai. I've developed a narrative voice
that's often nonplussed by members' quixotic intensity, at a time when
most people are griping about their mutual funds being shot to hell by
an increasingly lousy economy. My narrator is doing a heartfelt job of
managing grief in response to the loss of his wife, having become a
better man in the course of toughing it out. All in all, the book is shaping up to be a nice slice of globalizing middle-class spiritual life at the
start of a new century.

This tidy narrative package flies apart at the seams with the pancak-
ing down of the twin towers on September 11, 2001, when all bets are
suddenly off for the future of globalization, its course, and its meaning.
As the spectacle unfolds over the next days and weeks, first in lower

Manhattan and then in Afghanistan, I find I can't construct even a single sentence. After a month, I've lost my grip on my narrator because I can't recognize America. I'm back to having no plot for myself, much less for a book about the Buddhist Humanism of Daisaku Ikeda. I seem, he seems, Buddhism seems so tied to the '60s, at a time when the nation is racing back to the '50s to take on axes of evil and man the ramparts for homeland defense.

What to say about a Buddhist peace movement while public attention shifts to the Abrahamic religions and goes on a wartime footing is something I struggle with each day, as expressing dissent aloud over the nation's course of action begins to feel very dangerous. So from the security of my Deansboro refuge, I take up a new round of Gakkai watching. The movement's connections to the disaster are ongoing and intimate: David Seima Aoyama, an administrator in SGI-USA's Santa Monica headquarters, was on American Airlines' Boston-to-L.A. flight number 11, which smashed into the north tower. Ground zero is home turf for scores of Gakkai New Yorkers. Mariane Pearl, the wife of Daniel Pearl, the *Wall Street Journal* reporter who is killed in Pakistan, is in the Gakkai in France.

Caught off guard by resurgent American nationalism, I feel confusion and guilt over not being prepared to care less about Afghani lives than those of young Americans. As a historian of American religion, I get queasy witnessing the resurgence of a bellicose U.S. civil religion. So as I watch the Gakkai respond, I'm impressed by Ikeda's constancy, his message never veering from peace, culture, and education even as he negotiates the changing political climate.

Always pro-American and abhorring terrorism, he reiterates in his new Peace Proposal that the law of cause and effect demands nonviolence because "vengeance invites vengeance. Any act of reprisal will inevitably provoke a response and the cycle will continue without end."[7] As the United States digs into its old-style headstrong, go-it-alone mission, he also holds fast to institutional multilateralism—international law, tribunals, courts, the United Nations. With many American commentators going jingo, I'm reminded that Japan, however much an ally of the U.S., has more consistently styled itself Asian-European than Asian-American since the cultural revolutions of the Meiji Restoration.

As the Middle East erupts and Japan talks of rearming because North Korea talks of nuclear weapons, I decide to turn off the television, seeing no point in staying informed about all that when I'm powerless to alter the course of my own country. But I am again impressed, this time to see that Gakkai members are not disheartened, even as King's world house threatens to burn down around us. Far from an irrelevancy, they now see the kosen-rufu movement as an utter necessity, the logic of the age of mappo dictating that bad times must necessarily call forth the most determined responses.

As I cultivate indifference, I also come to appreciate that Ikeda is a deeply committed religious teacher, a person of genuine faith, not an easy idealist. He restates in a hundred ways his conviction that global kosen-rufu can result in a world at peace, but only by the awakening of the mystic law in individuals, person by person: "Altering the course of human history . . . will require of each individual a profound inner resolution, a truly existential determination to seek their fundamental, inherent humanity and to transform their entire being."[8] I am equally impressed that he makes no pronouncements on what his disciples should think or what they must do as the world begins to take shape post–September 11.

Unhappy as a new breed of neoconservatives proclaims the end of irony and the rebooting of the American imperium, I find I'm actually proud of Ikeda and the Gakkai for hanging in there with their humanistic liberalism, an existential outlook that seems to have all but disappeared in America. So when Rob calls with a new proposal, I jump at the chance to go look at the Gakkai in Brazil, thinking it also a good time to get out of the United States.

. . .

A thousand white towers, all some thirty stories tall, only one or two to a block, dominate the view of São Paulo from the plane, creating the impression of new construction stretching to a limitless horizon. This seemingly endless phalanx is broken by spots of verdant green and red-tiled roofs, many of them overcrowded favelas—squatters' slums and neighborhoods of the destitute—built chock-a-block up hillsides, which gives them the cubist look prominent in paintings bought by tourists. Like many cities in what was once called the Third World, São Paulo has seen a population explosion in the past three decades as people flocked from the countryside to the city in search of work, encouraged by a fitfully booming economy and a movement for democracy after two decades of military rule. By some reckoning, metropolitan São Paulo vies with Tokyo and Mexico City for the status of largest city in the world.

I've not flown since September 11, so the long flight from Miami becomes a time for reflection. "Do you recall the hot-button issues when we made our first flight to Tokyo?" I ask Rob, who's watching a movie. "It was the hazard posed by airline snacks to peanut-sensitive people and an air traveler's manifesto that claimed speedy luggage handling as an inalienable right of the American people," I say, inviting him to commiserate with me about how much the world, or America's relationship with the world, has changed. "Another Buddhist lesson in impermanence, my friend," he replies, slipping his earphones off momentarily.

Brazil is a good place to wrap up research because BSGI (Brazil Soka Gakkai International) is a zuiho-bini success story for a number of reasons. Acceptance of BSGI has been eased by its association with a large Japanese immigrant community that is highly regarded in Brazil, a nation with no history of struggle with Japan, unlike the United States, where ideas about Japaneseness remain conflicted and complex. More specifically, BSGI is recognized as a positive force in Brazil, its members working for kosen-rufu through a wide range of effective social programs designed to strengthen civil society. The movement has also been successful in adapting itself to an ethos shaped by Latin Catholicism and in moving out of the immigrant community to recruit members from multiethnic Brazil, some 80 percent of its 150,000 members now non-Japanese.

My first impression, however, is that BSGI is still quite Japanese. I am met at the airport by Eduardo Taguchi and Getulino Nakajima; get a briefing at the BSGI center in Liberdade Ward, a historic Japanese neighborhood; and eat sushi, sashimi, tempura, and miso soup at Suntory restaurant. In the morning, I see Josei Toda Viaduct and Makiguchi Road near an exit off the expressway that leads us to the Eternal Peace Memorial Palace, a mortuary in the Japanese style adjacent to the BSGI Nature Culture Center, an extensive parklike retreat twenty or so miles outside the city that was founded by Ikeda.

When Ikeda visited Brazil on his first trip in 1960, there were about 150 Gakkai members, all of whom had joined back in Japan. The next few years saw some growth, but in 1965 the membership exploded after Roberto (Yasuhiro) Saito and his wife, Silvia (Etsuko), arrived to lead the entire South American movement. Head of the Women's Division, Silvia energized the Brazilian organization, achieving its goal of adding ten thousand new members in one year in anticipation of Ikeda's next visit. She shakubukued the Japanese community with such intensity that sectarian conflicts flared between rival Nichiren groups and other new religions from Japan. These campaigns laid the foundation for the Gakkai's subsequent growth, but when Ikeda arrived in 1966 he urged moderation, calling for the movement to embrace non-Japanese and suggesting that leaders shift from Japanese to Portuguese as the movement's primary language. This opened up a new phase in the growth of BSGI, as second-generation Japanese Brazilians and people from other ethnic and racial groups began to alter its character.[9]

The Latin tempo and look of São Paulo are a real tonic to my spirits, and I begin to develop a whole new view of the Gakkai in conversation with Amaral Vieira, a noted composer around fifty.[10] We talk in his comfortable studio home in the hills on the eve of his departure for Japan, where he will tour under the auspices of the Min-On Concert Association. A lapsed old Catholic, Vieira now considers himself a Buddhist and a friend of BSGI but belongs to no religious organizations.

Vieira shares with me how he had read about Tibetan Buddhism and Zen in the past, but never took up meditation. In 1991, he happened upon *Before It Is Too Late*—Ikeda's dialogue with Aurelio Peccei, founder of the Club of Rome—in a European airport and was impressed by Ikeda's blend of spirituality and pragmatism. A year later, he was drawn to the Gakkai through events he now sees as karmically related: his consulting at São Paulo's art museum when Ikeda donated two grand pianos there; his discovery of "Dawn of the Century of Humanity," Ikeda's 1991 peace proposal, on the desk of the museum's secretary. Eventually, he composed several pieces inspired by Ikeda's Buddhist Humanism, discovered BSGI, and began to work with Min-On and a Gakkai student orchestra in Brazil. Over the years he has forged a friendship with Ikeda, whom he has met on ten different occasions and considers a great teacher.

Coming from the insecurity pandemic in middle-class America, I find it refreshing to hear Vieira talk of how BSGI works to address the very concrete needs of Brazil, which is torn between vast numbers of people who are desperately poor and the rich who dominate the country. He recalls being impressed to find ordinary people in BSGI practicing Buddhism to empower themselves, to solve immediate problems, to gain dignity and hope, while learning the value of contributing to the greater good through volunteerism, which they understand to be the work of a bodhisattva. He sees a similar populism at work in Min-On, whose tours allow him to play not only in fine concert halls in great cities but also in villages and towns in the Japanese hinterlands, for working-class men and women who know little about the classical tradition of Western music. Vieira sees this orientation to the grassroots as reflecting the spirit of the Gakkai's three presidents, all of whom taught that the cultural heritage of humankind is the possession of everyone, not simply elites, and propagated a spirituality that values beauty and art in the creation of a responsible citizenry, as did the ancient Romans and Greeks.

Like Dr. Gwee in Singapore, Vieira shows me new sides to the Gakkai, his view informed not by academics but by crypto-Catholic mysticism and art. When I express surprise at his calling Nam-myoho-renge-kyo "my most important prayer," he elaborates with enthusiasm. He compares chanting daimoku to reciting the paternoster in the days before the church abandoned Latin, a move he sees as wrongheaded because it severed a living connection between Catholics today and countless ones in the past. Nam-myoho-renge-kyo "is very powerful, very strong. How many billions of times has this been recited over time? There is an energy in that, just as in music. Something immaterial is present, which can bring you to tears, make you very happy. It can make you believe again in being human." A roomful of Gakkai members chanting is a transcendental experience, he tells me, likening it to an orchestra—each person a different instrument in a symphony, each reaffirming what they believe in, all of them connecting to one another in a single rhythm, revealing together a higher, abstract plan or the collective feeling of humanity today.

The populist tone of BSGI becomes more apparent to me that night when I visit a member's house to attend a shakubuku meeting that is part neighborhood social, part church meeting.[11] The ground-floor living room has been cleared to make room for long rows of plastic lawn chairs set facing the gohonzon. A crowd of about a hundred, thirty-eight of them guests, overflows into a rear garden and onto the front street, a welcome relief on a hot and humid night. Ten or so people are elderly, but many are in their thirties, among them lots of moms and dads with infants and kids.

In most respects, the setting could be Japan. Chanting is followed by *relatos*—members recounting their experiences—and educating one another about aspects of Nichiren's philosophy. Members of the local Youth Division, however, entertain with Brazilian pop tunes. Umbanda, a form of Afro-Caribbean spiritism, and Roman Catholicism factor into people's stories of their spiritual journeys. Buddhism teaches that religion shapes the environment, the Japanese Brazilian leader, Ieyasu Hase, notes in his brief teaching; the object you worship is what you become. He uses a familiar biblical illustration to make his point: "If I worship the golden calf, my life cannot become more than that. When I worship the gohonzon, however, my life can change because I have the benefit of the life force of the universe."

A Japanese-Brazilian fusion is more apparent the next morning, a quiet Sunday, when we drive across São Paulo to a south-side culture center to take part in a Youth Division celebration. They are commemorating Kosen-rufu Day, the day that Toda, in the final month of his life, seated on his palanquin on the grounds of Taisekiji, passed the baton to Gakkai youth.[12] It is also the fourth anniversary of the opening of the sleek new center, so it is a particularly festive occasion with some three hundred people attending, some black, some brown, others Japanese or Caucasian or mixes I can't identify.

In addition to chanting and relatos, the event is a kind of multiethnic mini–culture festival—older Japanese Brazilian women in kimonos doing folkloric dances with fans, a jazz combo playing "Século de Paz" (Age of Peace) and "Garota de Ipanema" (Girl from Ipanema). Nova Era Kotekitai, the girls' fife-and-drum corps, performs "Saudações a Sensei" (Greeting to Teacher), a BSGI standard. I don't speak Portuguese but know enough Spanish to catch the drift—"We receive you, we embrace you / We are happy in this age of mappo / Many thanks, teacher / We offer you these flowers with love." The wonder of this zuiho-bini success story is driven home when a multiethnic group of young women performs an interpretive dance based on the ten worlds, the philosophical framework of Nichiren practice that has its roots in ancient China.

Afterward, I chat with a group of young people in a comfortable, somewhat Japanese-Gakkai–looking reception room—spare, modern, and businesslike, with no religious adornments. Playing the now-familiar role of visiting scholar, I take the opportunity to gauge the degree to which the Gakkai experience in Japan lives in the imagination of young Brazilians.

"I am curious to know what, if anything, the phrase *Kansai spirit* means to you," I ask, referring to the triumph-over-all obstacles rallying cry that emerged in the course of the Osaka campaign of the 1950s. As enthusiastic as the young Singaporean Chinese I met in Singapore, they all have an opinion. One round-faced young brown girl offers, "It means all that human beings can achieve when they have a goal."

A burly black boy says, "It is the spirit of protecting people, of coming to the defense of sensei." It is the spirit of peace, I learn as we go from one to the next, of dedicating oneself to peace, of believing that there is hope in seeking world peace. The last one, a young woman I take to be Japanese Brazilian, recalls that "a few years ago, President Ikeda called Rio de Janeiro the Kansai of Brazil, because people in Rio are very persistent. Kansai spirit means perseverance."

That evening, after a full BSGI day, I want to experience São Paulo on foot, to absorb a sense of the chronic poverty apparent here in run-down shops and shabby apartment buildings, to escape for a moment the artificial needs of my thoroughly consumerist life in the States. But my translator, Sandra—a young Japanese Brazilian who has lived in both Tokyo and Los Angeles—tells me in no uncertain terms, "It's my job to keep an eye on you. Please don't leave the hotel. This is a very dangerous city."

How different to be in a world with highly tangible, desperate needs where kidnapping is an illicit growth industry, most victims returned quickly for cash. I explain to Sandra that, having just left the United States, where people now live with an unrealistic sense of imminent danger, I have a need not to be sequestered in the hotel. Eventually she relents but shepherds me to a bodega with tables on the street just a half-block from the hotel, where we enjoy the night air in safety.

Like many second-generation Gakkai, Sandra takes Buddhism for granted and seems immune to rhetoric about benefits and inner trans-formation. She chats instead about how Buddhism is used to discipline children in Gakkai families. "That action will bring consequence you'll regret, young woman," she says, teasingly paraphrasing her mother. "You don't want to do that! That cause is certain to have bad effects," as I picture a small, childish misdeed rippling throughout the universe with deep and dire consequences. She also regales me with stories of her experience with identity politics in Los Angeles. "People get the Japanese part. So they call me an Asia/Pacific Islander, as if I have something in common with people from Guam," she says with undisguised annoyance. "Or they get Brazil, but then they insist I am Latina. They just can't get Brazilian Japanese."

· · ·

As days in São Paulo unfold and I begin to dig into things Brazilian-Japanese, the diversity within King's world house begins to take on an unexpected meaning. My old take on pluralism was shaped by post–civil rights multiculturalism in the U.S. academy, a celebration of freedom and diversity that atrophied when ideologues took over and the whole thing went P.C. That culture-oriented view of planetary possibilities was supplanted by globalization conceived in terms of cheap labor and resources, universal consumerism, and high profits driven by visions of an unparalleled accumulation of wealth through the invisible hand of the market. As that view teetered and threatened to collapse, along came September 11, and a terror of terrorism took over, which now seems to dominate Americans' global thinking.

But here in Brazil I seem to have stepped across a geo-spiritual-political threshold to a place where September 11 doesn't count, where people say they are sorry about what happened but are focused on more immediate matters such as desperate poverty, crushing illiteracy, and creating a strong democracy. My sense of a new perspective owes a great deal to my being embedded once again in the Gakkai, a world of purpose, joy, and hope. It is also a world organized not around a Washington-London axis but around one that runs between São Paulo and Tokyo, a world that is not Anglo-American but Brazilian-Japanese or Japanese-Latin. And I find that I like it.

Eduardo Taguchi, BSGI's president, quite predictably attributes the unique spirit of the Brazilian Gakkai to Ikeda.[13] "I don't consciously try to carry on activities based on zuiho-bini," he tells me. "We have President Ikeda's guidelines. He is constantly urging us to be aware of the customs, traditions, culture, and people's hearts within each society where we practice. So zuiho-bini comes naturally."

When I ask him to describe how the Tokyo–São Paulo connection works, he sketches a collaborative relationship, with BSGI administratively and financially independent of Tokyo. Large-scale events such as traveling exhibits are funded, designed, and constructed in Japan but with room for local material, whether children's art from Brazilian schools or Amazon basin environmental issues. As he talks, I recall videos of the culture festival held to celebrate Ikeda's 1984 visit—the joyous energy of multiethnic Brazil, thousands dancing, their shouts of "Obrigado [thank you], sensei." "President Ikeda has said that Brazil is the farthest country from Japan, but is closest in terms of the heart," Taguchi says. "Members are very proud of the trust he shows our organization. They are struggling to make it the ideal he wants. We want to build the most friendly organization in the world, the most harmonious, where people can become happy."

The deeply personal nature of the bond between Japan and Brazil is revealed to me by Roberto Saito, the BSGI pioneer who, with his wife, Silvia, built the movement from the ground up back in the '60s.[14] Silvia died unexpectedly in 1993, an event that sent Roberto into a suicidal depression. She remains so powerful a presence that he circles and recircles her life in the course of our four-hour conversation, more than once bringing tears to my eyes as his admiration for his wife reminds me of my own for Ann. As he recounts their tale, I am struck by how zuiho-bini is less an abstract principle than a creative act at the point where two cultures meet in the life of a single disciple, in this case Silvia whose infusion of Japaneseness into Brazil was a passionate act all tied up with her love for Ikeda, her mentor.

I'm astonished by the personal details Saito shares with me—Silvia having been a youngest daughter, a pampered child, born Etsuko, whose mother taught her to love traditional dance, ikebana, the tea ceremony, and other refinements. He takes particular pleasure in talking of her "mystic" bond with Ikeda, whom she met when she was nineteen, when she was addressing envelopes during the Osaka campaign. It was only after Saito married Etsuko that he took Buddhism seriously, and it becomes apparent that his doting on her relationship with Ikeda is a key to his own spirituality. Each time I prompt him gently to talk about BSGI history, he assures me that each detail—the instant eye contact between Silvia and Ikeda when they met accidentally, how Ikeda prompted her to study *Gosho*, how she brought rice balls to him in prison and helped to care for young Hiromasa—is essential to understanding why she became a great Brazilian leader, a woman Ikeda praised at her death as "the mother of South American kosen-rufu." There is a Japanese expression, he tells me—"*ichigo ichie,* which means that one encounter can change everything. And for her, for Silvia Saito, that moment came when she and Ikeda met eye to eye; that moment changed her whole life."

After lunch, Saito returns with two photographs of Silvia that snap his story into perspective, two bookends of a life that epitomizes the fusion of Brazil and Japan. In the first, her wedding portrait, she is still Etsuko in Japan, twenty years old, clad in a kimono and *tsunokakushi,* the elaborate white hat worn in the wedding ceremony that is said to hide a woman's horns. This is the woman who packed up her life in a few weeks to take off with Roberto, then twenty-eight-year-old Yasuhiro, to propagate her mentor's Buddhism on the other side of the world. On arriving in Brazil, she began to shakubuku contract laborers on farms outside São Paulo, pregnant with their first child but riding long distances in beat-up trucks and slogging through torrential rains, shocked by the disheveled appearance, disheartened spirit, and poor living standards of Japanese immigrants. I now see what Saito wants me to see—Etsuko as a young woman infused with the Kansai spirit, charged up by the Osaka incident, full of love for her mentor, making it her business to enact a human revolution in Brazil. The second photo, a Polaroid snapshot he'd taken on their last vacation in Rio de Janeiro some thirty years later, was Brazilian Silvia—her hair cut short, wearing glasses, slacks, and sweater, the surf on Copacabana beach in the background.

Once I've comprehended Silvia's story, Saito can tell his own, sometimes harrowing one to me quickly, almost blasé about leading the movement under military dictatorship, about police interrogations when BSGI members were charged with being Castro sympathizers and terrorists. Saito recalls both DOPS and SNI, the Brazilian equivalents of the FBI and CIA, writing reports about BSGI that later became public. "I was so happy when I read them," he says in a rare moment in which he laughs openly. "They concluded that the Soka Gakkai was not a dangerous organization. That means they were really doing their research. We came out white—clean."

Many subsequent interviews focus on public service, BSGI's local work for global kosen-rufu, which Saito saw as the most important manifestation of the spirit of zuiho-bini. Flávio Fava de Moraes—former rector of São Paulo University and now executive director of SEADE, an office that does socioeconomic research for the state of São Paulo—is another friend of BSGI.[15] But unlike Vieira, he knows nothing about Buddhist spirituality: he is surprised to learn that members view their social programs as bodhisattva work. But he knows a great deal about BSGI's efforts as a nongovernmental organization (NGO) that works to strengthen Brazil's civil society.

The number of NGOs has skyrocketed in the past fifteen years, Moraes says, but many are *fantasmas,* ghost institutions that accomplish little and exist only on paper. In contrast, BSGI has a reputation for well-conceived projects and follow through, important qualities in a culture inclined to put things off *até amanhã,* until tomorrow. Moraes first came into contact with BSGI at the university, where many students, staff, and faculty are members. Its leaders often came to me for support, he recalls, "and to my wife too. She's always receiving calls—you must be there; you must be someplace; you must do this—she's not a member, but is happy to help." He tells me that BSGI consistently seeks out quality people, qualified people, to help direct their initiatives. In his opinion, it attracts people to Buddhism not because of its doctrine but by the example set by members who are always finding new ways to be socially engaged—conferences, programs for children, for the needy or the poor. I am astonished when Moraes suggests that BSGI must be among the top ten or twenty NGOs in Brazil.

I admire the way the Gakkai integrates itself into Brazilian culture in ways less overtly patriotic than the movement in the United States, a style that no doubt appeals because at the moment I'm wearied by America. Given my privileged indifference, I am surprised to find myself yearning to live in a society where "making a contribution" is not a vague abstraction but involves working with people who often must struggle to survive. The group conducts literacy campaigns, a pressing need in a country where an estimated one-third of its citizens, about 56 million people, are functionally illiterate. In response to a call for NGOs to address this public crisis, BSGI educators developed the Literacy Poles project for members whose inability to read, write, or do math adequately blocked their social and economic advancement. As of the year 2000, almost one thousand members had acquired the skills they needed to continue their education, compete more effectively in the job market, and function more effectively as responsible citizens.[16]

I am awestruck when I contemplate what Gakkai practice and culture mean for some of its Brazilian members. Masako Watanabe writes that after joining BSGI many learn for the first time to discipline themselves to be on time, to take on responsibility and fulfill expectations, and to internalize the patience they need to make these efforts consistent—all qualities tied up with a diligence that is very Japanese. Benefits from practice are inconspicuous but also highly tangible—improvements in speech, conduct, and grooming, all of which contribute to their sense of well-being, their happiness, and their upward mobility.[17]

But some BSGI projects are large-scale and dramatic, such as the Amazon Ecological Research Center (AERC) outside Manaus, which has pioneered reforestation, the creation of a regional seed bank, and experiments in sustainable agroforestry, in collaboration with the state of Amazonas and Soka University in Tokyo. Ikeda's 1992 essay, "A New Strategy for Environmental Protection," which he wrote in response to the Earth Summit in Rio de Janeiro that same year, serves as AERC's inspiration, as it does for what is reputed to be the first college-level Environmental Studies major in Brazil, in Timoteo in the state of Minas Gerais, which was started by a local BSGI leader.[18]

The showcase of BSGI's social action, however, is the Makiguchi Project in Action, a volunteer effort to revitalize education in public schools. It began in one classroom in one São Paulo school in 1994 but expanded to some fifty-five schools by the year 2000, aiding over a thousand teachers and enhancing the education of some thirty-four thousand students. The project was founded in response to two events: the translation of Makiguchi's pedagogy into Portuguese in 1994 and a new national educational initiative adopted in 1997, which called for strengthening Brazil's democracy through creativity in education. Volunteers from BSGI's Educators Division built a working relationship with federal, state, and municipal authorities to implement the project and fostered collaborations among school principals, teachers, families, and students to bring it to fruition.

Dilma de Melo Silva, a professor of Brazilian studies at São Paulo University and yet another friend of the Gakkai, discovered BSGI at a children's art exhibit sent from Tokyo to Brazil.[19] As she describes it, the pedagogy at the heart of the Makiguchi Project is elegant in its simplicity. It begins with creating an inviting classroom for students who often come from tough neighborhoods and poor families—clean, well ordered, a few flowers for decoration, a little snack. "These small details make a difference," she tells me. Lesson plans are designed to engage students in playful activities that also support interdisciplinary learning. A vegetable garden project, for instance, becomes an opportunity to learn about space and planning, ecology, teamwork, responsibility, nutrition, and health. An origami or gift-wrapping workshop is a vehicle for learning about geometry, mathematics, shapes, proportion, color, and aesthetics.

The underlying point, however, is to foster an awareness in students that learning is an enjoyable, continuous, internal process of engaging in life with others, be they friends, parents, or the larger community. Parental involvement has been one key to its success. Another has been raising the self-esteem of chronically underpaid, often beleaguered teachers. A decisive factor in its success is, however, the diligence of the some five hundred BSGI volunteers who administer the project, run pedagogical workshops, and aid public-school teachers.

I get a glimpse of BSGI's educators in action during a visit with Dirce Ivamoto, an older Japanese Brazilian who bristles with energy as she describes her experience with Makiguchi's pedagogy, while we tour the new Soka Kindergarten.[20] Having spent thirty-five years in the public schools, Ivamoto has firsthand knowledge of teachers' problems—low pay, poor facilities, large classes, broken families, poverty, violence, and drugs. As we stroll through the modern, somewhat spartan facility, Ivamoto talks of Makiguchi's philosophy but without tying it to Buddhism, seeing it as separable and independent from religion.

Even so, an understated, implicit spiritual dimension is clear in Ivamoto's commitment to education. She speaks of the cultivation of "a loving triangle" among students, parents, and teachers as being at the heart of the Soka education. When I ask about obstacles the project encounters—institutional inertia, bureaucratic hurdles, and the like—she admits they are formidable but whisks them away with the strength of her faith, which clearly owes much to Ikeda, whom she views as her mentor. "Dialogue solves many things, many problems," she tells me briskly; "there is resistance, but goodness wins." Ivamoto recalls her visit with Ikeda in Japan last year, noting, "The guidelines he gave us . . . well, he defined the dream this way—honesty; the dignity of children; make students happy when they study. Those are the main points." As she describes the Makiguchi Project spreading from one to fifty schools by "life-to-life contact," with no state funding and little institutional apparatus, I hear in her voice the determination of the shakubuku spirit and her assurance of the ultimate irresistibility of the kosen-rufu movement.

After our conversation, while stuck in unbelievable traffic by torrential rains that frequently immobilize the city, I ponder zuiho-bini, how Buddhist Humanism relates to Japaneseness, and how both work together in Brazil. It's hard not to see Japanese aesthetic concerns in origami and gift-wrapping workshops and in the attention to detail when creating an inviting classroom environment. The particular quality of BSGI's diligent energy—not really laid back, despite claims about the Gakkai mellowing in Brazil—seems also very Japanese. More concretely, I'm certain I see a familiar strategic and pragmatic intelligence at work in how the Gakkai views needs in Brazilian society as windows of opportunity: occasions to practice faith, strengthen democracy, better the world, advance kosen-rufu, and promote BSGI at the same time. This strikes me as a new twist on acting locally and thinking globally and a seamless approach to propagating what Ikeda teaches is the essence of Nichiren's Buddhism.

It also occurs to me that putting a good cause into effect may work like God helping those who help themselves. Ikeda writes a book that finds its way into Vieira's hands, which results in his touring Japan for Min-On. Gakkai professors seek support from the university rector, with the effect that the BSGI gets high scores as an NGO from Moraes.

Silva attends an exhibit sponsored by SGI, which leads her to support the Makiguchi Project.

Taken by the image of an endless cascade of good causes leading to good effects, I too might be persuaded of the irresistibility of global kosen-rufu but for my professional skepticism. More immediately wonderful to me is that these ripples radiate out from Japan to Brazil and then across the planet—a refreshing and hopeful new angle on what it means to live in our great world house.

. . .

On the short flight from São Paulo to Rio de Janeiro, I find my having likened cause and effect to Providence is more on the mark than I knew, when I skim Peter Clarke's "Buddhist Humanism and Catholic Culture in Brazil."[21] While the plane follows the Atlantic coast, passing over towns hemmed in by jungle and beaches, I'm struck again by the subtleties of zuiho-bini. Clarke writes that BSGI neither affirms nor denies monotheism but teaches that a Buddhist notion of God is expressed in Nam-myoho-renge-kyo, which is the power of awakening and the life force in the universe. This blunts the charge of atheism in a culture where theism is ubiquitous, whether in Catholicism or Afro-Brazilian Candomblé, while bringing Nichiren's first secret law into play with a profound, yet familiar, idea. Clarke's observation that traditional Christian belief in God threatens to undermine "the fundamental Nichiren Buddhist principle of self-responsibility" also rings true.[22] It echoes comments I heard from seasoned São Paulo Gakkai practitioners about new members, often steeped in Latin Catholic fatalism, who must learn to discipline themselves to look within, not without, to inner self, not transcendent deity, for the source of empowerment and transformation.

Our descent takes us inland over Ipanema and Copacabana beaches on a course between Sugarloaf and Guanabara Bay on one side, and Corcovado Mountain on the other with its soaring Cristo, his outstretched arms signaling our welcome in Rio. I'm soon wondering whether there might not be something to the Gakkai having mellowed in Brazil—at least here in this city a short hop but a world away from São Paulo, which is intense with hustle, bustle, and business. Here I begin research by chatting with local leaders over lunch with views of Sugarloaf and the bay. Then I'm checked into a hotel on Copacabana beach with time for a quick swim before touring the city, after which my schedule reads "relaxation and dinner." It may be that I am too easily swayed by the Carioca mystique, but the pace of the Rio BSGI seems geared to cool drinks and ocean breezes.

The working portion of the trip opens in a congenial way the next day with an amusing conversation with Cicero Sandroni, yet another influential friend of BSGI, in his home in one of Rio's many canyons.[23] Sandroni and his wife write, she children's literature, he fiction and biography; but our conversation revolves around his father-in-law, Austregésilo de Athayde—a renowned activist who for years opposed Brazil's dictatorship and helped to write the U.N.'s Universal Declaration of Human Rights—and his relationship with Ikeda.

Sandroni describes Athayde as taking to Ikeda immediately during his 1993 visit to Brazil, when they conducted a dialogue subsequently published under the title *Human Rights in the Twenty-first Century*. President of the Brazilian Academy of Letters, Athayde also sponsored Ikeda's election to one of twenty chairs reserved for corresponding members, which Sandroni recalls as having been a campaign of sorts because Ikeda was not well known in Brazil. Ikeda's books were distributed to academy members by BSGI, and Athayde himself lobbied each of them, persuading them to see in this unknown Japanese Buddhist a great humanitarian leader.

A cultured man in his sixties, Sandroni talks easily about topics from Catholic liberation theology to the reforming pharaoh Akhenaton, about whom he is currently writing a book for juveniles, and he readily admits to his own misconceptions about Buddhism. "I thought Dr. Ikeda would be one of these mystical men with a long beard and very thin, with deep eyes. When I first saw him here in Brazil, I thought he was a sympathetic man, but a little fat and—well, I was disappointed." Later, meeting him again in Japan after Athayde's death, he discovered Ikeda to be a man of wit, a spiritual leader by virtue of his intelligence and heart, not his appearance.

The next few days are productive but roll by at a lovely pace, the romance of Rio seemingly always present. I spend an entire morning with attractive, intelligent kids, white, black, brown, some poor, others rich. They talk of how the Gakkai links them together across class lines and enables them to work with different people, a middle-class kid from a well-educated family, for instance, learning to take guidance from an illiterate leader, and vice versa.

One afternoon I hear about volunteer work done by Gakkai professionals in the favelas—health care, literacy education, community organizing—some in BSGI communities, some not.

One memorable evening I sit in the dark under trees at the local center in Botafogo, one of Rio's charming older neighborhoods, engaged in a heady conversation with two high-powered women, a physician and a businesswoman, whose experiences with BSGI speak to the kind of struggles I have faced since Ann's death. For them, the practice of Buddhism is about finding existential meaning, not about boot strapping. Afterward, conversation rolls on over late-night drinks in a Botafogo watering hole with a German expatriate, her artist boyfriend, and a Brazilian man of about forty who lives in a beach community to the south but works in Rio real estate. Our discussion runs from Nam-myoho-renge-kyo as a source of creativity to Rio de Janeiro as a world-class real estate market, a place favored by Saudi princes and magnates.

At headquarters the next morning, however, I must make a gentle complaint to Júlio Kosaka, the soft-spoken Japanese Brazilian who has led the Rio organization for many years. "I'm meeting wonderful people who tell me great things about how BSGI has had great success recruiting the poor and the sick, just like in Japan when Toda was president after the war," I say, talking through Sandra because I speak no Portuguese and Júlio no English. "But I am not meeting any of them. I can't go back to the States without seeing the Gakkai in the favelas."

Despite protests about my safety, I know they will set wheels in motion—meeting needs, I've learned, is a Gakkai thing to do, whether in Japan or Brazil while I'm off interviewing Magdalena Landi, the "shakubuku queen of Copacabana."[24] A BSGI member for almost thirty years and a widow for three, Landi is an old-school Gakkai member in her sixties who is hard not to see as a Buddhist Carmen Miranda—dramatically expressive face, dark eyes that shift and flash with each syllable she speaks, hands that rarely rest. We talk together in a large gohonzon room used by area members in her modest walk-up apartment, where we sit before an immense, closed altar. The story she tells is as expansive as her personality, which means that precisely how chanting resolved a bankruptcy and healed a gangrenous leg is never crystal clear to me.

Landi, however, draws an indelible portrait of herself during her heyday as shakubuku queen—at work in her dress shop, healing leg propped up on a cushion, the other pedaling her sewing machine, all the while preaching the mystic law to anyone who came into the shop. She explains that shakubukuing someone is not simply a question of showing them that practice works. It is feeling compassion for what they are going through. It is being connected to Ikeda's heart and bringing it to them. After selling her shop, she found that shakubuku "has no hours, no days, no places. It doesn't matter if a person is black, white, yellow or rich or poor, ugly or beautiful, because everybody has Buddhahood in their hearts." She quickly describes her technique, whether used on the bus or on a bench in the park. "You might be talking about the weather. It's hot; it's cold. The sky is pretty. Eventually you ask, 'Are you happy?' And if the person says, 'No, I'm not,' then you say, 'I'll show you how to become happy.' If they answer, 'Yes, I'm happy,' then you say, 'I know a way you can be even happier.'"

Landi's expression shifts from light to dark and back as she speaks, like clouds in rapidly changing weather, but then she turns thoughtfully rapturous, hand clasped on her breast. "People say to me, 'Oh, dona Magdalena, aren't you sad living alone, all by yourself?' But I tell them I am living with the gohonzon. It is my happiness and my biggest treasure."

Later that same day arrangements have been made to see new-school Gakkai—Nam-myoho-renge-kyo in a socially engaged mode—so we head north from the central city, with its spectacular views of the sea, winding boulevards, and inviting promenades, through a graceless metro sprawl to Caju, an industrial district near the port of Rio. We find our way to a battered state hospital, where off a rear parking lot, through an opening in a graffiti-scrawled wall, we come upon Fabrica de Sonhos, the Dream Factory, where we spend the afternoon with Telma Lúcia Ferreira Moreira Martins, a slight, energetic *morena* of about fifty.[25]

Martins has practiced for thirteen years, having studied to become a Presbyterian minister until she discovered daimoku at a funeral for a young Caju boy, Fabio, a friend of her children, who died saving his brother's life. "They were chanting Nam-myoho-renge-kyo and there was something I felt, like a wave sound or something I can't explain, but it really shook me up. They were all very calm and, anyway, then I started practicing with them. I learned how to chant and to do gongyo with drums. I consider myself as being Fabio's shakubuku." When I ask her about the Presbyterian church, she says, "I just turned the page on that." Her husband and three children are now all Buddhist.

Fabrica de Sonhos (FASO) is a circus school for kids in the surrounding favelas. It sits on a steep hillside plot with views onto the kind of crowded, chock-a-block slums I'd seen from the plane, which was donated to the project by the hospital. Martins started it in 1993 with nineteen students but it now has four hundred. Mostly they come from one of nine nearby neighborhoods where poverty, hopelessness, drugs, and gang violence are rampant, a war zone in which FASO is what she calls "a safe haven" and "oasis," understood by gangs to be strictly off limits. We talk in FASO's main building, a cluster of squat, concrete-domed structures they built in 1997, roughly finished but clean and airy, with windows opening out to views of the city. A group of students work on art projects in one corner, while others mill about and Bruno, Martins's son who is in his twenties, pops in and out, adding bits to our conversation, while constantly talking on his cell phone.

"In Buddhism we say that no prayer goes unanswered," Martins says, a faith that sustains her every day, although it is clear that she is also a pragmatist with plenty of institutional savvy. The Fabrica was among forty-nine projects subsidized by the Inter-American Development Bank. It made a first cut to be among twenty-two finalists and was eventually chosen as one of two model projects for Brazil, recognized for its success in drug prevention and human development. Still, Martins sees FASO not as an institution but as a family (no one is allowed to curse on the grounds), where the benefits of chanting are manifest daily—as when Petrobras, Brazil's oil giant, became a FASO sponsor after a long funding drought during which thirty staff members worked for six months with no pay.

Martins explains the Fabrica's objectives as we tour the site—concrete slabs set into the hillside that support large red-and-blue circus tents housing wrestling mats, trampolines, and high-wire apparatus. "Kosen-rufu is not about propagating Nam-myoho-renge-kyo but about propagating humanism," she tells me, noting that sometimes kids and even their parents join her in chanting when they visit her at home, although she exerts no pressure on them and none have become BSGI members. Her main goal is to foster self-esteem and self-discipline in kids who otherwise tend to lead aimless lives, to encourage them to see themselves as capable people and valuable citizens.

As we talk, three young girls take turns practicing back flips and handstands, seemingly oblivious to visitors so intense is their concentration and discipline, while a young man walks the high wire, a long balance pole in hand. *It's a permanent culture festival,* I think, recalling Masako Watanabe's observation that the Gakkai teaches people to internalize patience and improve their carriage and comportment. These inner accomplishments notwithstanding, Martins also takes pride in the fact that a few students have budding professional lives that have grown out of their FASO training. Some have worked in local video productions, and several others have permanent positions in European circuses.

One such is Washington, a tall black juggler whom I meet briefly; he now lives in Europe, where he is a performer in Fantasyland, a German circus that recently toured Turkey. "The key word in Buddhist Humanism is *solidarity*," Martins says, her parting words as I leave, "for people to feel they are not alone but belong to a bigger collectivity. Humanism means not being selfish but being able to stand up when you see somebody who is really suffering and to be able to care about that person."

One night we drive past refineries and oil-related industrial plants over to Duque de Caxias, another tough area to the north of Rio, to attend a local meeting, a second last-minute addition to my schedule. We park in a poorly lit downtown center, its open-air stalls closed for the day, a few neon lights and music signaling a bar in the distance. Soon Marcio, a local group leader, appears on the darkened street to lead us to the area kaikan, which he says we could never find on our own.

Our van is soon lurching up steep unpaved streets wet and rutted from an afternoon rain, making turn after turn, passing walled yards and houses with steel garage doors pulled down over windows, the dank darkness unbroken by street lamps, lit only by the jostle of our headlights and the blue glow of an occasional TV. I remind myself that such favelas—however desperate-appearing and dangerous, no matter how bad the water, plumbing, and electricity—are the homes of people who struggle to raise kids and make ends meet, real communities under siege by a raft of urban dysfunctions. But I cannot help but be excited because this is a real frontier for me, a foray into a desolate, oftentimes desperate corner of the world house I would not have seen but for BSGI, a far cry from Shinanomachi, central Singapore, or Santa Monica, California.

Eventually we stop on a straightaway near the top of a substantial hill where the community center is located, leaving our vehicles to step gingerly through muck. We have arrived late and can hear the Japanese phonemes used to recite the Lotus Sutra—*Niji seson. Ju sanmai. Anjo ni ki Go sharihotsu*—from far down the street, favela dwellers recalling Shakyamuni on Eagle Peak just as he arises out of a deep trance to teach his wisdom to the world.[26]

Inside the kaikan it is very bright, some sixty people seeming to radiate both energy and light, some singles, others complete families, most of them black. They chant in a way identical to that of Gakkai members in Tokyo, Singapore, and Los Angeles, and I am struck by the fact that soulful variations and samba rhythms are not fair game for zuiho-bini as far as chant style is concerned. The format of the proceedings is identical too—chanting, relatos, teachings, inspiring entertainment—and for the first time I see clearly that Gakkai meetings are formal liturgies, no matter how lively and warmhearted.

But people's experiences fully reflect their cultural surroundings—stories about struggle with gangs, about putting drugs behind them, about finding a happiness they did not have the way they were raised, Catholicism too much a part of the woodwork of their lives to make much of a difference. Throughout the evening, a translator gives me a running commentary on calls to realize world peace, exhortations to victory, and poems about the spirit of Brazil while I take in details—a few neon decorations around the altar, a reproduction of Makiguchi Hall pinned to the wall, a portrait of Ikeda.

During refreshments after the formal part of the meeting, there is so much spirited conversation, with kids running to and fro and people spilling out onto the streets, that I can't gather much information. One older woman, a public-school principal, tells me about her problems with students as we drink punch and eat cookies, the two of us soon exchanging our impressions of the Makiguchi Project, which she hopes to start in her school. After we talk, I watch her tiptoe off, high heels sinking into the mud in the streets, toward her home in the darkened neighborhood. A man about forty stops to introduce his five children—three boys, two girls, all of them seeming to be between four and eleven—saying that he and his wife once lived in New York too. Some people give me small, very neatly wrapped gifts—a pen that says "Welcome to Brazil" on it, a small pin from BSGI, four postcards with views of Rio—a bit of the gift giving and receiving maybe learned from Japan.

Shortly thereafter we depart, lurching around in the van once again as we bounce back down the hill through drizzly, dismal streets, none of us talking but sharing, I think, a sense of well-being, having experienced the Gakkai functioning as an anchor for a troubled but vibrant community.

Early the next morning, Rob and I fly back to the States.

CHAPTER 9

Intrepid Navigators

Back on the ground in Miami, Rob and I plan to spend a day and a night gently decompressing from the purposeful intensity of the Gakkai in Brazil. But American TV is in our face before we've exited the airport, shrill sales pitches and droning debates about our homeland and its defense, paced to fill half a dozen news channels 24-7.

We go to take a look at the city, but deco-slick South Beach and the many lush, causeway-linked islands and marinas give both of us headaches.

So we are soon holed up in a hotel away from downtown, a Comfort or Ramada Inn near the airport whose pool and spa, however middle-class average and nondescript, seem unnecessarily posh. Poolside, I try to re-experience the feelings called up by the Gakkai in Caju and Duque de Caxias, but I am unsuccessful.

.   .   .

It's only back in the quiet shabbiness of central New York, while ordering BSGI notes and mementos on bookshelves in my basement, tucking them away among the gifts, books, articles, and notebooks I've collected in Singapore and Japan, in Tucson and Southern California, that I begin to put Brazil into perspective. What most powerfully links Brazil to all my other Gakkai experiences is the people: the Saitos, Telmas, Sandras, and Magdalena Landis I've met on three continents, whether pining for a lost wife, dedicated to social transformation, droll and ironic, or delightfully overdramatic, all of them modern lions of Nichiren each in their own way.

One Japanese Brazilian couple—married I think but I never knew for sure, whose names I cannot now remember—comes back to me to epitomize Gakkai spirituality in its valiantly mystical mode. In São Paulo they turned up repeatedly, silently but pleasantly looking on at the culture center where I interviewed young people; following us in their car to the university where I talked about the Makiguchi Project in Action with Dilma de Melo Silva. Eventually I asked Sandra to introduce us and, when I learned that they were rank-and-file members who simply had an interest in my work, I found time in the schedule to sit with them and chat.

I can still see Sandra, always a bit puzzled by my interest in how people imagine their inner life, roll her eyes when I asked her to inquire if they think of themselves as bodhisattvas arising from the earth. "Yes, they do," she told me, looking a bit surprised. "What does that mean?" I asked, to which the woman replied, "To work ceaselessly for global kosen-rufu," the man nodding his head in agreement. When I asked whether they believe in reincarnation, a notion by no means required of Gakkai members, they both nodded again, the man saying that they knew themselves to be coming back time and again, always to serve and to teach suffering people.

Such pristine piety is encouraged but not universally expected of Gakkai members, whose dedication, like that of Christians and Jews, runs the gamut from deeply committed to barely. Something more than 20 percent of members, I've heard it said, can be expected to show up for just about everything. Another 65 percent or so are consistent but average in their participation. Somewhere around 10 percent can't be bothered, ever. There are Gakkai Buddhists who primarily serve on boards, some who cook meals for get-togethers, others who drive young members here and there or visit shut-ins. There are many who are highly active in one or another Gakkai cause or organization, deeply committed to a peace group or to a musical ensemble, and others who attend only monthly meetings.

In other words, the Soka Gakkai is filled with members much like other religious people, their everydayness recalling to me the sameness/difference equation I began with, some two years in the past. "How much work!" I mutter aloud, as I make my way up the basement steps and into my study, where I am beginning to arrange mementos of my travels I may need to buoy me up during what I know will be a grueling stint of work. Such a steep learning curve to tread since that first Tokyo trip—Meiji Restoration; Japanese militarism; Japan's defeat, occupation, and phoenixlike rise—all to understand Ikeda and the Gakkai, only to come face-to-face with that familial resemblance which is the basis of all universal humanisms, Nichiren Buddhist or not.

This conviction of the Gakkai's sameness, however, only serves to remind me of how remote Japan once seemed, how much a scrim of romance and spiritual yearning, ignorance and phobia—all the Japan-envy and Japan-bashing in American culture—had made it hard for me to see clearly. How much more deeply I see into myself now, having shed a few distortions and illusions as I negotiated my own East-West encounter! How much more sense I can make now of a Japanese Buddhist Socrates, Hugo, Whitman, or Curie! How different Ikeda and the Gakkai look now than when I first posed questions to myself, mumbling aloud on a cold, gray, snowy morning among cherry blossoms in the garden of the Hotel New Otani!

For one, I now see historical and philosophical layers in the answer to the question of how SGI-USA can represent values typically American but also Buddhist and Japanese. As I think about the question now, it seems obvious that much of it goes back to Makiguchi and the liberal foundation of his modern-ancient, Western-Eastern, secular-Buddhist hybrid philosophy. But Toda clearly factors into it as well, with his regard for MacArthur and his seizing upon the American occupation as an opportunity for all sorts of freedoms. Ikeda the globalizer, of course, also has had a very big hand in it, with his liberalizing leadership and his championing of zuiho-bini. The work of the three presidents, however, would have meant little without bold members, those Caucasian, Japanese American, and African American GIs and their wartime brides who pioneered the movement in the United States, and then the people who made America's rainbow coalition ideal a Buddhist reality in the '60s and '70s.

I can also better grasp the movement's appeal for people in countries overseas. A knack for infusing the spirit of other cultures with a dose of Japaneseness—that diligence, a freshness in the nation's encounter with modernity, a Buddhist sense of mission, I'm still not sure just what—stands behind the Gakkai's success at globalization. Buddhism of all sorts is found almost everywhere today, but few groups equal the Gakkai in either its programmatic effort to adapt to new situations or its genius for organization. Despite its long alliance with priests, the Gakkai has been a lay group since its founding, always oriented to a shifting landscape of social realities that challenge ordinary people. Created in tandem with the rise of the Japanese middle class, unencumbered by the institutions and traditions of Buddhist monasticism, the Gakkai has a natural affinity for the needs and aspirations of regular working people in nations around the world.

Having had to wrestle my way through a difficult couple of years, struggling with loneliness, doubting my own ability to proceed in life, wondering often why I should even bother, I keenly appreciate a key element in the Gakkai's appeal—its teaching the empowerment of self and other to achieve happiness, a modernist spin on both Nichiren's three secret laws and the work of the bodhisattva. If one equates the dharma with quiet contemplation, it is easy to underestimate the energizing power of daimoku and gohonzon, the former the performance of Buddha nature, the latter its graphic representation, the two mirroring in each other what Buddhists understand to be a liberating power inherent in the fabric of the universe.

To grasp the Gakkai's appeal, one also needs to take seriously the third secret law—kaidan as place of practice. Home, school, zadankai, culture center, culture festival, symphony rehearsal, or meeting of professionals, whether physicians and lawyers or barbers and beauticians, are all opportunities for empowering practice. The power generated by this practice has been put to many ends in the history of the Gakkai, from resisting state tyranny under Makiguchi to Toda's high-energy campaigns of mass democratization. It is no wonder that some observers continue to find the movement both threatening and controversial.

It has been Ikeda's unique accomplishment to have globalized the Soka Gakkai and harnessed its energy to goals that suited new generations in different cultures, while maintaining its socially engaged and essentially political orientation. In Japan, Gakkai political activity is overt and has been expressed in electoral politics for decades in a way that it is not overseas, where the movement typically works to empower individuals and to foster peace, cultural, and educational activities, programs that tend to be uncontroversial and apolitical. And yet, something as apparently innocuous as peace work has taken on a political edginess since September 11, 2001—a reminder that the reality-transformative Buddhism Toda created in the wake of the war gives private aspiration and personal need a collective, social dimension that, under the right circumstances, cannot help but be political.

How the human revolution taught by Toda and after him by Ikeda will fare in the future is impossible to predict. But there are two challenges, one conjectural, the other inescapable, that the Gakkai may soon face, in which case the movement will have little choice but to reinvent itself again.

The first is tied to ongoing debates over the status of Japan's military and, more particularly, over Article Nine of its postwar constitution, which renounces war and the use of force in the settlement of international disputes. Since World War II, Japan's peace constitution has been a cornerstone of the nation's identity, the ideals of its people, and, more to the point here, the platform of the Soka Gakkai and its members. Throughout its history, the Gakkai has taken shape in response to developments in Japan's mainstream, at times resisting and at others embracing them. Should Japan repeal Article Nine or in some other way overtly recant its pacifist position, the impact on Gakkai institutions could be immense, most particularly on the Komeito party, which, while not a formal affiliate, continues to draw the bulk of its support from members. War and peace, arms and nonviolence can be reconciled to each other in many ways, but debates within Soka Gakkai–Japan over if and how to do so would have a major impact on the tenor and direction of the movement, both at home and overseas.

The second, more certain challenge is tied up with succession. Moving now into his late '70s, Ikeda has so defined the Gakkai's character and is so beloved by his disciples that his eventual passing has the potential to precipitate a major crisis. Unlike Makiguchi and Toda, Ikeda has no heir apparent to succeed him, which seems not to have been an accident but part of his effort to wean the organization off its dependence on charismatic leaders. According to President Akiya and others, discussions are under way about how best to institutionalize the philosophy and spirit embodied in the Gakkai's three presidents in a decentralized democracy or a consensus-oriented bureaucratic administration.

Any such development will require that the bond between mentor and disciple be recast insofar as the charisma of the presidents will be embodied in an institution, not a living representative. Such a shift, however daunting or traumatic it may be for disciples, is frequently made in the history of religion; this type of transition is almost a prerequisite for a movement if it is to ensure its continued existence. But one wonders how the Gakkai, both in the Japanese center and in the many movements on the overseas periphery, will proceed without Ikeda's personal touch and the warm affective bonds that tether him to his disciples and they to one another. On one hand, it is not clear that overseas members have the discipline to remain moored, however loosely, to Japan without Ikeda at the helm. On the other, Japanese leaders may not have the insight and savvy to negotiate the many cross-cultural shoals within Soka Gakkai International.

Though an outsider, I think I can see how each group needs and complements the other—large, powerful SG–Japan is both origin of and anchor for the globalizing movements; the smaller overseas movements are a source of the fresh inspiration that Ikeda has always sought to counterbalance Japan's strong parochial tendencies. To my mind, each group would become far less without all the others. Should members themselves decide this is the case, they will have to find ways to love Ikeda, once he is gone, by loving to develop his legacy, a major part of which is a globalizing and universalizing movement with currents that run deep—from Ikeda back through Toda and Makiguchi, through a long Nichiren tradition to the prophet himself, through China to ancient India and Shakyamuni. One hopes that these resources are sufficiently ample to keep a global alliance of Buddhist organizations lively, healthy, and happy enough to be able to work together for the greater good they see in the kosen-rufu movement.

My goal here has been to create an informed impression of Daisaku Ikeda as leader, president, and teacher and to explore the nature of some of the controversies that have surrounded the Gakkai since Makiguchi first refused to accept a talisman from the Ise shrine. By and large, the Gakkai's reputation as an overzealous, militant movement, deserved or not, is a thing of the past, although now and again the old skewed view of both it and Ikeda resurfaces. Consider this odd contrast.

On the second anniversary of September 11, Ikeda wrote for the editorial pages of the *Japan Times*, a highly respectable venue, reiterating his position that multilateralism and heart-to-heart understanding among people around the world are the only ways to build a stable, peaceful global society.[1] Quoting one of his dialogue partners, Iranian-born peace scholar Majid Tehranian, he called for us to step out of our isolation: "Without dialogue, we will have to walk in the darkness of our self-righteousness." The events of September 11 have made it imperative that we "look beyond questions of 'friend' or 'foe' and . . . learn to speak from the common ground of our shared humanity," Ikeda wrote. "Buddhism stresses that since war and violence are ultimately products of the human heart, the human heart is also capable of fostering peace and solidarity."

Just a year later, however, in September 2004, Ikeda was charged with being a self-aggrandizing, sometimes messianic empire builder in *Forbes* magazine of all places, in an article that knitted together old rumors, out-of-context quotes, and sinister allegations to attack tax exemptions for nonprofits, the case in point being the Soka Gakkai and Soka University of America.[2] President Akiya wrote to *Forbes*'s editors to point out the article's many inaccuracies—members do not tithe, Ikeda does not dictate policy, Tokyo courts had ruled years ago that the cited allegations were both unfounded and defamatory, and so on— charging in turn that the tax issue angle was a mere pretext for attacking the Gakkai.[3] Such an attack, however, may have been quite aside from the point of the article. In it Ikeda and the Gakkai function as symbols, scary because alien, powerful, and Japanese—*spooky* was editor William Baldwin's word—useful in riveting readers' attention to controversial tax-code issues, while standing so far beyond the ken of most American readers as to threaten no vested interests.

It would take a skilled Japanologist with the patience of Job and the instincts of a detective to sort through fact and fiction in the image of Ikeda and the ways both he and the Soka Gakkai are used in political discourse—a worthwhile, if daunting, endeavor. There are many other, more normative Gakkai-related topics that ought to be of interest to Japan-oriented historians of religion. One might look into Makiguchi's later years, for instance, as the State Shinto regime increasingly tightened its grip on the Japanese people. In Gakkai circles in Japan, Makiguchi is often portrayed as working with an increased urgency to take his religious resistance to the grass roots, to reach out beyond educators to the urban dispossessed and others, but I have not seen a sustained discussion of such episodes in scholarship in English.

Attention might also be given to Toda's amazing career, most especially to the postwar years and his attitudes toward MacArthur, the occupation, the new constitution, and the United States in general. The United States was, after all, not only responsible for Japan's new government but also for the use of atomic weapons at Nagasaki and Hiroshima, events that have given both America and Japan a singular status among the nations of the world. Much of Japan's modern history can be conceived in terms of a highly complex dialogue between it and the United States, a mutual exchange that was uniquely intense during the American occupation, the impact of which on Toda has yet to be explored.

An important religious figure, Ikeda deserves to have more serious scholarly attention devoted to his life and his work. One might explore his relationships with high priests or his doctrinal innovations, for instance, or his response to cultural change in Japan in the '60s and to being vilified in the press. For those with an interest in modern Asia,

Ikeda's longtime bridge building in northeast and south Asia and more recently in the Middle East should shed a new and interesting light on pan-Asian networking. Comparative work on Ikeda's Buddhist Humanism also needs to be done in order to understand the Gakkai's Nichiren-based spirituality alongside other expressions of Asia-based movements of modernist Buddhism.

My own hope is that scholars trained to think systematically about Japan will take up the question of how Japaneseness is manifest in the movement in both positive and negative ways. It is clear to me that its character—its intricate organization, idealism and intensity, preoccupation both with a charismatic mentor and with consensus among members, the discipline of disciples at home and overseas—owes a great deal to how groups get put together in Japan. At a time in which commentators routinely and far too easily equate globalization with Americanization, I found it inspiring and refreshing to wonder about Japanization as a productive spiritual, aesthetic, and social force in the contemporary world. It is a rich Buddhist topic—one not limited to the Soka Gakkai but extending to other forms of Japanese Buddhism, most especially Zen—that needs to be developed more deeply by Japanologists, who have the expertise to drive such questions home in a way I cannot.

Whatever topic one might pursue, however, I think it is time to dispense with at least one red herring that frequently is encountered when thinking about the Soka Gakkai. As we have all learned here in the United States, the relationship between church and state, between religion and politics, is hardly a simple matter of maintaining a stout wall of separation. That religions and religious people in this country have been and are still political no longer surprises us, whether one likes it or not. There is no reason to be particularly alarmed by Buddhists seeking to transform the world in accord with their principles, while expecting as much from religious Americans. Nor is there a reason to be troubled by the fact that church-state issues are negotiated differently in Japan or in any other modern country.

I think it is also time to cease being overly intrigued by the Soka Gakkai's history of controversy. Over the course of a relatively short period, the Soka Gakkai moved from the margins of Japanese society into its mainstream, at every step intimately a part of the emergence of Japan as a whole from its self-imposed isolation to its place at center stage in today's global society. Unlike Japan's ancient religious institutions, the Gakkai has made its steps and missteps, fashioned its dreams, and fought its many battles—all of them growing pains on the way to its maturity—more or less in the public eye. Through the skill of its leaders and the dedication of its members, it has become a formidable and, I think, quite admirable network of creative and productive institutions, however many youthful excesses are to be found in the historical record. As I see it, the real question now is whether the Gakkai and its people have the wherewithal to survive their great success.

· · ·

As I order my study—a memento from Dr. Gwee here, a plaque from the Soka schoolkids there, a photo of Copacabana beach, my Japanese Socrates—I'm made aware of just how healing it has been to voyage out from my sleepy Deansboro center to the Tokyo–Singapore–São Paulo/Rio periphery. Ann's picture, which I carried with me to Asia and South America, still has pride of place on my desk, but she now seems a bit distant from me, as if she has reincarnated someplace and is beginning to build a new life. Or perhaps she has nestled into a new abode near our cherry trees in the Makiguchi Memorial Garden. Wherever she is, I know she is pleased to know that I finally quit smoking, in Brazil of all places, where I found it easy to stop because no one there seems to see smoking as a P.C., moral reform issue, as it has become here in the U.S.

As I rifle through miscellaneous papers, I run across a crinkled pass-out I picked up in the Afro-Caribbean-Brazilian kaikan I was fortunate enough to visit in Duque de Caxias. I smooth it out, then pin it up over my computer—a reminder, in a way I do not yet fully understand, of the essential power in my encounter with the Gakkai and Ikeda. It is the lyric of a song, "Navegando com Sensei" (Sailing with Sensei), which was sung that night by the community, but was led by a thin black kid of twelve or fourteen.

"This is a hymn dedicated to Sensei / Because he gave me inspiration / I take this opportunity to say / I gave him my heart long ago," it begins, sentiments that strike me as Latinate and almost plaintive. As I puzzle out the Portuguese, the boy's image comes back to me: opening the lilting song with a cheer, seeming to be the community's cheerleader. He made a distinctive gesture—a swinging arm motion I assumed was Brazilian, something from soccer games perhaps, but later learned was Japanese in origin—which he used to punctuate each letter in an acrostic worked out on the word *gohonzon*. "With the letter *G*," he sang,

I go beyond any barrier
With the letter *O*, Open-hearted and with passion
With the letter *H*, Holding the banner high
With the letter *O*, Oh banner of love
With the letter *N*, Never be defeated
With the letter *Z*, Zealous I will always be
With the letter *O*, On and on working in the front lines
With the letter *N*, Navigating with Sensei.

Reliving the energy, light, and cheer generated in that dark, muddy hilltop slum, I'm genuinely moved, Gakkai stuff once again coaxing me out of my habitual cynicism and jaded consumerist mind-set. Dreading having to take up once again the very particular stress that comes with living in the United States, I long to stay at sea on this journey with Brazilian Buddhists, sweet Japanese schoolkids, intense old Gakkai pioneers, upwardly mobile Singapore professionals, and once-upon-a-time Santa Monica hippies.

But if I've learned anything over the past few years it is that I study religion, but am not very good at being religious myself. So for now, at least, I must stop sailing with sensei and make do instead with writing about him, his predecessors, and his disciples, all those crazy lions of Nichiren, the thirteenth-century prophet of Kamakura Japan.

Notes

Chapter 1. Mystic Opportunity

1. "Become Leaders of Conviction," *World Tribune,* 25 May 2001, 4–5. Field notes, entrance ceremony, Soka University, Hachioji, Japan, 2 April 2001.
2. William R. Hutchinson, *The Modernist Impulse in Protestantism* (Cambridge, MA: Harvard University Press, 1976).
3. Masaharu Anesaki, *Nichiren: The Buddhist Prophet,* repr. (Gloucester: Peter Williams, 1966 [orig. 1916]), p. 3.
4. Jacqueline I. Stone, *Original Enlightenment and the Transformation of Medieval Japanese Buddhism* (Honolulu: University of Hawaii Press, 1999), p. 241; Anesaki, *Nichiren,* p. 79.
5. John T. Brinkman, "The Simplicity of Nichiren," *Eastern Buddhist,* new ser. 28, no. 2 (1995): 261.

Chapter 2. Creating Value

1. Patrick Smith, *Japan: A Reinterpretation* (New York: Vintage Books, 1998), p. 28.
2. Shigeyoshi Murakami, *Japanese Religion in the Modern Century,* trans. H. Byron Earhart (Tokyo: Tokyo University Press, 1968), p. 20.
3. Masao Maruyama, *Thought and Behavior in Modern Japanese Politics,* ed. Ivan I. Morris (London: Oxford University Press, 1963), pp. 141, 144.
4. David M. O'Brien, *To Dream of Dreams: Religious Freedom and Constitutional Politics in Postwar Japan* (Honolulu: University of Hawaii Press, 1996).
5. Sharon A. Minichiello, "Introduction," in *Japan's Competing Modernities: Issues in Culture and Democracy 1900–1930,* ed. Sharon A. Minichiello (Honolulu: University of Hawaii Press, 1998), p. 12.

6. Heinz Bechert, "Buddhist Revival in East and West," in *The Worlds of Buddhism: Buddhist Monks and Nuns in Society and Culture,* ed. Heinz Bechert and Richard Gombrich (New York: Facts on File, 1984), pp. 273–85; idem, "Buddhist Modernism: Present Situation and Current Trends," in *Buddhism into the Year 2000: International Conference Proceedings* (Bangkok: Dhammakaya Foundation, 1994), pp. 251–60.

7. Polly Toynbee, "The Value of a Grandfather Figure," *Manchester Guardian,* 19 May 1984.

8. Quoted in Hiroo Sato, "Nichiren Thought in Modern Japan: Two Perspectives," *Journal of Oriental Studies* 10 (2000) [online: 23 February 2003]; Brian Daizen Victoria, "Engaged Buddhism: A Skeleton in the Closet?" *Journal of Global Buddhism* 2 (2001) [online: 23 February 2003]; Koichi Miyata, "Critical Comments on Brian Victoria's 'Engaged Buddhism: Skeleton in the Closet?'" *Journal of Global Buddhism* 3 (2002) [online: 23 February 2003].

Chapter 3. Mentor's Vision

1. Daisaku Ikeda, *The Human Revolution* (New York: Weatherhill, begins in 1972), vol. 2, pp. 129–57.

2. Quoted in Susumu Shimazono, "Soka Gakkai and the Modern Reformation of Buddhism," in *Buddhist Spirituality: Later China, Korea, Japan, and the Modern World,* ed. Takeuchi Yoshinori et al. (New York: Crossroads, 1999), p. 437.

3. Ibid., pp. 436–42; Michihito Tsushima, Shigeru Nishiyama, Susumu Shimazono, and Hiroko Shiramizu, "The Vitalistic Conception of Salvation in Japanese New Religions: An Aspect of Modern Religious Consciousness," *Japanese Journal of Religious Studies* 6, nos. 1–2 (1979): 139–61.

4. John Dower, *Embracing Defeat: Japan in the Wake of World War II* (New York: W. W. Norton, 1999), pp. 88–89.

5. Ibid., p. 105.

6. Ibid., p. 29.

7. Kyoko Inoue, *MacArthur's Japanese Constitution: A Linguistic and Cultural Study of Its Making* (Chicago: University of Chicago Press, 1991), pp. 2–3.

8. Ibid., p. 3.

9. H. Neill McFarland, *The Rush Hour of the Gods: A Study of New Religious Movements in Japan* (New York: Macmillan, 1967).

10. David M. O'Brien, *To Dream of Dreams: Religious Freedom and Constitutional Politics in Postwar Japan* (Honolulu: University of Hawaii Press, 1996), p. 61.

11. James White, *The Sokagakkai and Mass Society* (Stanford, CA: Stanford University Press, 1970), p. 303.

12. A comparison of two movements is found in Jacqueline I. Stone, "'By Imperial Edict and Shogunal Decree': Politics and the Issue of the Ordination

Platform in Modern Lay Nichiren Buddhism," in *Buddhism in the Modern World: Adaptations of an Ancient Tradition,* ed. Steven Heine and Charles S. Prebish (Oxford and New York: Oxford University Press, 2003), pp. 192–219.

13. Ibid., pp. 205–08.

14. Yasu Kashiwabara, interview by the author, Tokyo, Japan, 25 March 2001.

15. Einosuke Akiya, interviews by the author, Tokyo, Japan, 31 March 2001; 1 October 2000.

Chapter 4. Rising Star

1. James White, *The Sokagakkai and Mass Society* (Stanford, CA: Stanford University Press, 1970), p. 44.

2. Daniel Metraux, "The Soka Gakkai: Buddhism and the Creation of a Harmonious and Peaceful Society," in *Engaged Buddhism: Buddhist Liberation Movements in Asia,* ed. Christopher S. Queen and Sallie B. King (Albany: State University of New York Press, 1996), p. 371.

3. Andrew Gebert and Anthony George, "Josei Toda and the Growth of the Soka Gakkai" (Tokyo: Soka Gakkai International Office of Public Information, 2001, photocopy), p. 42.

4. *Global Citizens: The Soka Gakkai Buddhist Movement in the World,* ed. David Machacek and Bryan R. Wilson (Oxford and New York: Oxford University Press, 2000); Metraux, "The Soka Gakkai."

5. See, for example, Herbert J. Doherty, "Soka Gakkai: Religion and Politics in Japan," *Massachusetts Review* 4–5 (Winter 1963): 281–86; Nobusuke Kishi, "Political Movements in Japan," *Foreign Affairs* 44 (October 1965): 90–99; William Helton, "Political Prospects of Soka Gakkai," *Pacific Affairs* 38, nos. 3–4 (Autumn 1965–Winter 1965–66): 231–44.

6. White, *The Sokagakkai;* Arvin Palmer, *Buddhist Politics: Japan's Clean Government Party* (The Hague: Martinus Nijhoff, 1971).

7. Takesato Watanabe, "The Movement and the Japanese Media," in *Global Citizens,* ed. Machacek and Wilson, p. 228.

8. "A New Faith Called Soka Gakkai Raises Old Problems in Modern Japan," *Look* (10 September 1963): 19–26.

9. Ivan Morris, "Soka Gakkai Brings 'Absolute Happiness,'" *New York Times Magazine,* 18 July 1965, pp. 8–9 and 36–39.

10. Daisaku Ikeda, "How I Spent My Youth," in his *Glass Children and Other Essays,* trans. Burton Watson (Tokyo: Kodansha International, 1979), p. 58.

11. Idem, *My Recollections,* trans. Robert Epp (Santa Monica, CA: World Tribune Press, 1980), p. 35.

12. Ibid., p. 24.

13. Idem, *A Youthful Diary: One Man's Journey from the Beginning of Faith to Worldwide Leadership for Peace* (Santa Monica, CA: World Tribune Press, 2000), pp. 20, 29, 33–34, et passim.

14. Ibid., pp. 9, 21, 43, 55.

15. Ibid., pp. 6, 11.

16. "Morigasaki Beach," in idem, *Songs from My Heart: Poems and Photographs,* trans. Burton Watson (New York: Weatherhill, 1978), pp. 29–30.

17. Idem, "On the Path of My Mentor," *World Tribune,* 29 November 2002, p. 2.

18. Yasu Kashiwabara, interview by the author, Tokyo, Japan, 26 March 2001.

19. Einosuke Akiya, interview by the author, Tokyo, Japan, 31 March 2001.

20. White, *The Sokagakkai,* p. 48.

21. Winston Davis, "Fundamentalism in Japan: Religious and Political," in *Fundamentalisms Observed,* ed. Martin E. Marty and R. Scott Appleby (Chicago: University of Chicago Press, 1991), pp. 803–04.

22. White, *The Sokagakkai,* pp. 22–23.

23. Susumu Shimazono, "Soka Gakkai and the Modern Reformation of Buddhism," in *Buddhist Spirituality: Later China, Korea, Japan, and the Modern World,* ed. Takeuchi Yoshinori et al. (New York: Crossroads, 1999), p. 451.

24. Ian Reader and George J. Tanabe Jr., *Practically Religious: Worldly Benefits and the Common Religion of Japan* (Honolulu: University of Hawaii Press, 1998), p. 8.

25. Shimazono, "Soka Gakkai and the Modern Reformation," p. 452.

26. Daisaku Ikeda, *The Human Revolution* (New York: Weatherhill, begins in 1972), vol. 5, pp. 141–42.

27. Watanabe, "The Movement and the Japanese Media," p. 225.

28. Quoted in Gebert and George, "Josei Toda," pp. 61–62.

29. Quoted in Ikeda, *The Human Revolution,* vol. 6, pp. 182–83.

30. Ibid., vol. 6, p. 207.

31. Ibid., vol. 6, p. 201.

Chapter 5. Sea Change

1. James White, *The Sokagakkai and Mass Society* (Stanford, CA: Stanford University Press, 1970), p. 49.

2. Quoted in Jane D. Hurst, *Nichiren Shoshu Buddhism and the Soka Gakkai in America: The Ethos of a New Religious Movement* (New York: Garland Publications, 1992), pp. 140–41.

3. Daisaku Ikeda, *The New Human Revolution* (Santa Monica, CA: SGI-USA, 1995), vol. 1, p. 185.

4. Ibid., vol. 1, p. 144.

5. Yumiko Hachiya, interview by the author, Tokyo, Japan, 24 March 2001.

6. Einosuke Akiya, interview by the author, Tokyo, Japan, 3 March 2001.

7. Hiroshi Aruga, "Soka Gakkai and Japanese Politics," in *Global Citizens: The Soka Gakkai Buddhist Movement in the World,* ed. David W. Machacek and Bryan R. Wilson (Oxford and New York: Oxford University Press, 2000), p. 101.

8. Matsunami Michihiro, "Who's Who in Zengakuren & the Youth Movement in 1969: A Profile," in *Zengakuren: Japan's Revolutionary Students,* ed. Stuart J. Dowsey (Berkeley: Ishi Press, 1970), pp. 261–62.

9. Toru Shiotsu, interview by the author, Hachioji, Japan, 3 April 2001.

10. Minoru Harada, interview by the author, Tokyo, Japan, 31 March 2001.

11. Quoted in Kiyoaki Murata, *Japan's New Buddhism. An Objective Account of Soka Gakkai* (New York: Weatherhill, 1969), p. 134.

12. Jacqueline I. Stone, "'By Imperial Edict and Shogunal Decree': Politics and the Issue of the Ordination Platform in Modern Lay Nichiren Buddhism," in *Buddhism in the Modern World: Adaptations of an Ancient Tradition,* ed. Steven Heine and Charles S. Prebish (Oxford and New York: Oxford University Press, 2003), pp. 208–11.

13. Henry Scott-Stokes, "Quis Custodiet; The MOF: Plus Ça Change," *Tokyo Weekender,* 6 February 1998, www.weekender.co.jp/LatestEdition/980206/quiscustodiet.html (online: 5 October 2002).

14. Hirotatsu Fujiwara, *I Denounce Soka Gakkai,* trans. Worth C. Grant (Tokyo: Nisshin Hodo, 1970), pp. 36, 156, 73.

15. Lawrence Ward Beer, *Freedom of Expression in Japan: A Study of Comparative Law, Politics, and Society* (Tokyo: Kodansha International, 1984), p. 386.

16. Daisaku Ikeda, "An Address at the Thirty-Third General Meeting of Soka Gakkai May 3, 1970," trans. Soka Gakkai International Office of Public Information (Tokyo: Soka Gakkai International Office of Public Information, photocopy).

17. Ibid.

18. Field notes, Osaka, Japan, 7 April 2001.

19. Akiko Kurihara, interview by the author, Osaka, Japan, 7 April 2001.

20. Ryozo Nishiguchi, interview by the author, Osaka, Japan, 7 April 2001.

21. Kazuhito Fukunaka, interview by the author, Osaka, Japan, 8 April 2001.

22. Karel Dobbelaere, "Toward a Pillar Organization," in *Global Citizens: The Soka Gakkai Buddhist Movement in the World,* ed. David W. Machacek and Bryan R. Wilson (Oxford and New York: Oxford University Press, 2000), pp. 233–37.

23. Levi McLaughlin, "Faith and Practice: Bringing Religion, Music, and Beethoven to Life in Soka Gakkai," *Social Science Japan Journal* 6, no. 2 (2003): 161–79.

24. Toru Shiotsu, interview by the author, Hachioji, Japan, 3 April 2001.

25. Mitsunari Noguchi, interview by the author, Hachioji, Japan, 2 April 2001.

26. Hiroyasu Kobayashi, interview by the author, Tokyo, Japan, 5 April 2001.

27. José Casanova, *Public Religions in the Modern World* (Chicago: University of Chicago Press, 1994), pp. 5, 57–58, 65–66.

28. Toshiko Hamayotsu, interview by the author, Tokyo, Japan, 4 April 2001.

29. "Kansai Soka: Kansai Soka School System Campus Guide" (in English; n.p., n.d.), p. 4.

30. Kansai Soka schools, interview and notes by the author, Katano City, Osaka Prefecture, Japan, 9 April 2001.

Chapter 6. Countervailing Trends

1. See, for example, Yoshihiro Tsurumi, "An Unconventional Method for Killing America," *Tokuma Shoten* (October 1994): www.cebunet.com/cocaine .htm (online: 14 November 2004).

2. William Hardy McNeill, *Arnold Toynbee: A Life* (New York: Oxford University Press, 1989).

3. Quoted in Ann Kelly, "The Toynbee-Ikeda Dialogue," *Art of Living: A Buddhist Magazine* 11 (May 2002): 20.

4. Daisaku Ikeda, "Five Days with Arnold Toynbee," *Chuo Koron* (August 1973): 198–208, trans. Soka Gakkai International Office of Public Information (Tokyo: Soka Gakkai International Office of Public Information, photocopy), p. 2.

5. Arnold Toynbee and Daisaku Ikeda, *Choose Life: A Dialogue,* ed. Richard L. Gage (Oxford: Oxford University Press, 1989 [orig. 1976]), pp. 9–12.

6. McNeill, *Arnold Toynbee,* p. 273.

7. Ibid., pp. 272–73.

8. Ikeda, "Five Days," p. 4.

9. Kazuichi Namura, interview by the author, Tokyo, Japan, 30 March 2001.

10. Cai Delin, "Peace Bridge with China," *SGI Quarterly* 15 (January 1999): 12–13.

11. Daisaku Ikeda, "Education toward Global Citizenship, June 13, 1996, Teachers College, Columbia University," in his *Soka Education: A Buddhist Vision for Teachers, Students, and Parents* (Santa Monica, CA: Middleway Press, 2001), pp. 100–01.

12. Letter from Daisaku Ikeda to the author, 28 August 2003.

13. Ibid.

14. Daisaku Ikeda, interview and notes by the author, Tokyo, Japan, 23 March 2001.

15. Letter from Daisaku Ikeda to the author, 16 August 2001.

16. Rev. Nichijun Fujimoto, "The History Leading to the Split between the SGI and Nichiren Shoshu," www.cebunet.com/sgi/histsplit.htm (online: 26 July 2003).

17. Daniel A. Metraux, "Why Did Ikeda Quit?" *Japanese Journal of Religious Studies* 7, no. 1 (March 1980): 55–61.

18. *Issues between the Nichiren Shoshu Priesthood and the Soka Gakkai,* 5 vols. (Tokyo: Soka Gakkai International Headquarters, 1991–92).

19. Jane D. Hurst, "A Buddhist Reformation in the Twentieth Century: Causes and Implications of the Conflict between the Soka Gakkai and the

Nichiren Shoshu Priesthood," in *Global Citizens: The Soka Gakkai Buddhist Movement in the World,* ed. David W. Machacek and Bryan R. Wilson (Oxford and New York: Oxford University Press, 2000), pp. 67–96.

20. Rev. Shoshin Kawabe, "August Oko Lecture" (9 August 1998), Myosenji Temple: The Nichiren Shoshu Temple in Washington D.C., www.nstmyosenji org./sermons/1998/auguko98.htm (online: 27 July 2003).

21. Robert Eppsteiner, Joan Anderson, Mariko Imai, interview and notes by the author, Taisekiji, Fujinomiya city, Shizuoka Prefecture, Japan, March 2001.

22. Kimio Yokoyama, interview by the author, Tokyo, Japan, 28 March 2001.

23. Takudo Hosoi, interview by the author, Tokyo, Japan, 28 March 2001.

24. Hosho Shiina, interview by the author, Tokyo, Japan, 28 March 2001.

Chapter 7. Zuiho-bini

1. Catherine Cornille, "New Japanese Religions in the West: Between Nationalism and Universalism," in *Japanese New Religions in Global Perspective,* ed. Peter B. Clarke (Surrey, UK: Curzon Press, 1999), pp. 10–34.

2. Ibid., p. 14.

3. Quoted in Jeff Kriger, "The Precept of Adapting to Local Customs: Practice That Is Fitting for the Times and for Society," Lotus Sutra Study Center, www.buddhistinformation.com/the_lotus_sutra_study_center/precept_of_adapting_to_local_cus.htm (online: 25 October 2004).

4. Robert Epp, "Some Aspects of Daisaku Ikeda's Thought," in *Buddhism Today: A Collection of Views from Contemporary Scholars,* ed. Toyo Tetsugaku Kenkyujo (Tokyo: Institute of Oriental Philosophy, 1990), pp. 70–83.

5. Quoted ibid., p. 81.

6. Jacqueline I. Stone, *Original Enlightenment and the Transformation of Medieval Japanese Buddhism* (Honolulu: University of Hawaii Press, 1999), p. 68.

7. Dan Summers, notes and interview by the author, Tucson, AZ., 26 February 2001.

8. David W. Chappell, "Racial Diversity in the Soka Gakkai," in *Engaged Buddhism in the West,* ed. Christopher S. Queen (Boston: Wisdom Publications, 2000), p. 192.

9. Ibid., pp. 187–89.

10. James Allen Dator, *Soka Gakkai, Builders of the Third Civilization: American and Japanese Members* (Seattle: University of Washington Press, 1969), pp. 31–32.

11. Ibid., p. 32.

12. Ibid., p. 32 n. 6.

13. James Gardner, interview by the author, Chicago, IL, December 2000.

14. Patricia Walker, interview by the author, Chicago, IL, December 2000.

15. Chappell, "Racial Diversity," p. 198.

16. Ibid., p. 199.

17. Steven M. Tipton, *Getting Saved from the Sixties: Moral Meaning in Conversion and Cultural Change* (Berkeley: University of California Press, 1982).

18. *Hippy to Happy,* directed by Michael Elsey, Santa Monica, CA: Min-On of America, 1969, videocassette, 30 mins.

19. Larry Shaw, notes and interviews by the author, Los Angeles, CA, 25 March 2003; 24 July 2003.

20. Phillip E. Hammond and David W. Machacek, *Soka Gakkai in America: Accommodation and Conversion* (Oxford: Oxford University Press, 1999), p. 178.

21. George M. Williams, *Freedom and Influence: The Role of Religion in American Society, an NSA Perspective* (Santa Monica, CA: World Tribune Press, 1985), pp. 3–7, 197–222.

22. Daniel Golden, "Buddhism American Style," *Boston Globe Sunday Magazine,* 15 October 1989, pp. 18ff.

23. Hammond and Machacek, *Soka Gakkai in America,* p. 24.

24. Chappell, "Racial Diversity," p. 205.

25. *The Sun Rises: The Bell of Peace and Happiness,* Santa Monica, CA: NSA Video Productions, 1987, videocassette, 94 mins.

26. Matilda Buck, interview by the author, Santa Monica, CA, 6 November 2001; Danny Nagashima, interview by the author, Santa Monica, CA, 6 November 2001.

27. SGI-USA youth leaders, interview by the author, Santa Monica, CA, 5 November 2001.

28. Daisaku Ikeda, "Take the Next Great Step Forward," in *Wisdom for the New Era, Seikyo Times* special issue, March 1990 (Santa Monica, CA: World Tribune Press, 1990), p. 50.

29. Daisaku Ikeda, "Buddhism Is the Mirror That Perfectly Reflects Our Lives," in *Wisdom for the New Era, Seikyo Times* special issue, March 1990 (Santa Monica, CA: World Tribune Press, 1990), pp. 82–88.

30. Chappell, "Racial Diversity," p. 189.

31. Hammond and Machacek, *Soka Gakkai in America,* p. 90.

32. Benjamin R. Barber, *Jihad vs. McWorld* (New York: Ballantine Books, 1996), pp. 277–79.

33. Daniel Metraux, "The Expansion of the Soka Gakkai into Southeast Asia," in *Global Citizens: The Soka Gakkai Buddhist Movement in the World,* ed. David W. Machacek and Bryan R. Wilson (Oxford and New York: Oxford University Press, 2000), pp. 406, 405.

34. Singapore Soka Association leaders, interview by the author, Singapore, 11 April 2001.

35. Daniel Metraux, *The International Expansion of a Modern Buddhist Movement: The Soka Gakkai in Southeast Asia and Australia* (Lanham, MD: University Press of America, 2001), pp. 47–60.

36. Singapore Soka Association members, interview by the author, Singapore, 11 April 2001.

37. Angie Tay, interview by the author, Singapore, 11 April 2001.

38. Rev. Yuhan Watanabe, interview by the author, Singapore, 12 April 2001.

39. Gwee Yee Hean, interview by the author, Singapore, 11 April 2001. Additional material courtesy of Soka Gakkai International Office of Public Information and Singapore Soka Association.

40. "'Generation M, the Future Is Not Assured,'" *The Straits Times,* 13 April 2001.

Chapter 8. World House

1. Andrea Adelson, "Zen and the Liberal Arts," *New York Times,* Educational Life Supplement, 8 April 2001.

2. Daniel Habuki, interview by the author, Aliso Viejo, CA, 2 May 2001.

3. "Mottos and Principles, Soka University of America," www.soka .edu/soka_focus/mottos_principles.aspx (online: 27 December 2003).

4. Lawrence Carter, interview by the author, Aliso Viejo, CA, 3 May 2001.

5. Rabbi Abraham Cooper, interview by the author, Los Angeles, CA, 4 May 2001.

6. "Friedl and the Children of Terezin," Simon Wiesenthal Center, www.fujibi.or.jp/tfam/friedl/ (online: 2 January 2004); "Over 130,000 Visit Wiesenthal Center's Friedl Dicker-Brandeis Exhibition at Tokyo's Fuji Art Museum," Simon Wiesenthal Center, www.wiesenthal.com/social/press/ pr_item.cfm?itemID=5708 (online: 13 November 2004).

7. Daisaku Ikeda, *The Humanism of the Middle Way: Dawn of a Global Civilization* (Tokyo: Soka Gakkai International, 2002), p. 11.

8. Ibid., p. 13.

9. Masako Watanabe, "Soka Gakkai: From Shakubuku to Cultural Movement—the Changes and Their Cause," in her *Developmental Process of Japanese New Religions in Brazil: Tasks and Achievements of Missionary Work in Brazilian Culture,* trans. Soka Gakkai International Office of Public Information (Tokyo: Toshin do, 2001), Soka Gakkai International Office of Public Information, Tokyo, Japan, photocopy.

10. Amaral Vieira, interview by the author, São Paulo, Brazil, 16 March 2002.

11. Program and author's notes, Shakubuku Zadankai, São Paulo, Brazil, 16 March 2002.

12. Program and author's notes, Atividade Commerativa, São Paulo, Brazil, 17 March 2002.

13. Eduardo Taguchi, interview by the author, São Paulo, Brazil, 19 March 2002.

14. Roberto Saito, interview by the author, São Paulo, Brazil, 18 March 2002.

15. Flávio Fava de Moraes, interview by the author, São Paulo, Brazil, 18 March 2002.

16. Dilma de Melo Silva, "Makiguchi Project in Action—Enhancing Education for Peace," *Journal of Oriental Studies* 10 (2000): 82–88.

17. Watanabe, *Developmental Process,* n.p.

18. Mario Takao Inoue, "Amazon Ecological Research Center," Soka Gakkai International, www.sgi.org/english/SGI/infos/amazon.htm (online: 13 November 2004); "Founder of an Environmental Studies College: Luis Viera, Brazil," *SGI Quarterly* 8 (April 1997), www.sgi.org/english/archives/quarterly/ 9704/people1.html (online: 18 June 2003).

19. Dilma de Melo Silva, interview by the author, São Paulo, Brazil, 19 March 2002.

20. Dirce Ivamoto, interview by the author, São Paulo, Brazil, 19 March 2002.

21. Peter B. Clarke, "Buddhist Humanism and Catholic Culture in Brazil," in *Global Citizens: The Soka Gakkai Buddhist Movement in the World,* ed. David W. Machacek and Bryan R. Wilson (Oxford and New York: Oxford University Press, 2000), pp. 326–48.

22. Ibid., p. 345.

23. Cicero Sandroni, interview by the author, Rio de Janeiro, Brazil, 21 March 2002.

24. Magdalena Landi, interview by the author, Rio de Janeiro, Brazil, 22 March 2002.

25. Telma Lúcia Ferreira Moreira Martins, interview by the author, Caju, Rio de Janeiro, Brazil, 22 March 2002.

26. Program and author's notes, 21 Duque de Caxias, Rio de Janeiro, Brazil, 23 March 2002.

Chapter 9. Intrepid Navigators

1. Daisaku Ikeda, "Challenge of Building Peace," *Japan Times,* 11 September 2003.

2. Benjamin Fulford and David Whelan, "Sensei's World," *Forbes* (6 September 2004): 126–32.

3. Einosuke Akiya to the editor of *Forbes,* 27 August 2004.

Glossary

Amaterasu-kami	goddess of the Sun, the mythic progenitor of the imperial family.
Aum Shinrikyo	Japanese religious group responsible for the sarin gas attacks in the Tokyo subway in 1995.
Bodhisattva	"wisdom being"; a mythological being who passes through many lifetimes teaching the dharma to suffering people; a model for the ethical and spiritual practice of Mahayana Buddhists.
Dai-gohonzon	object of worship said to possess a special spiritual potency. It is housed at Taisekiji, the head temple of Nichiren Shoshu.
Daimoku	the chant "Nam-myoho-renge-kyo"; literally, "Hail to the Lotus Sutra of the dharma."
Dharma	the teachings or law discovered and taught by the Buddha.
Diet	Japan's parliament, established in 1890.
Gaijin	foreigner.
Gohonzon	"object of worship" devised by Nichiren that consists of the words "Nam-myoho-renge-kyo" surrounded by signs for bodhisattvas and lesser deities.
Gongyo	daily liturgy that consists of reciting selected portions of the Lotus Sutra.

Gosho	"writings"; the letters and treatises of Nichiren, considered authoritative scripture.
Hobobarai	the putting away of talismans and symbols of other religious traditions when choosing to practice Nichiren's Buddhism.
Jiriki	"self-power"; a practice in which one must exert oneself to effect an inner awakening.
Kaidan	ordination platform, seat of institutional religious authority, place of worship.
Kaikan	culture center, community meeting place used for both social and religious purposes.
Kami	deities of the Shinto tradition thought to be manifest in nature and social relations.
Kansai spirit	passionate sense of determination and commitment forged during the Osaka campaign in the 1950s.
Kokuritsu kaidan	national sanctuary, one established or sanctioned by the state.
Kosen-rufu	"to declare, spread, and flow"; a future era of harmony and peace prophesied by Nichiren; the progressive program of the Soka Gakkai.
Kyodatsu	a clinical term for depression, applied to the postwar psychosocial malaise in Japan.
Lotus Sutra	a foundational scripture in the Mahayana tradition, thought by the devout to contain the most complete teaching of Shakyamuni.
Mahayana	a tradition of Buddhist teachings influential throughout north and east Asia.
Mappo	the latter day of the dharma, an era of turmoil during which, it is thought, Shakyamuni's original teachings have become corrupt and need restatement.
Meiji Restoration	1868 coup d'état that restored the emperor, and the events of the next three decades under Emperor Meiji.
Nam-myoho-renge-kyo	the chant used in Nichiren Buddhist practice; referred to as *daimoku*.
Nichiren	thirteenth-century prophet and reformer, founder of the Nichiren tradition of Japanese Buddhism.
Nichiren Shoshu	a small priestly sect in the Nichiren tradition, once closely associated with the Soka Gakkai.

Rissho Ankoku Ron	"On Establishing the Correct Teaching for the Peace of the Land"; a treatise by Nichiren that became the platform of the Soka Gakkai under Toda.
Scikyo Itchi	unity of ritual and government, the fusing of ceremonial and political authority in the person of the emperor until the American occupation.
Seimei	"life force"; a modern vitalistic concept central to Josei Toda's Buddhism.
Sensei	spiritual teacher.
Shakubuku	traditional Buddhist style of refuting errors through vigorous debate, once used in Soka Gakkai as a strategy for mass propagation.
Shakyamuni	*muni* (sage) of the Sakya clan; among the names of Siddhartha Gautama, the Buddha.
Shinto	the ancient indigenous religious tradition of Japan, politicized and institutionalized during the prewar period in State or Shrine Shinto.
Shisohan	thought criminal.
Shoju	dialogue or conversation designed to persuade people to embrace Buddhist values.
Shoten zenjin	tutelary deity.
Soka Gakkai	Value Creation Society.
Soka Gakkai International	umbrella organization with some twelve million members, founded in 1975 to nurture national movements around the globe.
Soka Gakkai–Japan	the Japanese national movement, comprising some ten million members.
Soka Kyoiku Gakkai	Value Creating Education Society, the forerunner of today's Soka Gakkai.
Tariki	"other power"; a practice in which awakening is understood to be brought about by an external force.
Tatami mat	traditional woven floor covering used both in homes and in public places.
Tozan	pilgrimage, especially to Taisekiji, the head temple of Nichiren Shoshu.
Triple Gem	the Buddha, dharma, and sangha; a traditional formula expressing the essence of Buddhism.
Zadankai	small face-to-face meetings among Soka Gakkai members.

Zaibatsu   large family-owned industrial and financial combines that came to dominate Japan during the modernization era.

Zengakuren   Japanese student movement during the '60s and '70s.

Zuiho-bini   the principle of adapting Buddhist precepts to different cultures, said to have its source in Shakyamuni's original teachings.

Bibliography

Adelson, Andrea. "Zen and the Liberal Arts." *New York Times,* Educational Life Supplement, 8 April 2001.

Anesaki, Masaharu. *Nichiren: The Buddhist Prophet.* Gloucester, MA: Peter Williams, 1966 [orig. 1916].

Aruga, Hiroshi. "Soka Gakkai and Japanese Politics." In *Global Citizens: The Soka Gakkai Buddhist Movement in the World,* edited by David W. Machacek and Bryan R. Wilson, pp. 97–127. Oxford and New York: Oxford University Press, 2000.

Barber, Benjamin R. *Jihad vs. McWorld.* New York: Ballantine Books, 1996.

Bechert, Heinz. "Buddhist Revival in East and West." In *The Worlds of Buddhism: Buddhist Monks and Nuns in Society and Culture,* edited by Heinz Bechert and Richard Gombrich, pp. 273–85. New York: Facts on File, 1984.

———. "Buddhist Modernism: Present Situation and Current Trends." In *Buddhism into the Year 2000: International Conference Proceedings,* pp. 251–60. Bangkok: Dhammakaya Foundation, 1994.

"Become Leaders of Conviction." *World Tribune,* 2 April 2001.

Beer, Lawrence Ward. *Freedom of Expression in Japan: A Study in Comparative Law, Politics, and Society.* Tokyo: Kodansha International, 1984.

Brannen, Noah S. *Soka Gakkai: Japan's Militant Buddhists.* Richmond, VA: John Knox Press, 1968.

Brinkman, John T. "The Simplicity of Nichiren." *Eastern Buddhist,* new ser. 28, no. 2 (1995): 248–64.

Casanova, José. *Public Religions in the Modern World.* Chicago: University of Chicago Press, 1994.

Chappell, David W. "Racial Diversity in the Soka Gakkai." In *Engaged Buddhism in the West,* edited by Christopher S. Queen, pp. 184–217. Boston: Wisdom Publications, 2000.

Clarke, Peter B. "Buddhist Humanism and Catholic Culture in Brazil." In *Global Citizens: The Soka Gakkai Buddhist Movement in the World*, edited by David W. Machacek and Bryan R. Wilson, pp. 326–48. Oxford and New York: Oxford University Press, 2000.

———, ed. *Japanese New Religions in Global Perspective*. Surrey, UK: Curzon Press, 1999.

Cornille, Catherine. "New Japanese Religions in the West: Between Nationalism and Universalism." In *Japanese New Religions in Global Perspective*, edited by Peter B. Clarke, pp. 10–34. Surrey, UK: Curzon Press, 1999.

Dator, James Allen. *Soka Gakkai, Builders of the Third Civilization: American and Japanese Members*. Seattle: University of Washington Press, 1969.

Davis, Winston. "Fundamentalism in Japan: Religious and Political." In *Fundamentalisms Observed*, edited by Martin E. Marty and R. Scott Appleby, pp. 782–813. Chicago: University of Chicago Press, 1991.

Delin, Cai. "Peace Bridge with China." *SGI Quarterly* 15 (January 1999): 12–13.

Dobbelaere, Karel. "Toward a Pillar Organization." In *Global Citizens: The Soka Gakkai Buddhist Movement in the World*, edited by David W. Machacek and Bryan R. Wilson, pp. 233–56. Oxford and New York: Oxford University Press, 2000.

Doherty, Herbert J. "Soka Gakkai: Religion and Politics in Japan." *Massachusetts Review* 4–5 (Winter 1963): 281–86.

Dower, John W. *Embracing Defeat: Japan in the Wake of World War II*. New York: W. W. Norton, 1999.

Epp, Robert. "Some Aspects of Daisaku Ikeda's Thought." In *Buddhism Today: A Collection of Views from Contemporary Scholars*, edited by Toyo Tetsugaku Kenkyujo, pp. 70–83. Tokyo: Institute of Oriental Philosophy, 1990.

"Founder of an Environmental Studies College: Luis Viera, Brazil." *Soka Gakkai International Quarterly* 8 (April 1997), www.sgi.org/english/archives/quarterly/9704/people1.html (18 June 2003).

"Friedl and the Children of Terezin." Simon Wiesenthal Center, www.fujibi.or.jp/tfam/friedl (2 January 2004).

Fujimoto, Rev. Nichijun. "The History Leading to the Split between the SGI and Nichiren Shoshu." www.cebunet.com/sgi/histsplit.htm (26 July 2003).

Fujiwara, Hirotatsu. *I Denounce Soka Gakkai*. Translated by Worth C. Grant. Tokyo: Nisshin Hodo, 1970.

Fulford, Benjamin, and David Whelan. "Sensei's World." *Forbes* (6 September 2004): 126–32.

Gebert, Andrew, and Anthony George. "Josei Toda and the Growth of the Soka Gakkai." Tokyo: Soka Gakkai International Office of Public Information, 2001.

Golden, Daniel. "Buddhism American Style." *Boston Globe Sunday Magazine*, 15 October 1989, pp. 18ff.

Hammond, Phillip E., and David W. Machacek. *Soka Gakkai in America: Accommodation and Conversion*. Oxford: Oxford University Press, 1999.

Helton, William. "Political Prospects of Soka Gakkai." *Pacific Affairs* 38, nos. 3–4 (Autumn 1965–Winter 1965–66): 231–44.

Hippy to Happy. Directed by Michael Elsey. Santa Monica, CA: Min-On of America, 1969, videocassette, 30 mins.

Hurst, Jane D. *Nichiren Shoshu Buddhism and the Soka Gakkai in America: The Ethos of a New Religious Movement.* New York: Garland Publications, 1992.

————. "A Buddhist Reformation in the Twentieth Century: Causes and Implications of the Conflict between the Soka Gakkai and the Nichiren Shoshu Priesthood." In *Global Citizens: The Soka Gakkai Buddhist Movement in the World,* edited by David W. Machacek and Bryan R. Wilson, pp. 67–96. Oxford and New York: Oxford University Press, 2000.

Hutchison, William R. *The Modernist Impulse in American Protestantism.* Cambridge, MA: Harvard University Press, 1976.

Ikeda, Daisaku. "An Address at the Thirty-Third General Meeting of Soka Gakkai May 3, 1970." Translated by Soka Gakkai International Office of Public Information. Tokyo: Soka Gakkai International Office of Public Information, photocopy.

————. *The Human Revolution.* 6 vols. New York: Weatherhill, begins in 1972.

————. "Five Days with Arnold Toynbee." *Chuo Koron* (August 1973): 198–208. Translated by Soka Gakkai International Office of Public Information. Tokyo: Soka Gakkai International Office of Public Information, photocopy.

————. *Songs from My Heart: Poems and Photographs.* Translated by Burton Watson. New York: Weatherhill, 1978.

————. *Glass Children and Other Essays.* Translated by Burton Watson. Tokyo: Kodansha International, 1979.

————. *My Recollections.* Translated by Robert Epp. Los Angeles: World Tribune Press, 1980.

————. "Buddhism Is the Mirror That Perfectly Reflects Our Lives." In *Wisdom for the New Era, Seikyo Times* special issue, March 1990. Santa Monica, CA: World Tribune Press, 1990.

————. "Take the Next Great Step Forward." In *Wisdom for the New Era, Seikyo Times* special issue, March 1990. Santa Monica, CA: World Tribune Press, 1990.

————. *The New Human Revolution.* 6 vols. Santa Monica, CA: SGI-USA, begins in 1995.

————. *A Youthful Diary: One Man's Journey from the Beginning of Faith to Worldwide Leadership for Peace.* Santa Monica, CA: World Tribune Press, 2000.

————. "Education toward Global Citizenship, June 13, 1996, Teachers College, Columbia University." In his *Soka Education: A Buddhist Vision for Teachers, Students, and Parents.* Santa Monica, CA: Middleway Press, 2001.

————. *The Humanism of the Middle Way: Dawn of a Global Civilization.* Tokyo: Soka Gakkai International, 2002.

————. "On the Path of My Mentor." *World Tribune,* 29 November 2002.

————. "Challenge of Building Peace." *Japan Times,* 11 September 2003.

Inoue, Kyoko. *MacArthur's Japanese Constitution: A Linguistic and Cultural Study of Its Making.* Chicago: University of Chicago Press, 1991.

Inoue, Mario Takao. "Amazon Ecological Research Center." Soka Gakkai International, www.sgi.org/english/SGI/infos/amazon.htm (13 November 2004).

Issues between the Nichiren Shoshu Priesthood and the Soka Gakkai. 5 vols. Tokyo: Soka Gakkai International Headquarters, 1991–92.

Kawabe, Rev. Shoshin. "August Oko Lecture," 9 August 1998. Myosenji Temple: The Nichiren Shoshu Temple in Washington D.C., www.nstmyosenji.org/sermons/1998/augoko98.htm (27 July 2003).

Kelly, Ann. "The Toynbee-Ikeda Dialogue." *Art of Living: A Buddhist Magazine* 11 (May 2002): 19–23.

Kishi, Nobusuke. "Political Movements in Japan." *Foreign Affairs* 44 (October 1965): 90–99.

Kriger, Jeff. "The Precept of Adapting to Local Customs: Practice That Is Fitting for the Times and for Society." Lotus Sutra Study Center, www.buddhistinformation.com/the_lotus_sutra_study_center/precept_of_adapting_to_local_cus.htm (25 October 2004).

Machacek, David W., and Bryan R. Wilson, eds. *Global Citizens: The Soka Gakkai Buddhist Movement in the World.* Oxford and New York: Oxford University Press, 2000.

Maruyama, Masao. *Thought and Behavior in Modern Japanese Politics,* edited by Ivan I. Morris. London: Oxford University Press, 1963.

Matsunami, Michiro. "Who's Who in Zengakuren and the Youth Movement in 1960: A Profile." In *Zengakuren: Japan's Revolutionary Students,* edited by Stuart J. Dowsey. Berkeley: Ishi Press, 1970.

McFarland, H. Neill. *The Rush Hour of the Gods: A Study of New Religious Movements in Japan.* New York: Macmillan, 1967.

McLaughlin, Levi. "Faith and Practice: Bringing Religion, Music, and Beethoven to Life in Soka Gakkai." *Social Science Japan Journal* 6, no. 2 (2003): 161–79.

McNeill, William Hardy. *Arnold J. Toynbee: A Life.* New York: Oxford University Press, 1989.

Metraux, Daniel A. "Why Did Ikeda Quit?" *Japanese Journal of Religious Studies* 17, no. 1 (March 1980): 55–61.

———. "The Soka Gakkai: Buddhism and the Creation of a Harmonious and Peaceful Society." In *Engaged Buddhism: Buddhist Liberation Movements in Asia,* edited by Christopher S. Queen and Sallie B. King, pp. 365–400. Albany: State University of New York Press, 1996.

———. "The Expansion of the Soka Gakkai into Southeast Asia." In *Global Citizens: The Soka Gakkai Buddhist Movement in the World,* edited by David W. Machacek and Bryan R. Wilson, pp. 402–29. Oxford and New York: Oxford University Press, 2000.

———. *The International Expansion of a Modern Buddhist Movement: The Soka Gakkai in Southeast Asia and Australia.* Lanham, MD: University Press of America, 2001.

Minichiello, Sharon A., ed. *Japan's Competing Modernities: Issues in Culture and Democracy 1900–1930.* Honolulu: University of Hawaii Press, 1998.

Miyata, Koichi. "Critical Comments on Brian Victoria's 'Engaged Buddhism: A Skeleton in the Closet?'" *Journal of Global Buddhism* 3 (2002) (online: 23 February 2003).

Morris, Ivan. "Soka Gakkai Brings 'Absolute Happiness.'" *New York Times Magazine*, 18 July 1965, pp. 8–9 and 36–39.

Murakami, Shigeyoshi. *Japanese Religion in the Modern Century*. Translated by H. Bryon Earhart. Tokyo: University of Tokyo Press, 1968.

Murata, Kiyoaki. *Japan's New Buddhism: An Objective Account of Soka Gakkai*. New York: Weatherhill, 1969.

"A New Faith Called Soka Gakkai Raises Old Problems in Modern Japan." *Look* (10 September 1963): 19–26.

O'Brien, David M. *To Dream of Dreams: Religious Freedom and Constitutional Politics in Postwar Japan*. Honolulu: University of Hawaii Press, 1996.

"Over 130,000 Visit Wiesenthal Center's Friedl Dicker-Brandeis Exhibition at Tokyo's Fuji Art Museum." Simon Wiesenthal Center, www.wiesenthal .com/social/press/pr_item.cfm?itemID=5708 (13 November 2004).

Palmer, Arvin. *Buddhist Politics: Japan's Clean Government Party*. The Hague: Martinus Nijhoff, 1971.

Reader, Ian, and George J. Tanabe Jr. *Practically Religious: Worldly Benefits and the Common Religion of Japan*. Honolulu: University of Hawaii Press, 1998.

Sato, Hiroo. "Nichiren Thought in Modern Japan: Two Perspectives." *Journal of Oriental Studies* 10 (2000): 46–61.

Scott-Stokes, Henry. "Quis Custodiet; The MOF: Plus Ça Change." *Tokyo Weekender*, 6 February 1998, www.weekender.co.jp/LatestEdition/980206/ quiscustodiet.html (5 October 2002).

Shimazono, Susumu. "Soka Gakkai and the Modern Reformation of Buddhism." In *Buddhist Spirituality: Later China, Korea, Japan, and the Modern World*, edited by Takeuchi Yoshinori, James W. Heisig, Paul L. Swanson, and Joseph S. O'Leary, pp. 435–54. New York: Crossroads, 1999.

Silva, Dilma de Melo. "Makiguchi Project in Action—Enhancing Education for Peace." *Journal of Oriental Studies* 10 (2000): 82–88.

Smith, Patrick. *Japan: A Reinterpretation*. New York: Vintage Books, 1998.

Stone, Jacqueline I. *Original Enlightenment and the Transformation of Medieval Japanese Buddhism*. Honolulu: University of Hawaii Press, 1999.

———. "'By Imperial Edict and Shogunal Decree': Politics and the Issue of the Ordination Platform in Modern Lay Nichiren Buddhism." In *Buddhism in the Modern World: Adaptations of an Ancient Tradition*, edited by Steven Heine and Charles S. Prebish, pp. 192–219. Oxford and New York: Oxford University Press, 2003.

The Sun Rises, the Bell of Peace and Happiness. Santa Monica, CA: NSA Video Productions, 1987, videocassette, 94 mins.

Tipton, Steven M. *Getting Saved from the Sixties: Moral Meaning in Conversion and Cultural Change*. Berkeley: University of California Press, 1982.

Toynbee, Arnold, and Daisaku Ikeda. *Choose Life: A Dialogue*, edited by Richard L. Gage. Oxford: Oxford University Press, 1989 [orig. 1976].

Toynbee, Polly. "The Value of a Grandfather Figure." *Manchester Guardian*, 19 May 1984, 15.

Tsurumi, Yoshihiro. "An Unconventional Method for Killing America." To-kuma Shoten (October 1994). www.cebunet.com/cocaine.htm (14 November 2004).

Tsushima, Michihito, Shigeru Nishiyama, Susumu Shimazono, and Hiroko Shiramizu. "The Vitalistic Conception of Salvation in Japanese New Religions: An Aspect of Modern Religious Consciousness." *Japanese Journal of Religious Studies* 6, nos. 1–2 (1979): 139–61.

Victoria, Brian Daizen. "Engaged Buddhism: A Skeleton in the Closet?" *Journal of Global Buddhism* 2 (2001) (online: 23 February 2003).

Viera, Luis. "Founder of an Environmental Studies College." *SGI Quarterly* 8 (April 1997), www.sgi.org/english/archives/quarterly/9704/people1.html (18 June 2003).

Watanabe, Masako. "Soka Gakkai: From Shakubuku to Cultural Movement—the Changes and Their Cause." In her *Developmental Process of Japanese New Religions in Brazil: Tasks and Achievements of Missionary Work in Brazilian Culture*. Translated by Soka Gakkai International Office of Public Information. Tokyo: Toshin-do, 2001. Soka Gakkai International Office of Public Information Office, photocopy.

Watanabe, Takesato. "The Movement and the Japanese Media." In *Global Citizens: The Soka Gakkai Buddhist Movement in the World,* edited by David W. Machacek and Bryan R. Wilson, pp. 205–31. Oxford and New York: Oxford University Press, 2000.

White, James. *The Sokagakkai and Mass Society*. Stanford, CA: Stanford University Press, 1970.

Williams, George M. *Freedom and Influence: The Role of Religion in American Society, an NSA Perspective*. Santa Monica, CA: World Tribune Press, 1985.

Index

African Americans: and civil rights, 148, 157, 176–78; and SGI-USA, 147–50

African National Congress, 120

Akiya, Einosuke, 59 63, 70, 104; and *Forbes* article, 208; on Ikeda, 59, 72, 76–77; overseas trip of, 87–88, 91; on postwar years, 99; and succession to Ikeda, 206

Amaterasu, 40

Amazon Ecological Research Center (AERC), 192

American Buddhism (Seager), 146

Anesaki, Masaharu, 16, 17

anti-Semitism: global, 180; in Japan, 178

Aoyama, David Seima, 182

architecture: of Sho-Hondo, 134–35; of Soka University, 5, 6, 11–12; of Soka University of America, 171, 174

Arnold Toynbee (McNeill), 116–19

art, 104–5, 107. *See also* architecture; music

Artists' Group, 103

Asakusa, temple complex at, 24, 29–30

Athayde, Austregésilo de, 196

Athens Academy, Soka University, 7, 8, 61

Aum Shinrikyo, 179

Baggio, Roberto, 35, 38

Barber, Benjamin, 159–60

Bechert, Heinz, 32

Beer, Lawrence Ward, 97

Before It Is Too Late (Ikeda and Peccei), 185

benefits, gaining, 28–29, 36, 78, 177

Bergson, Henri, 55–56, 72

Bible, 15, 18, 19

bin Talal, El-Hassan, 175

blacks. *See* African Americans; South Africa

Bodhgaya, 90. *See also* Eagle Peak

bodhisattvas, 15–16, 19, 20; globalization and, 142, 146, 203; *gohonzon* and, 33; Kannon (Kuan Yin), 29; priests only as, 130, *shakubuku* and, 33; Toda and, 48–49

bombing of Japan (World War II): Hiroshima and Nagasaki, 51, 83, 143, 208; Tokyo, 30, 31, 71–72, 75–76. *See also* nuclear arms

Bonten, 52–53, 88

Boston: Quincy Market, 30, 169; SGI, 67, 148, 149

Boston Research Center, 67

Boys' Japan, 74

bozu, 136

Brazil: author's trip to, 183–201, 202–3, 210–11; DOPS and SNI investigations in, 191; Ikeda visits, 85, 87–88, 184, 185, 189, 196; Japanese immigrant community in, 141, 184; in videos, 102. *See also* BSGI (Brazil Soka Gakkai International); Rio de Janeiro; São Paulo

Brazilian Academy of Letters, 196

Britain: British businessmen's Japanese wives, 141; and Toynbee, 116, 117–18; utilitarians in, 28

BSGI (Brazil Soka Gakkai International), 141, 184–201, 202–3; Educators Division, 193; *kaikan* of, 200–1, 210–11; member numbers of, 184–85; Nature Culture Center, 184; in Rio de Janeiro, 195–201; in São Paulo, 184–95, 203

Buck, Matilda, 155–56

Buddha, 14–15, 18, 19; bodhisattva and, 16; Bonten as helper of, 52–53, 88; Buddhist Jews and images of, 179; chant awakening, 33, 145, 205; *gohonzon* and, 33, 205; Ikeda as, 128–29; life force and, 48–49, 53, 55–58, 78, 83; Makiguchi and, 78; mirror guidance and, 158; Nichiren Buddhism and, 31–32, 128, 130, 143; Toda and, 47–49, 53, 78. *See also* Shakyamuni

Buddhism: Carter's views of, 177–78; death rituals in, 60; evangelical, 55, 57–58; Jews embracing, 179; Mahayana, 15–16, 17, 18, 118, 121; Pure Land, 16–17, 30; reality-transformative, 78–79; Shinto and, 25, 29–30; in Tokugawa Japan, 25; in United States, 1–2; *zuiho-bini*, 89. *See also* Nichiren Buddhism; Zen

"Buddhism Is the Mirror That Perfectly Reflects Our Lives" (Ikeda), 158

Buddhist Humanism, Ikeda's, 1–2, 5, 12, 90–94, 97–98, 114; in Brazil, 185, 194, 195, 199, 200; collectivism and, 102–3; as evolving, 114, 115; as globalizing, 5, 97, 114–15, 120–21, 142, 144; liberalization and, 114, 115, 127–28, 144; Makiguchi's influence on, 21, 27; mentor-disciple relationship and, 125; September 11, 2001, and, 183; SGI-USA and, 154, 156–57; solidarity and, 200; SSA and, 164, 168, 170; SUA and, 173; three pillars of, 5, 87, 102, 107–8; Toda and, 48–49

"Buddhist Humanism and Catholic Culture in Brazil" (Clarke), 195

Buddhist modernism, 32, 82–83

Buddhist Reformation, 130

Candomblé, Afro-Brazilian, 195

Carson, Clayborne, 178

Carter, Lawrence, 175–78

Casanova, José, 105–6

Castro, Fidel, 115

Catholicism. *See* Roman Catholicism

Chang Shuhong, 11

Chappell, David, 146, 150, 154, 157

Chicago: Parliament of the World's Religions in (1993), 3; SGI in, 147–49

China: Confucianism from, 16; Japanese relationship with, 9–10, 11, 68, 120; Lotus Sutra in, 18; Sino-Japanese War (1937–45), 29; Zhou Enlai, 10, 11, 12, 20, 120

Choose Life (Toynbee and Ikeda), 118

Christianity: Bible, 15, 18, 19; Carter and, 177–78; fundamentalists, 105; globalization and, 163; Ikeda and, 124, 126; Lotus Sutra compared with, 18; Makiguchi's contact with, 31; missionary, 19; Mission San Xavier del Bac, 126, 145; and racism, 148; Reformation, 130; and right-wing politics, 13; and self-responsibility, 195; and SGI-USA members' backgrounds, 147; in Singapore, 165; and Tokugawa Japan, 25; and Toynbee, 116, 118. *See also* Protestantism; Roman Catholicism

Chuo Koron, 117–18

church-state separation, 105–6, 209. *See also* civil religion

civil religion, 25, 26–27, 28, 182. *See also* church-state separation; State Shinto

civil rights movement, 148, 157, 176–78

Clarke, Peter, 195

Club of Rome, 119, 175, 185

Cold War, 56; American scholars on, 68, 102; Ikeda presidency and, 86, 162; and SG as revolutionary force, 55, 93; Toda and, 53, 55, 83

collectivism, Japanese, 30, 52, 102–3

Columbine High School shootings (1999), 156–57

Communists, Japanese party, 53, 94, 96, 97. *See also* China

The Complete Works of Daisaku Ikeda (Ikeda), 151

Confucianism, 15, 16, 25

Cooper, Abraham, 175, 178–81

Cornille, Catherine, 142

critics, 37, 67–69, 80, 101–2, 139, 209–10; of Ikeda, 3–6, 23, 37, 49, 54, 63, 67–69, 80, 96, 106, 115, 119, 127–28, 168, 207–8; Japan-bashing, 70, 204;

of Makiguchi, 69; Metraux vs.,
65; and Osaka incident, 80, 98–99;
of SG aggressiveness, 62, 80, 99–101;
of SG politics, 69, 105–6; of SG
youth, 58; of Toda, 54, 55, 58, 66, 67;
Toynbee's defense against, 119. *See
also* media
culture, 107, 200–1; multiculturalism,
188–89; '60s-era, 3, 50, 61, 93, 150–52,
182. *See also* art; culture festivals;
Min-On Concert Association; *zuiho-
bini*
culture festivals, 132, 153–54, 156–57, 189,
199
Curie, Marie, 20; and Soka University, 6,
8, 12

dai-gohonzon, 34, 95, 131, 132
daimoku. See Nam-myoho-renge-kyo
Dator, James, 147
Davis, Winston, 77
Deansboro, 66–67, 81, 168, 210; author
working on book in, 67–70, 81–82,
181–82, 202, 203–4; and September 11,
2001, 181–82
democracy: Brazilian, 193; Japanese, 61,
68–69, 79, 95–96; SG internal, 97,
206. *See also* rights
deprivatization of religion, 105–6
Dewey, John, 28
dharma, 19; Makiguchi and, 32; as mystic
law, 16–17; Shakyamuni and, 14–15;
zuiho-bini and, 89. See also *mappo*
Dicker-Brandeis, Friedl, 181
Diet (Japanese parliament): establishment
of (1890), 26; peace constitution
submitted to, 52; SG members in, 56,
69, 79, 96, 106
Dobbelaere, Karel, 102–3
Dower, John, 51
dukkha, 14–15, 140. *See also* suffering
Duque de Caxias, 200–1, 210–11

Eagle Peak, 20, 142, 146; Shakyamuni on,
18–19, 33, 39, 48, 200; Toda with
Nichiren on, 83–84; trip to, 92
Earth Summit (Rio de Janeiro), 192
economy, 181; consumerism, 159–60, 163;
global, 82, 168, 169, 174–75; Japan's,
53, 86, 87, 93, 175; and urban poor,
40. *See also* markets, financial
Edo, 2, 29, 30, 123. *See also* Tokyo

Edokko, Ikeda as, 123, 124
Edo-Tokyo Museum, 24, 30–31
education: BSGI and, 193–94, 198–201;
FASO circus school, 198–200, Ikeda
and, 107–8, 173–74; Kansai SG
schools, 108–13; Makiguchi and, 5, 10,
21–22, 27–29, 107–8, 166, 173, 193–94;
SG centrality of, 8–9, 28, 107–8;
Shinto taught in, 27; Singapore Soka
Kindergarten, 166; Soka Kyoiku
Gakkai (Value Creating Education
Society), 21; and spirituality, 37, 108;
Toda and, 46–47, 53, 78, 142, 173.
See also Kansai Soka schools; Soka
University; SUA (Soka University of
America)
Embracing Defeat (Dower), 51
emperor: divinity of, 24, 142; Makiguchi
and, 29, 40–41; Meiji-era, 25–27, 106;
stripped of divinity, 32
Epp, Robert, 144
ethnic composition: of BSGI, 141, 184,
185, 187, 188–89; and Los Angeles
identity politics, 188; and multiculturalism, 188–89; of SGI-USA, 146–50;
of SSA, 141, 164, 165
evangelical Buddhism, 55, 57–58. See also
shakubuku

Fabrica de Sonhos (FASO, the Dream
Factory) circus school, 198–200
"Faith and Practice" (McLaughlin), 103
favelas in Rio de Janeiro, 196, 197,
198–201
55 System, 53
Forbes magazine, 207–8
Ford, Ann, 176
Frank, Anne, 180
Freedom and Influence (Williams), 154
Friedl and the Children of Terezin
(exhibit), 181
Friedman, Thomas, 159
Fujimoto, Nichijun, 128
Fujiwara, Hirotatsu, 95, 96, 105
Fukunaka, Kazuhito, 100–1
fukusa, 89

Gakkai. *See* Soka Gakkai
Galtung, Johan, 115
Gandhi, Mohandas, 156–57, 174, 175–77
Gandhi Institute for Reconciliation
(Morehouse), 176

Gandhi-King-Ikeda Community Builders Prize (Morehouse), 175–77
Gardner, James, 147–48
gays, Ikeda's gesture in support of, 49, 50
gender roles: globalization and, 143. *See also* Women's Division (SG); women's rights in Japan
Germany: Nazis in, 180; neo-Kantians in, 28
Glass Children (Ikeda), 71, 120
Global Citizens (Hammond and Machacek), 67
globalization, 2, 22, 24, 87–93, 114–21, 204–7; of author, 66, 70, 181; of Buddhist Humanism, 5, 97, 114–15, 120–21, 142, 144; economic, 82, 168, 169, 174–75; vs. insularity, 11–12, 91–92; Japaneseness and, 143–44, 148, 160, 164–65, 184, 192, 194, 204–5; Japanization/ Americanization, 209; liberalization and, 114, 115, 127–28, 143–44, 204; Makiguchi and, 29, 160, 204; multilateralism and, 182–83, 207; Parliament of the World's Religions and, 3; by rank-and-file Japanese SG, 141; September 11, 2001, and, 181–82, 189; SG break with Nichiren Shoshu and, 127–28, 130, 137, 157; SUA and, 175; *zuiho-bini* and, 89, 140–70, 184, 189–90, 191, 194. *See also* global *kosen-rufu;* networking, Ikeda's; peace; SGI (Soka Gakkai International)
global *kosen-rufu,* 85, 88, 143, 160, 183; in Asia, 90; and BSGI, 184, 191, 194, 199, 203; and SSA, 164, 169; in United States, 88, 149
gohonzon, 33, 78, 79, 205; Buddhist Jews and, 179; *dai-gohonzon,* 34, 95, 131, 132; globalization of, 142; vs. human image, 135; Landi's, 197, 198; mirror guidance and, 158; priest-laity break and, 131; song about, 210–11; visualizing, 47
Golden, Daniel, 154
gongyo, 33, 78, 133
Gosho (Nichiren), 16, 32, 94, 105; global-ization of, 142, 157, 158; Nichiren Shoshu–SG break and, 129, 130; Toda and, 53
Gwee Yee Hean, 167–68

Habuki, Daniel, 172–73
Hachioji (Tokyo), 5–6
Hachiya, Yumiko, 91
Hamayotsu, Toshiko, 106–7
Hamilton College (NY), 6
Hammond, Phillip, 153, 154, 158–59
happiness, 79, 81–82, 99, 140, 205; Akiya on, 60–61; in BSGI, 201; Ikeda on, 158; Makiguchi on, 25, 28–29, 32, 78, 104; media on SG and, 69, 151–52, 155; mirror guidance and, 158; Nichiren Shoshu–SG break and, 128; Sho-Hondo and, 135; street shakubuku and, 151; TFAM and, 104
Harada, Minoru, 94, 124
Hase, Ieyasu, 187
Hawaii, Ikeda's trip to, 85, 87–88, 91
Hinduism, 165
Hippy to Happy (1969), 151–52
Hiroshima, bombing of, 51, 83, 143, 208
Hispanic Americans and SGI-USA, 149–50
hobobarai, 99–100
Holocaust exhibit, 180
Hosoi, Takudo, 136–37
Hugo, Victor, and Soka University, 6, 7–8, 12, 22, 91
humanism, 20, 91, 94; Makiguchi's, 21, 27, 28, 103, 121. *See also* Buddhist Humanism, Ikeda's
The Human Revolution (Ikeda), 47, 56–57, 62, 79, 83–84, 128–29
The Human Revolution (Toda), 47
Human Rights in the Twenty-First Century (Ikeda and Athayde), 196
Hurst, Jane, 130
Huyghe, René, 119

ichigo ichie, 190
ichinen sanzen, 81
I Denounce Soka Gakkai (Fujiwara), 95, 96
Ikeda, Daisaku, 1, 5, 43, 71–98, 115–20, 175, 206–9; Akiya and, 59, 72, 76–77; and art, 104, 105; author meeting, 35–38, 121–26, 162–63; *Before It Is Too Late* (with Peccei), 185; and Brazil, 85, 87–88, 184, 185, 188, 189, 190, 192, 194, 196; brothers of, 71, 92, 124; "Buddhism Is the Mirror That Perfectly Reflects Our Lives," 158; childhood of, 71–72, 74, 88; *The*

Complete Works of Daisaku Ikeda, 151; contemporary middle way of, 160; critics of, 3–6, 23, 37, 49, 54, 63, 67–69, 80, 96, 115, 119, 127–28, 168, 207–8; diaries of, 72–73, 125, 165; and education, 107–9, 173–74; generous gestures of, 17, 43, 49–50, 124; *Glass Children*, 71, 120; Gwee and, 167–68; home of, 23; as honorary president of SG, 128; *The Human Revolution*, 47, 56–57, 62, 79, 83–84, 128–29; innovations of, 86–87, 88, 127; institutions founded by, 102–3, 107; joining SG, 76; and Kashiwabara, 56–57, 76; and Kurihara, 99; leaders' meeting with, 38–39; and liberalization of SG, 100, 114, 115, 127–28, 143–44, 204; and Makiguchi Hall, 34–38; Makiguchi's influence on, 9–10, 21–22, 27, 32, 87, 92, 114, 121; Makiguchi Memorial Garden monument to, 44; marriage of (1952), 72; mentor-disciple relationship with SG members, 92–93, 106–7, 125, 156, 166, 173–74, 194, 206; and modernism, 87, 131; Morehouse College and, 175–78; "Morigasaki Beach," 74; *The New Human Revolution*, 88, 90, 91–92; "A New Strategy for Environmental Protection," 192; Nichiren's influence on, 16, 37, 80, 94, 97–98; and Osaka incident, 79–80, 98; peace proposals of, 182, 185; in photos/videos, 56, 75, 102, 119; poetry by, 9, 71–72, 73–74, 84, 144–45; and politics, 5, 23, 77–80, 95–96, 150, 162, 182; presidency of SG, 1, 5, 21–22, 36, 43, 44, 76–97, 107, 114–20, 125, 128, 130, 180, 186, 206, 207; presidency of SGI, 128; and priests, 90, 92, 95–96, 115, 127–28, 132, 135–38; and Rabbi Cooper, 179–81; and racism in United States, 149; reading list of, 73; and September 11, 2001, 182, 207; and *shakubuku*, 79–80, 86, 87–90, 93, 100; and Sho-Hondo, 95, 115, 127, 132, 135; at Soka University, 4–12, sons of, 35–36, 168, SSA and, 161–63, 164, 165, 166; style of, 9, 11, 37, 59, 77, 89, 122–24; and SUA, 171–72, 174, 175; succession to, 36, 206–7; and Toda, 37, 42, 55–56, 60–66, 72–77, 83–84, 88, 92, 114,

123–25; and Toynbee, 34–35, 116–19; *Unlocking the Mysteries of Birth and Death*, 145; U.S. visits of, 85, 87–90, 91, 121, 146, 157–58; *The Wisdom of the Lotus Sutra*, 145; and *zuiho-bini*, 89, 143–44, 204. See also Buddhist Humanism, Ikeda's; globalization; networking, Ikeda's

Ikeda, Hiromasa, 35–36, 168, 174
Ikeda, Kaneko: home of, 23; at Makiguchi Hall, 35, 36–37, 38; marriage of (1952), 72; paintings of, 35–36, 177; and SUA library, 174; and Toynbees, 35, 117–18; in videos, 102
Ikeda, Takahiro, 35–36
Imperial Rescript on Education, 27
India, 90, 160; Gandhi, 156–57, 174, 175–77
Inoue, Kyoko, 52
Institute of Oriental Philosophy (IOP), 3, 102, 103, 120
insularity, Japan's, 9–12, 91–92. See also nationalism
internationalism. See globalization
Ise shrine, 40–41, 100, 207
Islam. See Muslims
Ivamoto, Dirce, 193–94

Japan-bashing, 70, 204
Japanese constitutions: Meiji-era, 26; peace, 51–52, 53, 55, 95–97, 100–1, 106, 206
Japanese immigrant community in Brazil, 141, 184
Japanese militarism (1930s), 3, 10; Ikeda's childhood and, 71, 121; Makiguchi and, 22, 40; occupation by United States and, 52; Toda and, 37, world peace commitment and, 143
Japanese nationalism, 9–10, 25. See also insularity, Japan's; Japaneseness
Japaneseness, 1, 6, 209; globalization and, 143–44, 148, 160, 164–65, 184, 192, 194, 204–5; priest-laity conflicts and, 128; real estate and, 155; Sensoji temple and, 29–30. See also Japanese nationalism
Japanese parliament. See Diet
Jiba, 142
Jihad vs. McWorld (Barber), 159–60
jiriki, 33
Jisshuji, 136
Jodo sect, 16–17

kaidan, 33–34, 205; globalization of, 142; *kokuritsu kaidan,* 54, 95; Nittatsu and Ikeda and, 95, 96, 115, 129, 130, 135; priest-SG break and, 34, 129–35; Sho-Hondo as, 84–85, 95, 115, 129, 130, 131, 135

kaikans, 129, 200–1, 210–11

Kamakura Japan, 3, 14, 16–17, 34, 37, 75

kami, 25, 30, 40

Kannon (Kuan Yin), 29, 30

Kansai Soka schools, 108–13

Kansai spirit, 99, 187–88, 191

karma, 15; changing, 78, 89, 99, 146; of house of Toda-Ikeda meeting, 75–76; and Ikeda overseas trip, 88; negative, in United States, 154; Toynbee and, 118

Kashiwabara, Yasu, 56–59, 76, 87–88

Kawabe, Shoshin, 131

Kawada, Yoichi, 103

King, Martin Luther Jr., 156, 175–77; and world house, 178, 183, 188–89

Kishi, Nobusuke, 83

Kobayashi, Hiroyasu, 104–5

Komei, 23. *See also* Komeito

Komeito, 23, 95–96, 102; elections, 38, 49, 96; Hamayotsu and, 106–7; and Japan's pacifism, 206; separated from SG, 97; Zhou and, 120

Korea: Korean War, 53, 73; North, 182; South, 141

Kosaka, Júlio, 197

kosen-rufu, 36, 79, 80, 97–98, 133–34; as flow, 99; Nichiren and, 44, 94, 139; priest-laity conflicts and, 137, 139; after September 11, 2001, 183; at Sho-Hondo, 134; Toda and, 44, 61, 83–84, 88, 99, 136, 187. *See also* global *kosen-rufu*

Kosen-rufu Day, 187

Kuan Yin, 29, 30

Kurihara, Akiko, 98–99

kyodatsu condition, 51, 78

Kyoto Sangyo University, 117

Landi, Magdalena, 197–98

laws. *See* mystic law; secret laws

Lee Kuan Yew, 161

Leonardo da Vinci, 20; and Soka University, 6, 8, 12, 107

lesbians, Ikeda's gesture in support of, 49, 50

The Lexus and the Olive Tree (Friedman), 159

liberalism: nineteenth-century Protestant, 12–13; September 11, 2001, and, 183

liberalization, SG, 100, 114, 115, 127–28, 143–44, 204

life conditions, 81

life-force philosophy, 48–49, 53, 55–58, 78, 83

lions of Nichiren, 163, 175, 202, 211

Literacy Poles project (BSGI), 192

Look magazine, 68–69

Los Angeles: identity politics in, 188; Ikeda visits, 88, 89, 157; SGI-USA in, 89, 152–53, 155

Lotus Sutra, 15, 18–19, 32; Bonten, 52–53, 88; chant from, 2, 17; egalitarian readings of, 157; Ikeda and, 72, 87, 157; IOP course on, 157; Makiguchi and, 21, 31–32; Nichiren and, 17, 32–33; recitation of, by SG members, 78; secret laws of, 32–34, 90, 95, 129, 131, 145, 195; Toda and, 47, 48, 53

Luther, Martin, 130

Lu Xun, 10

MacArthur, Douglas, 51, 52–53, 88, 106

Machacek, David, 153, 154, 158–59

magical worldview, 76

Mahayana Buddhism, 15–16, 17, 18, 118, 121

Mahikari, 142

Mainichi Shimbun, 117

Maintenance of Religious Harmony Act (Singapore), 165

Makiguchi, Tsunesaburo, 5, 9–10, 28–34, 40–41, 42; critics of, 69; and deprivatizing religion, 106; and education, 5, 10, 21–22, 27–29, 107–8, 166, 173, 193–94; on faith and disaster, 75–76; and globalization, 29, 160, 204; and humanism, 21, 27, 28, 103, 121; imprisonment/death of, 9, 21, 22, 25, 38, 41, 47, 48, 54, 84; influence of, on Ikeda, 9–10, 21–22, 27, 32, 87, 92, 114, 121; and Ise shrine, 40–41, 100, 207; Kashiwabara and, 56, 57; Makiguchi Memorial Garden monument to, 44; and modernism, 21, 25, 27–28, 32, 82–83, 87; politics of, 5, 9–10, 29, 40–41, 208; SG presidency of, 5, 21–22, 40, 43, 44, 76, 84, 107, 125, 186, 206; Toda and, 21–22, 32, 42–49,

53–55, 82–83, 125; and value creation, 21, 28–29, 31–32, 104
Makiguchi Hall, 34–38, 70, 174, 179
Makiguchi Memorial Garden, 43–46; cherry tree for Ann in, 43, 45–46, 67, 121–22, 126–27, 210; cherry tree for author in, 126–27, 210
Makiguchi Project in Action, 193–95, 201
Manchester Guardian, 34–35
Mandela, Nelson, 119–20
mappo: Nichiren and, 16, 33, 90, 128, 143; after September 11, 2001, 183; Toda and, 53–54; Toynbee and, 118
markets, financial, 160, 163; bull, 2, 22, 63, 82, 189; collapse of, 82, 159, 168, 174–75, 189
Martins, Telma Lúcia Ferreira Moreira, 198–200
Maruyama, Masao, 27
Massey, Walter, 176
Matsuda, Shigeyuki, 108, 112
McLaughlin, Levi, 103
McNeill, William H., 116–19
media: on Ikeda, 4–5, 37, 49, 80, 179, 207–8; and Ikeda's May 1970 speech, 97; Japanese TV, 14, 50–51, 159; of modern Japan, 69–70; after September 11, 2001, 182; vs. SG, 37, 68–69; SGI-USA Hispanic, 149; SG's *Seikyo Shimbun*, 7, 23, 59–60, 77, 115–16, 120; on Singapore caning incident, 160; after Toda's death, 85; and Toynbee, 117; understanding of Buddhism in United States, 172; and videos, 102, 135–36, 151–52. *See also* critics
Meiji Restoration, 3, 25–27, 106, 182; Makiguchi and, 21, 25, 28, 29, 87
mentor-disciple relationship, 63, 103–4; of Ikeda–SG members, 92–93, 106–7, 125, 156, 166, 173–74, 194, 206; of Makiguchi-Toda, 42; of Toda-Ikeda, 42, 63, 66, 72, 76–77, 84, 124–25
Metraux, Daniel, 65, 128, 160
militarism. *See* Japanese militarism (1930s); wars
Min-On Concert Association, 23, 102, 104–5, 107; and Ikeda's networking dialogues, 115, 120; and Vieira tour, 185–86, 194
mirror guidance, 158
Mission San Xavier del Bac, 145

modernism, 30–31, 98, 137; Asia and, 168; Buddhist, 32, 82–83; Ikeda and, 87, 131; Makiguchi and, 21, 25, 27 28, 32, 82–83, 87; and SG appeal to East Asian countries, 160; and Sho-Hondo architecture, 135; and Soka University's architecture, 5, 11 12; and Taisekiji facilities, 79; Toda and, 53, 78 79, 82–83, 87. *See also* Meiji Restoration; westernization
Moraes, Flávio Fava de, 191–92, 194
Morehouse College, 175–78
"Morigasaki Beach" (Ikeda), 74
Mtshali, Oswald, 120
multiculturalism, 188–89. *See also* ethnic composition
multilateralism, 207; institutional, 182–83
music, 104–5, 185–86, 194, 210–11. *See also* Min-On Concert Association
Muslims, 159–60; fundamentalist, 105; Malay, 165
Myoshinko, 129
mystic law, 16–17, 97–98. See also *dharma*
mystic opportunity, learning as, 8 9

Nagasaki, bombing of, 51, 83, 143, 208
Nagashima, Danny, 155–56, 176
Nakajima, Getulino, 184
Nam-myoho-renge-kyo, 224; author experimenting with, 2, 81, 145; and BSGI, 186–87, 195, 198, 199, 200–1; critics vs., 69; globalization of, 142, 151; in *gohonzon*, 33; on knees, 143; *kosen-rufu* and, 139; at leaders' meeting, 39; mirror guidance and, 158; Nichiren and, 17, 32–33, 145; performance of Buddha nature and, 33, 145, 205; and GI-USA, 148–51; and SSA members, 165–66; Toda and, 47, 48, 78
Namura, Kazuichi, 119 20
nationalism: globalization and, 142; Japanese, 9–10, 25; U.S., 24, 182. *See also* insularity, Japan's; Japaneseness; patriotism
Nellis, Darin, 157
networking, Ikeda's, 114–16, 119, 121, 160, 168, 180; and Buddhist Humanism, 114–15, 120–21, 142, 144; pan-Asian, 208–9. *See also* globalization
"The New Common Sense" (Williams), 154

New Freedom Bell tour (1987), 154–55
The New Human Revolution (Ikeda), 88,
    90, 91–92
"New Japanese Religions in the West"
    (Cornille), 142
"A New Strategy for Environmental
    Protection" (Ikeda), 192
New York City: Ikeda visits, 88, 91, 121;
    September 11, 2001, 181–84, 189, 205,
    207; SGI-USA in, 121, 137–38, 156
Nichijun, 84
Nichikan, 131
Nichiko, Hori, 79
Nichiren, 3, 14–17, 32–34; and Buddha,
    128, 130, 143; collection of writings
    by, 79; globalization and, 90, 143;
    hobobarai, 100; Ikeda influenced by,
    16, 37, 80, 94, 97–98; and *kaidan*, 33,
    84–85, 95, 115, 129; and *kosen-rufu*,
    44, 94, 139; lions of, 163, 175, 202,
    211; Makiguchi and, 16; and *mappo*,
    16, 33, 90, 128, 143; on Mount Hiei,
    18; and Nam-myoho-renge-kyo,
    17, 32–33, 145; poems by, 122,
    126–27; *Rissho Ankoku Ron*, 17, 34,
    88; on Sado Island, 75; Toda and, 16,
    47, 48, 53, 65, 79, 80, 84, 92–93, 95,
    115, 131; U.S. media and, 172; and
    zuiho-bini, 141–42. See also *Gosho*;
    secret laws
Nichiren Buddhism, 14–15, 18, 30, 47, 94;
    and art, 104; globalization and, 90,
    92, 115, 194; *Gosho* as scriptural
    authority for, 16, 32; Ikeda innova-
    tions and, 87, 127; and *kaidan*, 33–34,
    54, 129, 130; Kurosawa's *Dodes'ka-
    Den* on, 69; and Makiguchi, 28,
    29, 31–32; sects of, 21, 32; and self-
    awakening education, 173; and SG vs.
    seminary education, 166; Toda and,
    47, 48, 54, 92, 94; *zuiho-bini* and,
    143–44. See also Nichiren; Nichiren
    Shoshu; Soka Gakkai
Nichiren Shoshu, 21, 22, 128–29, 138;
    aniconic sensibility of, 135; Ikeda criti-
    cized by, 127–28; Ikeda joining SG in
    temple of, 76; Lotus Sutra and, 32;
    Makiguchi joining, 21, 22, 32, 46;
    priests leaving, 136–39, 166–67; Sho-
    Hondo architect and, 134, 135; Toda
    and, 42–43, 46, 53, 78, 79, 83, 84.
    See also Nichiren Shoshu–SG break

(1991); priests; Taisekiji temple
    complex
Nichiren Shoshu of America (NSA),
    146–47, 150, 155, 157
Nichiren Shoshu–SG break (1991), 5, 23,
    42, 79, 127–39; Ikeda's U.S. visit on
    eve of, 146, 157–58; *kaidan* and, 34,
    129–35; Nikken Abe excommunicates
    SG, 32, 114–15, 129–31, 138–39; SSA
    members and, 165, 166, 168
Nichiren: The Buddhist Prophet (Anesaki),
    16
Nikken Abe, 128, 137; demolition of
    SG structures by, 131–37, 168; excom-
    munication of SG by, 32, 114–15,
    129–31, 138–39; personal psychology
    of, 129, 136, 137, 138; priests leaving
    Nichiren Shoshu because of, 136–39,
    166–67
Nikko, 132
Nisei in SGI-USA, 147
Nishiguchi, Ryozo, 99–100
Nittatsu: Asian trip of, 90, 92; daughter
    and sons of, 134, 136; Ikeda's
    relationship with, 90, 92, 95, 96, 115,
    127, 132, 135–38; and *kaidan*, 95, 96,
    115, 129, 130, 135; Myoshinko
    disbanded by, 129; Nikken vs., 129,
    130, 132; and Sho-Hondo, 115, 127,
    132, 135
Noguchi, Mitsunari, 104
nondualism, Buddhist, 19, 32, 135
nongovernmental organizations (NGOs),
    121, 191–92, 194
nonviolence: and college programs,
    176–77; Japan's pacifism and, 206;
    September 11, 2001, and, 182; VOV
    campaign, 156–57, 176. See also
    pacifism; peace
Noriega, Manuel, 115
North Korea, 182; Korean War, 53, 73
nuclear arms: Hiroshima and Nagasaki, 51,
    83, 143; North Korea and, 183; race,
    83; Toda calls for abolition of (1957),
    83, 107, 121

O'Brien, David M., 30, 52
occupation of Japan, U.S., 3, 42–43, 49,
    51–53, 86, 92, 106, 208
Ong Bon Chai (B.C.), 160–61, 164,
    166, 169
Operation C, 129

organizations: nongovernmental (NGOs), 121, 191–92, 194; in SG, 3, 23, 102–6. *See also* political parties
orientalism, 35
Osaka incident, 79–80, 98, 190, 191
Ota Ward (Tokyo), 70–76, 123–24
out-of-placeness, 6, 12. *See also* sameness/difference
Ozu, Yasujiro, 69

pachinko, 139
pacifism: Japanese, 52, 71, 206; Nichiren's message of, 98. *See also* peace
Panama, 115
Parks, Rosa, 157
Parliament of the World's Religions, Chicago (1993), 3
patriotism: and BSGI, 192; and SGI-USA, 154–55, 192. *See also* nationalism
Pauling, Linus, 115, 174
peace, 159; Ikeda's proposals for, 182, 185; Min-On and, 105; Morehouse College and, 175–77, 178; September 11, 2001, and, 182, 183, 205; SG missionary impulse for, 143; SGI-USA and, 155; Sho-Hondo dedicated to, 115, 133–34; Toda and, 83, 107; Toynbee and, 118; U.N. and, 121. *See also* pacifism
peace constitution, Japanese, 51–52, 53, 55, 95–97, 100–1, 106, 206
Pearl, Daniel and Mariane, 182
Peccei, Aurelio, 119, 185
Perry, Matthew, 25
pilgrimage sites: Bodhgaya, 90; Taisekiji temple complex, 79, 83, 131–35
pillarization, 102–3
Plato and Soka University, 7, 8, 61
poetry: Ikeda's, 9, 71–72, 73–74, 84, 144–45; Nichiren's, 122, 126–27
political parties: Japanese Communist party, 53, 94, 96, 97; Komei, 23; Liberal Democratic Party (LDP), 23. *See also* Komeito
politics, 37, 205; Buddhist Humanism overseas and, 144; civil religion and, 25, 27; critics of SG's, 69, 105–6; global, 114, 119–20, 205; Ikeda and, 5, 23, 77–80, 95–96, 150, 162, 182; Makiguchi and, 5, 9–10, 29, 40–41, 208; Nichiren and, 34; *shakubuku* and, 55, 150; '60s-era, 3, 50, 61, 93,

150–52, 182; SUA and, 172; Toda and, 5, 56, 61, 77–80, 150; U.S. right-wing, 13, 183. *See also* democracy; Diet (Japanese parliament); emperor; globalization; Japanese militarism (1930s); nationalism; political parties; wars
populism and BSGI, 185–86
Poseidon and Soka University, 6, 7–8, 10
priests: *bozu*, 136; Christian Reformation and, 130; conflicts between laity and, 32, 114–15, 127–39; first priesthood issue, 114, 128–29; *gosoryo*, 136; Ikeda and, 90, 92, 95–96, 115, 127–28, 132, 135–38; leaving Nichiren Shoshu, 136–39, 166–67; Nichijun, 84; Nikken reasserting authority of, 128; second priesthood issue, 114, 129; Shoshinkai, 129, 137. *See also* Nichiren Shoshu; Nichiren Shoshu–SG break (1991); Nikken Abe; Nittatsu
prison: Makiguchi in, 9, 21, 22, 25, 38, 41, 47, 48, 54, 84; Toda in, 47–49, 51, 53, 54, 66
Protestantism: nineteenth-century liberal, 12–13; Puritan, 24–25, 177; Reformation, 130; and SGI-USA members' backgrounds, 147; Shinto comparison with, 24–25, 30; in Singapore, 164; and Toynbee, 116
The Protocols of the Elders of Zion, 178
Public Security Preservation Law (1925), 40
Pure Land Buddhists, 16–17, 30

racism: anti-Semitism, 178, 180; Christianity and, 148; SGI-USA and, 148–49
Raphael, 7, 11, 12, 107
Reader, Ian, 78
Reformation, Buddhist, 130
reincarnation, 84, 203
religious freedom: in Japan, 30, 52–53, 79, 88, 95, 97, 100–1, 106; in Singapore, 164, 165
rights: African American civil rights, 148, 157, 176–78; collectivism vs. personal, 30; equal, 157–58; free speech, 95–97; global issues and, 176; human, 106, 178, 180; Meiji-era, 26, 106; religious freedom, 30, 52–53, 79, 88, 95, 97, 100–1, 106; religious postwar movements and, 52; women's, 51, 77

Rio de Janeiro, 195–201; Earth Summit in, 192
Rissho Ankoku Ron (Nichiren), 17, 34, 88
Roman Catholicism: and author's upbringing, 18, 134, 163; in Brazil, 184, 186–87, 195; in Philippines, 160; Reformation, 130; and SGI-USA members' backgrounds, 147; and Toynbee, 116

Sado Island, 75
Saicho, 18
Saito, Roberto (Yasuhiro), 184, 190–91
Saito, Silvia (Etsuko), 184–85, 190–91
sameness/difference, 12; Edo-Tokyo Museum, 30–31; everydayness of members, 203–4; movies, 69–70; religion in politics, 23; Soka University, 5–6, 7–8; videos of '70s SG, 102. *See also* Japaneseness
Sandroni, Cicero, 196
Santa Monica, SGI-USA headquarters in, 155, 182
São Paulo, 183–95, 203
São Paulo University, 191–92
Scott-Stokes, Henry, 96
secret laws, 32–34, 90, 95, 129, 131, 145, 195. See also *gohonzon; kaidan;* Nam-myoho-renge-kyo
seikyo itchi, 27
Seikyo Shimbun, 7, 23, 59–60, 77, 115–16, 120
seimei, 48–49. *See also* life-force philosophy
Sensoji temple, 29–30
September 11, 2001, 181–84, 189, 205, 207
SG. *See* Soka Gakkai
SGI (Soka Gakkai International), 174; in Britain, 141; building of, 23–24; Ikeda presidency of, 128; Ikeda succession in, 206–7; Sho-Hondo attendees, 134; Singapore Soka Association (SSA), 141, 160–70; in South Africa, 141; and U.N. Economic and Social Council, 121. *See also* BSGI (Brazil Soka Gakkai International); globalization; SGI-USA; SG-Japan
SGI-USA, 23, 146–59, 204; in Boston, 67, 148, 149; Ikeda visits, 85, 87–90, 91, 121, 146, 157–58; member numbers of, 150, 158; in New York City, 121, 137–38, 156; Nichiren Shoshu of

America (NSA), 146–47, 150, 155, 157; and patriotism, 154–55, 192; period of dialogue, 146, 157; period of evangelism, 146; Santa Monica headquarters of, 155, 182; SUA, 171–76, 208; war brides in, 141; and *zuiho-bini,* 89, 141, 146–59
SG-Japan, 1–66, 70–80, 82–86, 205, 207; Akiya presidency of, 59–60; Carter visits, 176–77; headquarters of, 23; main constituency of, 78; member numbers of, 23, 53, 77, 84, 86; schools of, 108–13, 173. *See also* education; politics; Soka Gakkai
shakubuku, 55; aggressive, 62, 80, 99–101; of Akiya, 60; BSGI and, 184–85, 186–87, 190–91, 194, 197–98; chant behind, 145, 150; Ikeda and, 79–80, 86, 87–90, 93, 100; moderating, 97; priest-laity conflicts and, 138; SGI-USA and, 89, 147–54; and *shoju,* 169–70; SSA, 166, 169–70; street, 151–53; Toda campaigns, 55, 57–58, 77, 78–80, 86, 138, 151
Shakubuku Dai-Koshin (Great Propagation Drive), 77
Shakubuku Kyoten (Propagation Handbook), 77
Shakyamuni, 14–16, 33, 48; birthday observances for, 80; at Bodhgaya, 90; on Eagle Peak, 18–19, 33, 39, 48, 200; Nichiren supplanting, 128; and *zuiho-bini,* 141
Shaw, Larry, 152–53
Shibata, Koji, 43–46
Shiina, Hosho, 136, 137–38
Shimazono, Susumu, 78
Shinanomachi (Tokyo), 23–24, 106–10; Akiya interview, 59–63; Kashiwabara interview, 56–59; and Nichiren Shoshu–SG break, 130, 131; Ota Ward, 70–76, 123–24
Shingakudo (New Student League), 93–94
Shinto, 24–25; Buddhism and, 25, 29–30; *kami,* 25, 30, 40; Nichiren and, 16; shrines, 24, 40–41, 100; in Tokugawa Japan, 25. *See also* State Shinto
Shiotsu, Toru, 94, 103
Shiraki, Giichiro, 79–80
shishin-sou-o, 132
shisohan, 41

Sho-Hondo, 132–34; architect Yokoyama, 134–35; demolished by Nikken, 115, 131–37, 168; as *kaidan*, 84–85, 95, 115, 129, 130, 131, 135; Nittatsu and Ikeda work toward, 115, 127, 132

shoju, 169–70

Shoshinkai, 129, 137

shoten zenjin, 53

Silk Road, 10, 11

Silva, Dilma de Melo, 193, 195

Simon Wiesenthal Center, 178, 180

Singapore, 159–70

Singapore Soka Association (SSA), 141, 160–70

Singh, Karan, 115

Sino-Japanese War (1937–45), 29

sociology of demand and supply, 158–59

Socrates, 20, 28; and Soka University, 7, 8, 22, 61, 91

Soka Gakkai, 23; education as central to, 8–9, 28, 107–8; esoteric side of, 81; formal incorporation of (1937–40), 40; gender separation and, 143; history of, 1, 3, 5, 9, 14–15; Ikeda as honorary president of, 128; Ikeda presidency of, 1, 5, 21–22, 36, 43, 44, 76–97, 107, 114–20, 125, 128, 150, 180, 186, 206, 207; liberalization and, 100, 114, 127, 143–44; Makiguchi presidency of, 5, 21–22, 40, 43, 44, 76, 84, 107, 125, 186, 206; member numbers of, 23, 53, 77, 84, 86, 150, 158, 184–85; organizations in, 3, 23, 102–6; Overseas Affairs Section, 88; *Seikyo Shimbun*, 7, 23, 59–60, 77, 115–16, 120; and "sevens," 84, 88; Study Department, 77; Toda presidency of, 5, 21–22, 43, 44, 66, 75–77, 82–84, 107, 125, 150, 186, 197, 206; Young Men's Division, 101. *See also* globalization; Ikeda, Daisaku; Makiguchi, Tsunesaburo; Nichiren Shoshu–SG break (1991); SGI (Soka Gakkai International); SG-Japan; Toda, Josei; Women's Division (SG); Youth Division (SG)

The Sokagakkai and Mass Society (White), 68

"Soka Gakkai Brings 'Absolute Happiness,'" 69

"The Soka Gakkai: Buddhism and the Creation of a Harmonious and Peaceful Society," 67

Soka Gakkai, Builders of the Third Civilization (Dator), 147

Soka Gakkai in America (Hammond and Machacek), 153, 154, 158–59

Soka Kyoiku Gakkai (Value Creating Education Society), 21

Soka University, 4–12; architecture of, 5, 6, 11–12; and China, 11, 120; founding of, 5, 9, 22; Gwee and, 167; IOP, 3, 102, 103, 120; and Jewish issues, 178–79, 180; Makiguchi as guiding spirit of, 28; Western figures represented at, 6, 7–8, 10, 11, 12, 22, 61, 91, 107

Soka University of America (SUA), 171–76, 208

South Africa, 119–20, 141

South Korea: Korean War, 53, 73; SG in, 141

SSA (Singapore Soka Association), 141, 160–70

State Shinto, 27; Akiya and, 60; Ikeda and, 10; Makiguchi vs., 29, 54, 208; occupation and, 52

Stone, Jacqueline, 17, 145

Straits Times newspaper, 169

A Study of History (Toynbee), 116, 117

SUA (Soka University of America), 171–76, 208

succession to Ikeda, 36, 206–7

suffering, 14–15, 16, 18, 19. *See also dukkha*

Sugihara, Chiune, 186

Suiko-kai leadership group, 61

Summers, Dan, 146

The Sun Rises (1987), 155

Taguchi, Eduardo, 184, 189

Taisekiji temple complex, 92, 131–34, 138; *dai-gohonzon*, 34, 95, 131, 132; demolitions of SG structures by Nikken, 115, 131–37, 168; *kaidan*, 34, 84–85, 95, 115, 129, 130, 131, 135; Makiguchi refusing to recant at, 40–41; Mieido, 132, 133; pilgrimages to, 79, 83–84, 131–35; SG banned/excommunicated from, 23, 32, 79, 114–15, 129–31, 138–39; SG building projects, 79, 92, 95, 115, 129–37, 168. *See also* Sho-Hondo

Tanabe, George J. Jr., 78

Taoism, 15

tariki, 33

Tehranian, Majid, 207

temples: Asakusa complex, 24, 29–30; Jisshuji, 136; Soka AnLe Temple (Singapore), 166. *See also* Taisekiji temple complex
Tenrikyo, 142
ten worlds, 81, 187
terrorism, 182–83, 189; September 11, 2001, 181–84, 189, 205, 207
Thoreau, Henry David, 176
Thurman, Howard, 176
Tipton, Steven, 151
Toda, Josei, 5, 42–66, 77–83, 174, 208; Akiya and, 59, 60, 61–62, 76–77; and *Boys' Japan,* 74; critics of, 54, 55, 58, 66, 67; death of, 9, 47, 83–85; and education, 46–47, 53, 78, 142, 173; funeral of, 65, 84; and globalization, 92, 121, 160, 204; *The Human Revolution,* 47; Ikeda and, 37, 42, 55–56, 60–66, 72–77, 83–84, 88, 92, 114, 123–25; Kashiwabara and, 56, 57–59, 76; and *kosen-rufu,* 44, 61, 83–84, 88, 99, 136, 187; and Makiguchi, 21–22, 32, 42–49, 53–55, 82–83, 125; Makiguchi Memorial Garden monument to, 44; and modernism, 53, 78–79, 82–83, 87; and Nichiren, 16, 47, 48, 53, 65, 79, 80, 84, 92–93, 95, 115, 131; vs. nuclear arms, 83, 107, 121; peace principle associated with, 83, 107; personal style of, 65; in photos/videos, 56, 75, 102; and politics, 5, 56, 61, 77–80, 150; and priests, 136, 138; prison experiences of, 47–49, 51, 53, 54, 66; *Seikyo Shimbun* founded by, 7; SG presidency of, 5, 21–22, 43, 44, 66, 75–77, 82–84, 107, 125, 150, 186, 197, 206; *shakubuku* campaigns, 55, 57–58, 77, 78–80, 86, 138, 151; *sokoto,* 84; and Taisekiji temple complex, 79, 83–84, 92, 95, 115, 131, 132
Toda Institute for Global Peace and Policy Research, 107
To Dream of Dreams (O'Brien), 30
Tokugawa Japan, 25, 29, 30, 72
Tokyo, 1–4, 24–25, 31, 70–75, 123–24, 139; bombing of (World War II), 30, 31, 71–72, 75–76; as Edo, 2, 29, 30, 123; Edo-Tokyo Museum, 24, 30–31; and emperor household, 26; and

Holocaust exhibit, 180; Hotel New Otani, 1–2, 159, 204; Keihin Industrial Zone, 71; Makiguchi in, 28; Ota Ward, 70–76, 123–24; sarin gas release on subway in, 179. *See also* SG-Japan; Soka University
Tokyo Fuji Art Museum (TFAM), 102, 104, 107, 120, 180–81
Tokyo Orchestra, 103
Tokyo Story (Ozu), 69
Tolstoy, Leo, and Soka University, 6, 7–8, 107
Toynbee, Arnold, 34–35, 116–19
Toynbee, Polly, 34–35, 37, 116
Toynbee Society (Japan), 117
tozan. See pilgrimage sites
Triple Gem, 130
Tucson, 126, 145–46

Umbanda, 186–87
unions, Japanese postwar, 51, 53; Tanro, 79
United Nations, 107, 121; Economic and Social Council, 121; Universal Declaration of Human Rights, 196
United States: Buddhists (general) in, 1–2; Hispanic culture as dominant in, 150; Ikeda visits, 85, 87–90, 91, 121, 146, 157–58; and Japaneseness, 148, 184; nationalism in, 24, 182; occupation of Japan by, 3, 43, 49, 51–53, 86, 92, 106, 208; Matthew Perry, 25; right-wing politics in, 13, 183; Security Treaty with Japan, 93, 117; September 11, 2001, 181–84, 189, 205, 207; SUA, 171–76, 208; Toynbee and, 116; in World War II, 29, 30, 31, 51, 71–72, 75–76, 83, 92, 143, 208. *See also* Boston; Chicago; Los Angeles; New York City; SGI-USA; Tucson
universe, Buddhism on, 15, 18–19, 121
Unlocking the Mysteries of Birth and Death (Ikeda), 145

Value Creating Society, 21, 23. *See also* Soka Gakkai
value creation: Makiguchi and, 21, 28–29, 31–32, 104; *shakubuku* on, 166
via negativa, 48
Victory over Violence (VOV) campaign, 156–57, 176
Vieira, Amaral, 185–86, 194

Vietnam War, 69, 93, 117, 159
violence: VOV campaign, 156–57, 176.
    See also nonviolence; nuclear arms;
    terrorism; wars
vitalistic philosophy, 48–49, 55–56. See also
    life-force philosophy

Wakaizumi, Kei, 117
Walker, Patricia, 148–49
wars: Korean, 53, 73; Sino-Japanese
    (1937–45), 29; Vietnam, 69, 93, 117,
    159. See also Cold War; World War II
    (Pacific)
Watanabe, Masako, 192, 199
Watanabe, Takesato, 68, 80
Watanabe, Yuhan, 166
westernization, 163; Makiguchi and,
    21–22, 29; Meiji-era, 26; and Soka
    University, 12. See also modernism;
    sameness/difference
White, James, 65, 68, 77, 78, 86
Whitman, Walt, 20; and Soka University,
    6, 7–8, 10, 11, 12, 22, 91, 107
"Why Did Ikeda Quit?" (Metraux), 128
Wiesenthal, Simon. See Simon Wiesenthal
    Center
Williams, George (Masayasu Sadanaga),
    147, 150, 152, 154, 155
Wilson, Bryan, 115
The Wisdom of the Lotus Sutra (Ikeda), 145
Women's Division (SG), 77; in Brazil, 184;
    Chorus of, 103; Ikeda's guidance to,
    158; Kashiwabara as chief of, 56–59,

87–88; Shinanomachi building, 23; in
    United States, 143, 146, 155–56, 158
women's rights in Japan, 51, 77
world house, 178, 183, 188–89
world peace. See peace
World Peace Culture Festival, 132
World War II (Pacific), 29, 92; and global
    ization of SG, 141; and Sensoji
    temple, 30; surrender by Japan, 21, 51;
    United States in, 29, 30, 31, 51, 71–72,
    75–76, 83, 92, 143, 208; U.S. occupa
    tion of Japan after, 3, 43, 49, 51–53,
    86, 92, 106, 208. See also bombing
    of Japan

Yokoyama, Kimio, 134–35
Young Men's Division (Soka Gakkai), 101
Youth Division (SG): of BSGI, 186–88;
    and disarmament and U.N. support,
    121; and Ikeda teachings, 157; leader
    ship of, 61, 72, 77, 87–88; and Osaka
    incident, 80; and Toda's death, 83;
    VOV campaign, 156–57, 176

zadankai, 77, 89
zaibutsu, 26, 51
Zen, 17, 30, 33, 143, 172, 209
"Zen and the Liberal Arts," 172
zengakuren, 93
Zhou Enlai, 10, 11, 12, 20, 120
zuiho-bini, 89, 140–70, 204; BSGI and,
    184, 187, 189–90, 191, 194, 195, 200–1;
    SGI-USA and, 89, 141, 146–59

Text:	Galliard
Display:	10/13 Galliard
Compositor:	International Typesetting and Composition
Printer and Binder:	Edwards Brothers, Inc.